So You Think You Know Baseball

So You Think You Know Baseball

David Parks

Writers Club Press
San Jose New York Lincoln Shanghai

So You Think You Know Baseball

Writers Club Press
an imprint of iUniverse, Inc.

For information address:
iUniverse, Inc.
5220 S. 16th St., Suite 200
Lincoln, NE 68512
www.iuniverse.com

ISBN: 0-595-20300-0

Printed in the United States of America

To my loving wife, Patricia

ACKNOWLEDGEMENTS

Thanks to my wife, Patricia, for proofreading; my son Christopher for testing; and my son Michael for helping me find all the right words.

INTRODUCTION

I am just an ordinary guy who likes baseball. As a kid growing up in the late 1950's and the early 1960's baseball was my game. I loved it. I loved the statistics and trivia that go with the game. The stats on the backs of my baseball cards were committed to memory. I have always enjoyed having conversations about baseball; people I know come to me with questions about trivia, statistics, and players. Sometimes I knew the answers and many times I didn't. But I always found it fun.

Baseball is a game that is ready-made for statistics; how many; the most; the fewest; the worst; etc. It is a sport that is unlike any other in that you can compare a player in 2000 with a player in 1975, 1950, 1925 or 1900. Yes, the approach to the game has changed through the years. The 1990's saw home runs as the main attraction led by players such as Ken Griffey, Jr., Mark McGwire, and Sammy Sosa. The stolen base was king in the 1960's, 1970's and the early 1980's, from Lou Brock and Maury Wills to Rickey Henderson. Some claim that the 1940's and 1950's were the Golden Age of Baseball with Joe DiMaggio, Stan Musial, and Ted Williams as legends who were larger than life. The year 1947 was not only a landmark year in Major League Baseball, but in America itself. Jackie Robinson stepped onto a Major League diamond and baseball was changed forever. Hank Aaron, Roberto Clemente, Willie Mays, Frank Robinson and a whole new generation could now be included in The National Pastime. The 1920's and 1930's gave us an era in which batting averages, base hits and RBI's came at a record pace. The record setting performances from Jimmie Foxx, Lou Gehrig, Rogers Hornsby, Babe Ruth, and Hack Wilson still stand at the turn of the new millennium. The early part of the 1900's gave baseball the untouchable pitching stats—victories, shutouts and complete games from Grover Alexander, Walter Johnson, Christy Mathewson, and Cy Young.

Although the approach to the game has changed throughout the years, baseball is still nine innings long, three outs per inning, four balls for a walk, and three strikes and you're out. A ball a fielder can't get is still a hit and over the fence is still a home run. I believe that the great players in any era would shine just as brightly in any other era. Babe Ruth, Hank Aaron and Mark McGwire would hit home runs regardless of the year. Walter Johnson, Sandy Koufax and Nolan Ryan would strike out batters. Ty Cobb, Ted Williams and Pete Rose would get their base hits. Willie Mays, Brooks Robinson and Ken Griffey Jr. would catch anything hit their way. Lou Gehrig and Cal Ripken Jr. would play all those games. Baseball transcends time.

It has always been fun to compare players from one era with those of another, but a fan will always think that the players he or she grew up with are the best. That's what makes baseball so great and so much fun: you can actually compare Mark McGwire to Babe Ruth, Pete Rose to Ty Cobb, Nolan Ryan to Walter Johnson and so on. Baseball is the only sport that allows fans the opportunity to accurately compare players from different generations.

In this book, I have tried to focus on the games, events, teams and players that most fans are familiar with: the Hall of Famers, star players, World Series that fans remember, the games that really stand out, and so on. Hopefully when you read a question it rings a bell, that the players and their accomplishments are something you know about. You might not know the answer, but the achievement, the player or the event is something that you will find interesting. There are some questions that I think you will find easy, where you'll say, "I know that." Many will require some thought and baseball knowledge. Some are difficult; please don't get too discouraged. Unless otherwise stated, all information and statistics are from the 1901 season to the start of the 2001 season. Enjoy.

Dave Parks

Contents

SECTION 1—GENERAL QUESTIONS

I. Feats and Accomplishments

1. All baseball fans know that Pete Rose is the career hits leader and that he broke Ty Cobb's record. But who is third on the all-time hit list?
A. Willie Mays   B. Stan Musial   C. Hank Aaron
D. Ted Williams   E. Frank Robinson

2. Which hitter has the distinction of being the only player in Major League history to win batting titles in three different decades?
A. George Brett   B. Paul Molitor   C. Ted Williams
D. Al Kaline   E. Roberto Clemente

3. One of the more exciting plays in baseball is a three-base hit. It is something that catchers are not associated with, yet one Hall of Fame catcher can claim that he lead his league in triples. Who is this fleet footed backstop?
A. Mickey Cochrane   B. Carlton Fisk   C. Yogi Berra
D. Johnny Bench   E. Ernie Lombardi

4. Only in one other season did a catcher lead his league in triples and that occurred in 1966 when this backstop lashed out 13 three-base hits. Who is this catcher?
A. John Roseboro   B. Jerry Grote   C. Bob Uecker
D. Elston Howard   E. Tim McCarver

5. Three Hall of Famers have a unique hitting accomplishment. At some point in his career, each has been his league's season leader in batting average, hits, doubles, triples and home runs. Ty Cobb and Rogers Hornsby are two of these three. Who is the other well-rounded batsman? Note that these hitting accomplishments did not have to occur in the same season.
A. Lou Gehrig   B. Carl Yastrzemski   C. Hank Aaron
D. Pete Rose   E. Roberto Clemente

6—8. It takes a very special kind of player to be a successful pinch-hitter: a player must sit on the bench all game and then produce in the clutch. The next three questions deal with these clutch players.

6. Who is the career record holder with 150 pinch-hits?
A. Smoky Burgess   B. Cliff Johnson   C. Jerry Lynch
D. Manny Mota   E. John Vander Wal

7. Who is the career record holder with 20 pinch-hit home runs?
A. Smoky Burgess   B. Cliff Johnson   C. Jerry Lynch
D. Manny Mota   E. John Vander Wal

8. Who is the single season record holder with 28 pinch-hits?
A. Smoky Burgess   B. Cliff Johnson   C. Jerry Lynch
D. Mannt Mota   E. John Vander Wal

9. Only 13 pitchers have won 30 games in a single season and the last pitcher to join this elite group was Denny McLain in 1968. The following Hall of Fame pitchers all won 300 games but one of them did not have a 30-win season. Who?
A. Eddie Plank   B. Christy Mathewson   C. Walter Johnson
D. Lefty Grove   E. Grover Alexander

10—11. Even less frequent than a 30-win season is a Triple Crown season. To lead the league in average, home runs and runs batted in is truly a daunting task. Only a dozen players have been Triple Crown winners and one player from each league has had two Triple Crown seasons.

10. Who is the two-time American League Triple Crown winner?
A. Mickey Mantle   B. Frank Robinson   C. Carl Yastrzemski
D. Ted Williams   E. Joe DiMaggio

11. Who is the two-time National League Triple Crown winner? ·
A. Hank Aaron   B. Jackie Robinson   C. Honus Wagner
D. Mel Ott   E. Rogers Hornsby

12. Cumulatively, there have been 14 Triple Crown seasons; nine in the AL and five in the NL Surprisingly, in one season, both leagues had a Triple Crown winner. Which year was it?
A. 1924   B. 1933   C. 1942   D. 1956   E. 1966

13. Baseball has many milestones to measure a player's success and place him in the game's history. Only 20 pitchers have reached 300 victories and only 16 sluggers have hit 500 home runs. Perhaps the most select is the 400 home run/400 stolen base club, which boasts only one member. Who is this lone player?
A. Andre Dawson   B. Rickey Henderson   C. Bobby Bonds
D. Barry Bonds   E. Joe Morgan

14. To some, base stealing is considered an art form and in the Major Leagues only four artists have ever had 100 thefts in a single season. Which one of the following fell short of the century mark?
A. Maury Wills   B. Rickey Henderson   C. Tim Raines
D. Lou Brock   E. Vince Coleman

15. Babe Ruth has the highest single season slugging percentage of .847 (1920). The Bambino also places second, third and fifth on the all-time list. Who is the only other hitter to place in the top five?
A. Mickey Mantle   B. Ralph Kiner   C. Mark McGwire
D. Sammy Sosa   E. Lou Gehrig

16. Babe Ruth's 714 career home runs are the most by a left-handed hitter. Who is a distant second to the Babe?
A. Mel Ott   B. Stan Musial   C. Reggie Jackson
D. Eddie Mathews   E. Ted Williams

17. Hitting .400 for a season is truly special accomplishment and only eight players have ever reached this lofty plateau. Which of the following batsman is not one of the magnificent eight?
A. Ty Cobb   B. Tris Speaker   C. George Sisler
D. Napoleon Lajoie   E. Rogers Hornsby

18. Name the Hall of Famer who hit .422 in 1901 to become the first player of the modern era to bat over .400.
A. Ty Cobb   B. Tris Speaker   C. George Sisler
D. Napoleon Lajoie   E. Rogers Hornsby

19. In 1911 Shoeless Joe Jackson hit .408 and finished second in the batting race. Whom did he lose the batting title to?
A. Ty Cobb   B. Tris Speaker   C. George Sisler
D. Napoleon Lajoie   E. Rogers Hornsby

20. The National League has had its share of great pitchers, but only four times in its long history has a hurler thrown a perfect game. These four aces are listed here along with a fifth who never achieved perfection. Which pitcher did not throw a perfect game?
A. J.R. Richard   B. Sandy Koufax   C. Tom Browning
D. Dennis Martinez   E. Jim Bunning

21. The American League has had ten perfect games, including the most famous (Don Larsen in the 1956 World Series). Four of the five pitchers listed can claim perfection. Who is the AL odd man out?
A. Kenny Rogers   B. Len Barker   C. David Wells
D. Cy Young   E. Bret Saberhagen

22. Nolan Ryan pitched a Major League record seven no-hitters in his Hall of Fame career. How many did he toss while he was in the National League?
A.1   B. 2   C. 4   D. 5   E. 7

23. Aside from the Ryan Express, since 1901 six other Hall of Fame pitchers have thrown at least two no-hitters. Which one of the following hurlers cannot claim this distinction?
A. Bob Feller   B. Christy Mathewson   C. Warren Spahn
D. Sandy Koufax   E. Catfish Hunter

24. In the history of the Major Leagues, only one pitcher has been fortunate enough to throw a no-hitter on Opening Day. Who is this Hall of Famer.
A. Jim Palmer   B. Tom Seaver   C. Walter Johnson
D. Ferguson Jenkins   E. Bob Feller

25. At the other end of the season, only once has a pitcher tossed a no-hitter to clinch the pennant.
Who was this pitcher?
A. Don Sutton   B. Mike Scott   C. Dave Righetti
D. Jim Lonborg   E. Doyle Alexander

26. Which slugger holds the record for multiple home run games in a career? (72)
A. Mark McGwire   B. Hank Aaron   C. Babe Ruth
D. Jimmie Foxx   E. Mickey Mantle

27. One player has a rather unique accomplishment on his career stat sheet, that of having 500 hits with four different teams. Who?
A. Rusty Staub   B. Joe Carter   C. Harold Baines
D. Pete Rose   E. Paul Molitor

28. Only one current member of Baseball's Hall of Fame can claim the distinction of hitting a home run in his first Major League at-bat. Oddly enough it was a pitcher. Which pitcher?
A. Hoyt Wilhelm   B. Gaylord Perry   C. Don Drysdale
D. Whitey Ford   E. Nolan Ryan

29. Hitting four home runs in a game is an awesome display of power. On June 3, 1932 Lou Gehrig was the first to do so and on September 7, 1993 Mark Whiten became the seventh player to hit four home runs in a nine-inning game. Listed below are four of the five other sluggers. Who does not belong in this group?
A. Willie Mays   B. Rocky Colavito   C. Gil Hodges
D. Joe Adcock   E. Dave Kingman

30. Only one of these five Hall of Famers ever hit three home runs in a game and he accomplished this feat a Major League record six times. Who is this slugger?
A. George Kell   B. Brooks Robinson   C. Tony Perez
D. Charlie Gehringer   E. Johnny Mize

31. One player amassed over 500 home runs in his career, but his single season best was a mere 33. This single season total is the lowest for any player with 500 home runs. Who is this slugger?
A. Mel Ott   B. Eddie Murray   C. Reggie Jackson
D. Ernie Banks   E. Babe Ruth

32. In 1934, future Hall of Fame pitcher Carl Hubbell turned in one of the most memorable performances in All-Star history. Hubbell struck out in succession five future Hall of Fame sluggers. One of the victims was Babe Ruth and the other four are listed here. Which slugger was not one of Hubbell's victims?
A. Joe Cronin   B. Lou Gehrig   C. Jimmie Foxx
D. Tony Lazzeri   E. Al Simmons

33. One hundred extra base hits in a season is a remarkable demonstration of power that has only been accomplished eleven times by nine different players. Which of the following Hall of Famers never had 100 extra base hits in one season?
A. Babe Ruth   B. Willie Mays   C. Stan Musial
D. Hank Greenberg   E. Rogers Hornsby

34. Which player listed below holds the Major League record with 119 extra-base hits in one season?
A. Babe Ruth   B. Willie Mays   C. Stan Musial
D. Hank Greenberg   E. Rogers Hornsby

35. Who was the only active player at the start of the 2000 baseball season to have belted 100 extra-base hits in one season?
A. Sammy Sosa   B. Cal Ripken, Jr.   C. Alex Rodriguez
D. Albert Belle   E. Edgar Martinez

36. Which player joined this elite group with 103 extra-base hits in the 2000 season?
A. Derek Jeter   B. Mike Piazza   C. Todd Helton
D. Darin Erstad   E. Chipper Jones

37. This recent addition to the 3000 hit club is the only player to have a home run as his 3000th hit. Who?
A. Robin Yount   B. Dave Winfield   C. Paul Molitor
D. Wade Boggs   E. George Brett

38. Fred McGriff had the distinction of being the only player in Major League history to lead both leagues in home runs. His home run titles came in 1992 with the San Diego Padres of the National League and in 1989 with the Toronto Blue Jays of the American League. Since then, another player has duplicated McGriff's feat. Who?
A. Sammy Sosa…B. Greg Vaughn…C. Mark McGwire…
D. Matt Williams…E. David Justice

39. One Hall of Fame pitcher known for his strikeouts has the dubious distinction of issuing 208 bases on balls in a single season, a Major League Record. Who?
A. Steve Carlton   B. Bob Feller   C. Walter Johnson
D. Bob Gibson   E. Tom Seaver

40. On September 25, 1984 Rusty Staub became only the second Major League player to hit a home run in his teens and in his 40's. Who was the first?
A. Ty Cobb   B. Al Kaline   C. Joe DiMaggio
D. Jackie Robinson   E. Hank Aaron

41. Some rookies are awestruck in their first big league game and others respond with the confidence of a seasoned veteran. Casey Stengel was one of the latter group, as he had four hits in his first ML game. There is another Hall of Famer who, like Stengel, lashed out four hits in his debut. Who got this great start to his career?
A. Mike Schmidt   B. Reggie Jackson   C. Harmon Killebrew
D. Willie McCovey   E. Willie Stargell

42. On September 16, 1975 Rennie Stennett of the Pittsburgh Pirates became the first and only player to get seven hits in seven at-bats in a nine-inning game. Whether it is a regulation game or an extra inning affair, only a handful of players ever had six hits in a game. Listed below are five active players, four of whom have done so. Who is the odd man out?
A. Sammy Sosa   B. Cal Ripken, Jr.   C. Tony Gwynn
D. Andres Galarraga   E. Larry Walker

43. Which Hall of Famer cannot claim a six hit game?
A. Jackie Robinson   B. Paul Waner   C. Lloyd Waner
D. Ernie Lombardi   E. Ty Cobb

44. Which National League team was the first in the Major Leagues to hit four consecutive home runs? They accomplished this feat on June 8, 1961.
A. New York Mets   B. Chicago Cubs   C. Milwaukee Braves
D. Pittsburgh Pirates   E. Houston Colt 45's

45—46. In this day and age, it is indeed an oddity for a player to spend his entire career with one franchise. At the conclusion of the 2000 season, which player (in each league) has served his respective team for the longest consecutive span?

45. National League:
A. John Franco   B. Mark Grace   C. Barry Larkin
D. John Smoltz   E. Tony Gwynn

46. American League:
A. Frank Thomas   B. Harold Baines   C. Edgar Martinez
D. Cal Ripken, Jr.   E. Paul O'Neill

47. Who holds the record for most seasons played in the Major Leagues (27)?
A. Pete Rose   B. Nolan Ryan   C. Willie Mays
D. Carl Yastrzemski   E. Stan Musial

48. Two players share the Major League record for most seasons played with one team (23). One was Brooks Robinson and the other played a Major League best 3,308 games with one team. Who was this Hall of Famer?
A. Carl Yastrzemski   B. Lou Gehrig   C. Hank Aaron
D. Johnny Bench   E. Willie Stargell

49. How was Harvey Haddix's famous 12-inning perfect game broken up?
A. Single   B. Home Run   C. Walk   D. Error   E. Hit Batsman

50. In the 1950's the New York Yankees won the American League pennant eight times. Preventing the Yanks from sweeping the decade were the 1954 Cleveland Indians and the 1959 Chicago White Sox, both of whom were managed by the same person. Which skipper was it?
A. Bucky Harris   B. Paul Richards   C. Jimmy Dykes
D. Fred Hutchinson   E. Al Lopez

51. Which first baseman of the late 1970's was the only player in Major League history to hit for the cycle in both the National and American Leagues? He accomplished this feat as a member of the Houston Astros (NL) on June 24, 1977 and the Boston Red Sox (AL) on September 15, 1979.
A. Bob Watson   B. John Mayberry   C. Bill Buckner
D. Tony Perez   E. Dan Driessen

52. He was George Steinbrenner's favorite manager, but Billy was not Billy "The Kid" Martin's real first name. What was?
A. Dean   B. Mary   C. Alfred   D. Martin   E. Pepper

53. The Chicago Cubs, Slammin' Sammy Sosa has always found Wrigley Field to be very friendly. In the 1998 season, he found many friendly ballparks as well, as he hit 66 home runs but finished second to Mark McGwire's total of 70. However, he did break a different Major League record: most different parks to have hit a home run in for a single season. How many?
A. 13   B. 14   C. 16   D. 18   E. 19

54. In the 2000 season, this player walked passed Babe Ruth (2,056) to become the career leader in free passes (2,060). Who is this new king of the walks?
A. Mark McGwire   B. Tony Gwynn   C. Barry Bonds
D. Cal Ripken, Jr.   E. Rickey Henderson

55. Who holds the National League record for walks in a career (1,799)?
A. Joe Morgan   B. Mike Schmidt   C. Willie McCovey
D. Gil Hodges   E. Dave Kingman

56. Some players will do anything to get on base, including taking one for the team. Who holds the career record for being hit by a pitch (267)?
A. Don Baylor   B. Craig Biggio   C. Brady Anderson
D. Ron Hunt   E. Don Zimmer

57. Whether it's a straight steal or the back end of a double steal, the theft of home is bold act. Which Hall of Famer was the boldest of them all and the all-time leader in stealing a run?
A. Jackie Robinson   B. Lou Gehrig   C. Ty Cobb
D. Rod Carew   E. Frankie Frisch

58. How many times did the above thief steal home?
A. 20   B. 30   C. 40   D. 50   E. 60

59—60. On a baseball diamond the difficulty level for fielding varies from position to position. Based upon a minimum of 1,000 games played, three first basemen have tied for the highest percentage of all-time (.996). All had careers spent entirely in one league; two in the National, the other in the American. Although not as well publicized, Wes Parker of the Los Angeles Dodgers is one of the three.

59. Who is the other National Leaguer?
A. Steve Garvey   B. Dave Kingman   C. Keith Hernandez
D. Willie Stargell   E. Gil Hodges

60. Who is the American Leaguer?
A. Rod Carew   B. Kent Hrbek   C. Eddie Murray
D. Boog Powell   E. Don Mattingly

61. Which Hall of Famer is the all-time leader in shutouts by a lefthander (69)?
A. Steve Carlton   B. Warren Spahn   C. Whitey Ford
D. Sandy Koufax   E. Eddie Plank

62. Fans know that Hank Aaron is the career leader in home runs (755) and Pete Rose is the career leader in base hits (4,256). But which Hall of Famer is the career leader in doubles (792)?
A. George Brett   B. Sam Crawford   C. Rogers Hornsby
D. Tris Speaker   E. Stan Musial

63. Which Hall of Famer is the career leader in triples (309)?
A. George Brett   B. Sam Crawford   C. Rogers Hornsby
D. Tris Speaker   E. Stan Musial

64. The single season record for base hits (257) was established over 80 years ago (1920). Which Hall of Famer holds this long-standing record?
A. Jimmie Foxx   B. Ty Cobb   C. George Sisler
D. Hank Greenberg   E. Joe Cronin

65. The record for the most games by a pitcher in a season is 106. This was the only time a pitcher has topped the century mark in appearances and it occured in 1974. Who was this bullpen workhorse?
A. Dan Quisenberry   B. Hoyt Wilhelm   C. Mike Marshall
D. Bruce Sutter   E. Kent Tekulve

I. Feats and Accomplishments—Answers

1. C Hammerin' Hank finished his career with 3771 hits.

2. A George Brett   Hit .333 in 1976, .390 in 1980 and .329 in 1990

3. B In 1972; Boston's Carlton Fisk was tied with Joe Rudi of the Oakland A's for the league lead with nine triples.

4. E Tim McCarver   St. Louis Cardinals

5. A Lou Gehrig   Batting Average: 1934
Hits: 1931
Doubles: 1927, 1928
Triples: 1926
Home Runs: 1931, 1934, 1936

Ty Cobb   Batting Average: 1907-15, 1917, 1918, 1919
Hits: 1907, 1908, 1909, 1911, 1912, 1915, 1917, 1919
Doubles: 1908, 1911, 1917
Triples: 1908, 1911, 1917, 1918
Home Runs: 1909

Rogers Hornsby   Batting Average: 1920, 1921, 1922, 1923, 1924, 1925, 1928
Hits: 1920, 1921, 1922, 1924
Doubles: 1920, 1921, 1922, 1924

Triples: 1917, 1921
Home Runs: 1922, 1925

6. D Manny Mota

7. B Cliff Johnson

8. E John Vander Wal 1995—Colorado Rockies

9. A Eddie Plank Christy Mathewson: 1903, 1904, 1905, 1908
Walter Johnson: 1912, 1913
Lefty Grove: 1931
Grover Alexander: 1915, 1916, 1917

10. D Ted Williams Boston Red Sox: 1942, 1947

11. E Rogers Hornsby St. Louis Cardinals: 1922, 1925

12. B 1933 AL: Jimmie Foxx—Philadelphia Athletics
NL: Chuck Klein—Philadelphia Phillies

13. D Barry Bonds At the conclusion of the 2000 season Bonds had 494 home runs and 471 stolen bases

14. C Tim Raines His best season was 1983 with 90 stolen bases
Maury Wills: 1962
Rickey Henderson: 1980, 1982, 1983
Lou Brock: 1974
Vince Coleman: 1985, 1986, 1987

15. E Lou Gehrig
1927—.765 SA   Babe Ruth: 1920—.847 SA
                                      1921—.846 SA
                                      1927—.772 SA
                                      1923—.764 SA

16. C Reggie Jackson   563 Home Runs

17. B Tris Speaker   Best average was .389 in 1925

18. D Napoleon Lajoie 1901—.422

19. A Ty Cobb   .420

20. A J.R. Richard
Jim Bunning, Philadelphia at New York, June21, 1964   6—0
Sandy Koufax, Los Angeles vs. Chicago, Sept. 9, 1965   1—0
Tom Browning, Cincinnati vs. Los Angeles, Sept. 16, 1988   1—0
Dennis Martinez, Montreal at Los Angeles, Jul 28, 1991   2—0

21. E Bret Saberhagen
Cy Young, Boston vs. Philadelphia, May 5, 1904   3—0
Len Barker, Cleveland vs. Toronto, May 15, 1981   3—0
Kenny Rogers, Texas vs. California, July 28, 1994   4—0
David Wells, New York vs. Minnesota, May 17, 1998   4—0

22. A   Only one no-hitter came while Ryan was in the NL; it occurred on Sept. 26, 1981 while he was a member of the Houston Astros. He defeated the Los Angeles Dodgers 5—0.

23. E   Catfish Hunter—Oakland Athletics—pitched a perfect game on
May 8, 1968 against Minnesota

Christy Mathewson	Bob Feller	Warren Spahn	Sandy Koufax
July 15, 1901	April 16, 1940	Sept. 15, 1960	June 30, 1962
June 13, 1905	April 30, 1946	April 28, 1961	May 11, 1963
	July 1, 1951		June 4, 1964
			Sept. 9, 1965
			Perfect Game

24. E   Bob Feller
Cleveland Indians on April 16, 1940 at Chicago   1—0

25. B   Mike Scott
Houston Astros on Sept. 25, 1986 vs. San Fran.   2—0
Also, Allie Reynolds of the New York Yankees pitched a no-hitter on
September 28, 1951, an 8—0 victory over the Boston Red Sox to clinch a
tie for the AL pennant.

26. C   Babe Ruth

27. A   Rusty Staub
He finished his career with 2716 hits: 792 Hits—Houston Colt 45's/Astros
531 Hits—Montreal Expos
709 Hits—New York Mets
582 Hits—Detroit Tigers
(and for good measure) 102 Hits—
Texas Rangers

28. A   Hoyt Wilhelm With the New York Giants on April 23, 1952

29. E   Dave Kingman
Gil Hodges—Brooklyn Dodgers on August 31, 1950
Joe Adcock—Milwaukee Braves on July 31, 1954
Rocky Colavito—Cleveland Indians on June 10, 1959
Willie Mays—San Francisco Giants on April 30, 1961
also, Bob Horner—Atlanta Braves on July 6, 1986

30. E Johnny Mize	St. Louis Cardinals	July 13, 1938
		July 20, 1938 (2nd game)
		May 13, 1940 (14 innings)
		Sept. 8, 1940 (1st game)
	New York Giants	April 24, 1947
	New York Yankees	Sept. 15, 1950

31. B   Eddie Murray   Baltimore Orioles—1983—33 Home Runs

32. D   Tony Lazzeri

33. B   Willie Mays   His best total was 90 extra base hits in 1962
Babe Ruth—1921—119 Hits   The other Hall of Fame players are:
Stan Musial—1948—103 Hits   Lou Gehrig—1930—117 Hits & 1930—100 Hits
Hank Greenberg—1937—103 Hits Chuck Klein—1930—107 Hits & 1932—103 Hits
Rogers Hornsby—1922—102 Hits Jimmie Foxx—1932—100 Hits

34. A   Babe Ruth
New York Yankees—1921   Had 204 total base hits, which included:
   44 Doubles   16 Triples   59 Home Runs=119 Extra base hits

35. D   Albert Belle   Cleveland Indians—1995   Had 173 total base hits which included:
   52 Doubles   1 Triple   50 Home Runs=103 Extra base hits

36. C   Todd Helton   Colorado Rockies Had 214 total base hits which included:
   59 Doubles   2 Triples   42 Home Runs=103 Extra base hits

37. D   Wade Boggs   Tampa Bay Devil Rays—August 7, 1999 vs. Cleveland Indians

38. C   Mark McGwire   Oakland Athletics—1987 & 1996
   St. Louis Cardinals—1998 & 1999

39. B   Bob Feller   Cleveland Indians issued 208 walks in 1938

40. A   Ty Cobb

41. D   Willie McCovey   San Francisco Giants—July 30, 1959: two singles and two triples

42. E   Larry Walker   Sammy Sosa—July 7, 1993
   Tony Gwynn—August 4, 1993
   Andres Galarraga—July 3, 1995
   Cal Ripken, Jr.—June 13, 1999

43. A   Jackie Robinson   Ty Cobb—May 5, 1925
                          Paul Waner—August 26, 1926
                          Lloyd Waner—July 15, 1929
                          Ernie Lombardi—May 9, 1937

44. C   Milwaukee Braves 7th inning at Cincinnati: Eddie Mathews, Hank Aaron, Joe Adcock and Frank Thomas

45. E   Tony Gwynn—San Diego Padres—1982—2000

46. D   Cal Ripken, Jr.—Baltimore Orioles—1981—2000

47. B   Nolan Ryan—1966—1993, except 1967

48. A   Carl Yastrzemski—Boston Red Sox—1961—1983

49. D   The perfect game was lost when third baseman Don Hoak committed a throwing error.

50. E   Al Lopez

51. A   Bob Watson

52. C   The perennial Steinbrenner scapegoat's real name was Alfred Manuel Martin.

53. D   18   16 N. L. and 2 A. L. parks

54. E   Rickey Henderson

55. A   Joe Morgan

56. A Don Baylor

57. C Ty Cobb

58. D 50

59. A Steve Garvey

60. E Don Mattingly

61. E Eddie Plank

62. D Tris Speaker

63. B Sam Crawford

64. C George Sisler St. Louis Browns

65. C Mike Marshall Los Angeles Dodgers

II. Awards

1. In 1956 the Cy Young Award was instituted to honor pitching excellence, and until 1966 there was only one recipient for all of baseball. The first Award went to a right-handed pitcher. Who was this inaugural Cy Young winner?
A. Don Larsen   B. Herb Score   C. Frank Lary
D. Don Newcombe   E. Robin Roberts

2. Who was the first lefty to win the Cy Young?
A. Sandy Koufax   B. Johnny Podres   C. Steve Carlton
D. Whitey Ford   E. Warren Spahn

3. The following pitchers are all multiple Cy Young Award winners. Only one of these pitchers won his Awards with the same team. Which pitcher?
A. Pedro Martinez   B. Roger Clemens   C. Tom Seaver
D. Randy Johnson   E. Gaylord Perry

4. Four hurlers have managed to capture the Cy Young in successive seasons. Which of the following pitchers does not have back-to-back awards?
A. Steve Carlton   B. Roger Clemens   C. Sandy Koufax
D. Greg Maddux   E. Jim Palmer

5. One of these pitchers claimed back-to-back Cy Young Awards on two separate occasions. Who has this distinction?
A. Steve Carlton   B. Roger Clemens   C. Sandy Koufax
D. Greg Maddux   E. Jim Palmer

6. Using these same pitchers, one has gone a step further with back-to-back-to-back-to-back Cy Young's. Who has this unprecedented four-peat?
A. Steve Carlton   B. Roger Clemens   C. Sandy Koufax
D. Greg Maddux   E. Jim Palmer

7. Only eight relief pitchers have been Cy Young Award winners. The first year a reliever captured this pitching trophy was in 1974. Name the first Cy Young fireman.
A. Mike Marshall   B. Rollie Fingers   C. Hoyt Wilhelm
D. Bruce Sutter   E. Sparky Lyle

8—12. In 1957 the Gold Glove Award was created to honor fielding excellence. The top player at each position was now recognized for his defensive skill. In this initial season Gold Gloves were given to only one player at each position. Starting in 1958 Gold Gloves were awarded to the top fielders in each league. The following questions will deal with Gold Glove Award winners.

8. A successful baseball team must have a top fielding shortstop. Which shortstop has won the most National League Gold Gloves?
A. Larry Bowa   B. Dave Concepion   C. Ozzie Smith
D. Maury Wills   E. Barry Larkin

9. Which shortstop has won the most American League Gold Gloves?
A. Cal Ripken, Jr.   B. Luis Aparicio   C. Mark Belanger
D. Alan Trammell   E. Tony Fernandez

10. The record for the most Gold Gloves in a career (16) is shared by two players. One is a pitcher and the other an infielder. First, who is the pitcher?
A. Bobby Shantz   B. Greg Maddux   C. Ron Guidry
D. Jim Kaat   E. Lee Smith

11. Who is the infielder?
A. Mike Schmidt   B. Nellie Fox   C. Mark Grace
D. Joe Morgan   E. Brooks Robinson

12. Willie Mays has won 12 Gold Gloves. Which other outfielder has matched his record?
A. Paul Blair   B. Roberto Clemente   C. Curt Flood
D. Ken Griffey, Jr.   E. Fred Lynn

13—14. Most Valuable Player Awards for the regular season began in 1911, but it was not until 1931 that the Award became an annual event. From that date to the present, The Baseball Writers Association of America has named the MVP for each league. No player in either league has ever been named MVP for three successive seasons. However, each league does have five players with back-to-back honors.

13. Which National Leaguer does not have back-to-back honors?
A. Steve Garvey   B. Ernie Banks   C. Joe Morgan
D. Dale Murphy   E. Mike Schmidt

14. Which American Leaguer does not have back-to-back honors?
A. Frank Thomas   B. Roger Maris   C. George Brett
D. Jimmie Foxx   E. Mickey Mantle

15. Eight players (four from each league) have won MVP honors on three occasions. Which of the following National Leaguers does not have three MVP Awards?
A. Barry Bonds   B. Hank Aaron   C. Roy Campanella
D. Stan Musial   E. Mike Schmidt

16. Which of the following American Leaguers does not have three MVP Awards?
A. Mickey Mantle   B. Jimmie Foxx   C. Yogi Berra
D. Joe DiMaggio   E. Cal Ripken, Jr.

17. Which of the following Hall of Fame catchers never won a regular season MVP Award?
A. Bill Dickey   B. Ernie Lombardi   C. Mickey Cochrane
D. Roy Campanella   E. Johnny Bench

18. Which of the following Hall of Fame outfielders never won a regular season MVP Award?
A. Roberto Clemente   B. Frank Robinson   C. Paul Waner
D. Al Kaline   E. Robin Yount

19. Which of the following middle infielders never won a regular season MVP Award?
A. Frankie Frisch   B. Tony Lazzeri   C. Lou Boudreau
D. Nellie Fox   E. Charlie Gehringer

20. There are some voters and fans that do not think that a pitcher should be considered an MVP candidate. They do not consider a pitcher an everyday player, and therefore, a pitcher should not be considered an MVP candidate. Despite these objections, pitchers, on occasion, come away with MVP honors. Four of the five pitchers below were named MVP. Which one was not?
A. Carl Hubbell   B. Bob Feller   C. Vida Blue
D. Rollie Fingers   E. Dizzy Dean

21. In 1944 & 45 this pitcher had the distinction of being named MVP in successive seasons. Who was the only pitcher to be so honored?
A. Allie Reynolds   B. Johnny Vander Meer   C. Ewell Blackwell
D. Preacher Roe   E. Hal Newhouser

22. Over the years, the regular season has seen numerous New York Yankees win the American League's MVP trophy. Which of the following Yankees was not named MVP?
A. Don Mattingly   B. Phil Rizzuto   C. Bernie Williams
D. Spud Chandler   E. Elston Howard

23. Which player from the Boston Red Sox was not named regular season MVP?
A. Mo Vaughn   B. Fred Lynn   C. Jim Rice
D. Wade Boggs   E. Jackie Jensen

24. Which player from the Philadelphia/Kansas City/Oakland Athletics was not named regular season MVP?
A. Mark McGwire   B. Lefty Grove   C. Jose Canseco
D. Reggie Jackson   E. Rickey Henderson

25. Which player from the St. Louis Browns/Baltimore Orioles was not named regular season MVP?
A. Boog Powell   B. Brooks Robinson   C. Frank Robinson
D. George Sisler   E. Rafael Palmeiro

26. Which player from the Detroit Tigers was not named regular season MVP?
A. Cecil Fielder   B. Hank Greenberg   C. Denny McClain
D. Mickey Cochrane   E. Willie Hernandez

27. Which player from the Brooklyn/Los Angeles Dodgers was not named regular season MVP?
A. Dolph Camilli   B. Duke Snider   C. Kirk Gibson
D. Jackie Robinson   E. Maury Wills

28. Which player from the St. Louis Cardinals was not named regular season MVP?
A. Ozzie Smith   B. Marty Marion   C. Joe Medwick
D. Joe Torre   E. Stan Musial

29. Which player from the New York/San Francisco Giants was not named regular season MVP?
A. Willie Mays   B. Mel Ott   C. Kevin Mitchell
D. Barry Bonds   E. Willie McCovey

30. Which player from the Chicago Cubs was not named regular season MVP? (Yes, the Cubs have had MVP players)
A. Sammy Sosa   B. Hank Sauer   C. Andre Dawson
D. Billy Williams   E. Ryne Sandberg

31. Which player from the Cincinnati Reds was not named regular season MVP?
A. Pete Rose   B. George Foster   C. Johnny Bench
D. Joe Morgan   E. Tony Perez

32. Which player from the Pittsburgh Pirates was not named regular season MVP?
A. Ralph Kiner   B. Dick Groat   C. Roberto Clemente
D. Willie Stargell   E. Dave Parker

33. Which player from the Boston/Milwaukee/Atlanta Braves was not named regular season MVP?
A. Chipper Jones   B. Eddie Mathews   C. Dale Murphy
D. Terry Pendleton   E. Hank Aaron

34—36. In 1955 Major League Baseball finally decided to honor the top performer in the World Series. After all, each league honored their top regular season performer and the top performer in the All-Star Game, so the decision made sense. Three players have accomplished a unique trifecta in their careers; at some point they have been named league MVP, All-Star MVP and World Series MVP. In each of the next three questions, select the player who has accomplished this feat.

34. A. Roger Maris   B. Steve Garvey   C. Brooks Robinson
D. Mickey Lolich   E. Bob Gibson

35. A. Ray Knight   B. Joe Morgan   C. Bobby Richardson
D. Rollie Fingers   E. Roberto Clemente

36. A. Frank Robinson   B. Willie Stargell   C. Alan Trammell
D. Jack Morris   E. Joe Carter

37. Baseball's inaugural All-Star game was played at Chicago's Comiskey Park on July 6, 1933, with the American League defeating the National League 4 to 2. Who was named MVP of that first All-Star Classic?
A. Lou Gehrig   B. Bill Terry   C. Carl Hubbell
D. Tony Lazzeri   E. Babe Ruth

38. Only four players have been named MVP of the All-Star Game more than once. Which one of the following is not one of the four?
A. Willie Mays   B. Gary Carter   C. Jim Rice
D. Ted Williams   E. Steve Garvey

39. The first year that managers received an award was in 1983. One manager has been honored with three Manager of the Year Awards. Who is this dugout leader?
A. Jim Leyland   B. Whitey Herzog   C. Tony LaRussa
D. Mike Hargrove   E. Lou Piniella

40. Many great managers never received an award for their managerial skills. Based upon a minimum of 1000 games managed, name the field boss who has the best winning percentage.
A. John McGraw   B. Walter Alston   C. Earl Weaver
D. Joe McCarthy   E. Leo Durocher

II. Awards—Answers

1. D   Don Newcombe—Brooklyn Dodgers

2. E   Warren Spahn—Milwaukee Braves—1957

3. C   Tom Seaver—New York Mets: 1969, 1973, 1975
   Pedro Martinez: 1997—Montreal Expos
   1999, 2000—Boston Red Sox
   Roger Clemens: 1986, 1987, 1991—Boston Red Sox
   1997, 1998—Toronto Blue Jays
   Randy Johnson: 1995—Seattle Marineers
   1999, 2000—Arizona Diamondbacks
   Gaylord Perry: 1972—Cleveland Indians
   1978—San Diego Padres

4. A   Steve Carlton—Philadelphia Phillies: 1972, 1977, 1980, 1982
   Sandy Koufax—Los Angeles Dodgers: 1963, 1965, 1966
   Jim Palmer—Baltimore Orioles: 1973, 1975, 1976
   Roger Clemens: 1986, 1987, 1991—Boston Red Sox
   1997, 1998—Toronto Blue Jays
   Greg Maddux—Chicago Cubs: 1992
   Atlanta Braves: 1993, 1994, 1995

5. B   Roger Clemens

6. D   Greg Maddux

7. A   Mike Marshall—Los Angeles Dodgers

8. C   Ozzie Smith—St. Louis Cardinals: 1980-92   13 Consecutive Gold Gloves

9. B   Luis Aparicio—Chicago White Sox: 1958-1962, 1968, 1970
Baltimore Orioles: 1964, 1966   9 Gold Gloves

10. D   Jim Kaat—Minnesota Twins: 1962-1972
Chicago White Sox: 1973-1975
Philadelphia Phillies: 1976, 1977
16 Consecutive Gold Gloves

11. E   Brooks Robinson—Baltimore Orioles: 1960-1975
16 Consecutive Gold Gloves

12. B   Roberto Clemente—Pittsburgh Pirates: 1961-1972
12 Consecutive Gold Gloves

13. A   Steve Garvey   Los Angeles Dodgers was MVP in 1974
Ernie Banks—Chicago Cubs: 1957 & 1958
Joe Morgan—Cincinnati Reds: 1975 & 1976
Mike Schmidt—Philadelphia Phillies: 1980 & 1981, 1986
Dale Murphy—Atlanta Braves: 1982 & 1983

14. C   George Brett   Kansas City Royals was MVP in 1980
Jimmie Foxx—Philadelphia Athletics: 1932 & 1933
Boston Red Sox: 1938
Mickey Mantle—New York Yankees: 1956 & 1957, 1962
Roger Maris—New York Yankees: 1960 & 1961
Frank Thomas—Chicago White Sox: 1993 & 1994

15. B   Hank Aaron
Only one MVP Award in 1957 with the Milwaukee Braves
Stan Musial—St. Louis Cardinals: 1943, 1946, 1948
Roy Campanella—Brooklyn Dodgers: 1951, 1953, 1955
Mike Schmidt—Philadelphia Phillies: 1980 & 1981, 1986
Barry Bonds—Pittsburgh Pirates: 1990, 1992 San Francisco Giants: 1993

16. E   Cal Ripken, Jr. Has two MVP Awards: 1983, 1991 with the
        Baltimore Orioles
Jimmie Foxx—Philadelphia Athletics: 1932 & 1933   Boston Red Sox: 1938
Joe DiMaggio—New York Yankees: 1939, 1941, 1947
Yogi Berra—New York Yankees: 1951, 1954, 1955
Mickey Mantle—New York Yankees: 1956 & 1957, 1962

17. A   Bill Dickey—New York Yankees
Yogi Berra—New York Yankees: 1951, 1954, 1955
Roy Campanella—Brooklyn Dodgers: 1951, 1953, 1955
Mickey Cochrane—Philadelphia Phillies: 1928
Ernie Lombardi—Cincinnati Reds: 1938

18. D   Al Kaline—Detroit Tigers
Paul Waner—Pittsburgh Pirates: 1927
Frank Robinson—Cincinnati Reds: 1961 Baltimore Orioles: 1966
Roberto Clemente—Pittsburgh Pirates: 1966
Robin Yount—Milwaukee Brewers: 1982, 1989

19. B   Tony Lazzeri—New York Yankees
Frankie Frisch—St. Louis Cardinals: 1931
Charlie Gehringer—Detroit Tigers: 1937
Lou Boudreau—Cleveland Indians: 1948
Nellie Fox—Chicago White Sox: 1959

20. B   Bob Feller—Cleveland Indians was never named MVP
Carl Hubbell—New York Giants: 1933
Dizzy Dean—St. Louis Cardinals: 1934
Vida Blue—Oakland Athletics: 1971
Rollie Fingers—Milwaukee Brewers: 1981

21. E   Hal Newhouser—Detroit Tigers

22. C   Bernie Williams
Spud Chandler: 1943
Phil Rizzuto: 1950
Elston Howard: 1963
Don Mattingly: 1985

23. D   Wade Boggs
Jackie Jensen: 1958
Fred Lynn: 1975
Jim Rice: 1978
Mo Vaughn: 1995

24. A   Mark McGwire
Lefty Grove: 1931
Reggie Jackson: 1973
Jose Canseco: 1988
Rickey Henderson: 1990

25. E   Rafael Palmeiro
George Sisler: 1922
Brooks Robinson: 1964
Frank Robinson: 1966
Boog Powell: 1970

26. A Cecil Fielder
Mickey Cochrane: 1934
Hank Greenberg: 1935, 1940
Denny McClain: 1968
Willie Hernandez: 1984

27. B Duke Snider
Dolph Camilli: 1941
Jackie Robinson: 1949
Maury Wills: 1962
Kirk Gibson: 1988

28. A Ozzie Smith
Joe Medwick: 1937
Stan Musial: 1943, 1946, 1948
Marty Marion: 1944
Joe Torre: 1971

29. B Mel Ott
Willie Mays: 1954, 1965
Willie McCovey: 1969
Kevin Mitchell: 1989
Barry Bonds: 1993

30. D Billy Williams
Hank Sauer: 1952
Ryne Sandberg: 1984
Andre Dawson: 1987
Sammy Sosa: 1998

31. E Tony Perez
Johnny Bench: 1970 & 72
Pete Rose: 1973
Joe Morgan: 1975 & 76
George Foster: 1977

32. A Ralph Kiner
Dick Groat: 1960
Roberto Clemente: 1966
Dave Parker: 1978
Willie Stargell: 1979

33. B Eddie Mathews
Hank Aaron: 1957
Dale Murphy: 1982, 1983
Terry Pendelton: 1991
Chipper Jones: 1999

34. C Brooks Robinson Baltimore Orioles: 1964 (AL), 1966 (All-Star), 1970 (WS)

35. E Roberto Clemente Pittsburgh Pirates: 1961 (All-Star, Game 1), 1966 (NL), 1971 (WS)

36. A Frank Robinson Cincinnati Reds: 1961—NL MVP
Baltimore Orioles: 1966—AL MVP
1966—World Series MVP
1971—All-Star MVP

37. E Babe Ruth

38. C   Jim Rice was never All-Star Game MVP
                        Ted Williams: 1941, 1946
                        Willie Mays: 1960 (both games), 1963, 1968
                        Steve Garvey: 1974, 1978
                        Gary Carter: 1981, 1984

39. C—Tony LaRussa   Chicago White Sox—1983
                        Oakland Athletics—1988 & 92
   Dusty Baker of the San Francisco Giants now has three Manager of the
Year Awards: 1993, 1997, 2000

40. D—Joe McCarthy   2125 Wins   1333 Losses   .615 Pct.

IIIa. Post-Season: Players

1. Babe Ruth and Lou Gehrig played together for ten seasons (1925-34). How many World Series titles did the Yankees win during that time?
A. 3   B. 4   C. 6   D. 7   E. 8

2. In the 1966 World Series the Baltimore Orioles used only four pitchers in their four game sweep of the Los Angeles Dodgers: 5—2, 6—0, 1—0 and 1—0. Who was the only Oriole pitcher with an ERA over 0.00?
A. Dave McNally   B. Jim Palmer   C. Wally Bunker
D. Moe Drabowsky   E. Steve Barber

3. Everyone knows that Don Larsen threw the only perfect game in World Series history. Can you name the pitcher who took the loss (2—0) in that historic game?
A. Carl Erskine   B. Sal Maglie   C. Don Newcombe
D. Sandy Koufax   E. Don Drysdale

4. It is not uncommon for baseball fans to boo the players of opposing teams, but in the 1934 World Series the people of Detroit did more than heckle one member of the St. Louis Cardinals. In Game 7, Tiger fans pelted this player with fruit and bottles and he was removed for his own protection. Who was this thorn in the side of the Motor City?
A. Joe Medwick   B. Pepper Martin   C. Dizzy Dean
D. Leo Durocher   E. Frankie Frisch

5. One of the most famous highlights in baseball is Willie Mays making his over-the-shoulder catch of a long fly ball in the 1954 World Series. What team were Mays and the Giants playing?
A. New York Yankees   B. Detroit Tigers   C. Chicago White Sox
D. Cleveland Indians   E. Boston Red Sox

6. Who was the batter?
A. Mickey Mantle   B. Al Kaline   C. Ted Kluszewski
D. Vic Wertz   E. Ted Williams

7. Only one manager in Major League history has had the good fortune and the managerial abilities to pilot World Series champions in both leagues. Who was this manager?
A. Casey Stengel   B. Sparky Anderson   C. Dick Williams
D. Joe Torre   E. John McGraw

8. Many pitchers have starred in the World Series, and there have been quite a few who have won a game in two decades. But only one pitcher has ever won a Series game in three different decades. Who?
A. Whitey Ford   B. Rollie Fingers   C. Catfish Hunter
D. Johnny Podres   E. Jim Palmer

9. The words "The Giants win the pennant! The Giants win the pennant!" immediately bring to mind visions of Bobby Thomson's game winning home run. Ralph Branca was the Dodger pitcher who surrendered the blast, but do you know which Giant pitcher was credited with the victory?
A. Jim Hearn   B. Sal Maglie   C. Johnny Antonelli
D. Sam Jones   E. Larry Jansen

10. Bob Gibson of the St. Louis Cardinals holds the World Series records for strikeouts in one game (17) and strikeouts in one Series (35). Which team did Gibson victimize? A curious note about this World Series is that

even with Gibson's strikeout records, the Cardinals lost the Series four games to three.
A. Baltimore Orioles   B. New York Yankees   C. Oakland Athletics
D. Detroit Tigers   E. Minnesota Twins

11. One of the most storied individual World Series performances occurred on October 18, 1977 when Reggie Jackson hit three home runs to clinch the series for the Yanks. In doing so, Jackson became only the second player to hit three home runs in a single World Series game. Who was the first to do so?
A. Bill Terry   B. Mickey Mantle   C. Lou Gehrig
D. Duke Snider   E. Babe Ruth

12. The 1975 World Series, between the Boston Red Sox and the Cincinnati Reds, gave fans one of baseball's most memorable images: Carlton Fisk standing at home plate, waving his arms in hopes that his long fly ball down the left-field line would stay fair. It did, and Boston won the game 7-6 and evened the Series at three games. Fisk's heroics were made possible by a pinch-hit three run homer in the bottom of the 8th to tie the score, 6-6. Who was that pinch-hitter?
A. Cecil Cooper   B. Juan Beniquez   C. Rick Wise
D. Bernie Carbo   E. Dick Drago

13. Middle infielders are not generally associated with power hitting statistics, yet the World Series record for most RBI's in a game (6) is held by one. Who holds this record?
A. Pee Wee Reese   B. Bert Campaneris   C. Bobby Richardson
D. Dick Groat   E. Barry Larkin

14. Which Hall of Fame slugger holds the all-time World Series slugging average (.755). (Minimum 20 games)
A. Duke Snider   B. Reggie Jackson   C. Johnny Bench
D. Frank Robinson   E. Stan Musial

15. One of the greatest rivalries in baseball was between the New York Yankees and the Brooklyn Dodgers. From 1941 to 1956, these teams met in the Series seven times. One player appeared in all 44 games. Who was this player?
A. Phil Rizzuto   B. Yogi Berra   C. Gil Hodges
D. Joe DiMaggio   E. Pee Wee Reese

16. Collecting four hits in a World Series game has been accomplished 50 times. Bret Boone of the Atlanta Braves was the most recent on October 26, 1999. Only one player ever had two such four hit games and oddly enough he did this in the same Series. Who is this batsman?
A. Robin Yount   B. Kirby Puckett   C. Pete Rose
D. Steve Garvey   E. Mark McGwire

17. One player did even better, as he is the only player in Series history to have a five hit series game. Who?
A. Derek Jeter   B. Andruw Jones   C. Roberto Alomar
D. Paul Molitor   E. Will Clark

18. It is not surprising that the career leader in RBI's in World Series play is a New York Yankee (40). Which Yankee slugger holds this record?
A. Mickey Mantle   B. Babe Ruth   C. Bill Skowron
D. Roger Maris   E. Yogi Berra

19. On the career RBI list in World Series play there is only one player who was not a Yankee to appear in the top ten; he is seventh with 26 RBI's. Who is this intruder to Yankee dominance?
A. Gil Hodges   B. Frank Robinson   C. Sal Bando
D. Duke Snider   E. Chipper Jones

20. Whitey Ford holds numerous career pitching records in World Series play. One record he does not hold is most home runs allowed (9). Who holds this record?
A. Don Drysdale   B. Greg Maddux   C. Catfish Hunter
D. Bob Turley   E. Tom Glavine

21. The 2000 World Series was the 37th appearance in the Fall Classic for the Bronx Bombers. Which Yankee manager has piloted the team in their most appearances?
A. Billy Martin   B. Casey Stengel   C. Miller Huggins
D. Ralph Houk   E. Joe McCarthy

22. Which player has appeared in more World Series (14) and in more games (75) than any other player?
A. Babe Ruth   B. Mickey Mantle   C. Joe DiMaggio
D. Yogi Berra   E. Hank Bauer

23. Which player has appeared in more League Championship Series (11) and in more games (45) than any other player?
A. Rickey Henderson   B. Hal McRae   C. Joe Morgan
D. Chipper Jones   E. Reggie Jackson

24. Which Hall of Famer leads all players with nine home runs in L.C.S. play?
A. Mike Schmidt   B. Harmon Killebrew   C. Willie Stargell
D. Johnny Bench   E. George Brett

25. In five L.C.S. this pitcher has compiled a perfect record of 8 wins and 0 losses—the best mark for any pitcher in L.C.S. play. Who was this pitcher?
A. Tom Glavine   B. Dave Stewart   C. Don Sutton
D. Bob Welch   E. John Candelaria

IIIa. Post-Season: Players—Answers

1. A Gehrig, Ruth and the Yanks won the Series in 1927, 1928 and 1932

2. A Dave McNally had a 1.59 ERA

3. B Maglie was the only Brooklyn pitcher that day. He pitched 8 innings and gave up 5 hits, losing 2-0

4. A Medwick was removed in the 6th inning. Already having built a healthy lead, his departure didn't hurt St. Louis much; the Cardinals won the game 11-0 to win the Series.

5 & 6. D Cleveland Indians The catch was made in the 8th inning, off the bat of Vic Wertz. The Giants swept the Indians four games to none.

7. B Sparky Anderson Cincinnati Reds—NL: 1975 & 1976 Detroit Tigers—AL: 1984

8. E Palmer won Game 2 in 1966, Game 1 in 1970, Game 2 in 1971 and Game 3 in 1983

9. E Larry Jansen He pitched the 9th inning in relief of starter Sal Maglie.

10. D Detroit Tigers—1968

11. E   Babe Ruth   Ruth actually accomplished this feat twice:
October 6, 1926 at St. Louis Cardinals
October 9, 1928 at St. Louis Cardinals

12. D—Bernie Carbo

13. C—Bobby Richardson   New York Yankees—on October 3, 1960 in game 3 against Pittsburgh.

14. B—Reggie Jackson   Oakland Athletics 1973, 1974   New York Yankees 1977, 1978, 1981
30 Games   98 At Bats   35 Hits   74 Total Bases (7 Doubles, 1 Triple, 10 Home Runs)

15. E—Pee Wee Reese

16. A—Robin Yount   Milwaukee Brewers—October 12 & October 17, 1982 vs. the St. Louis Cardinals.

17. D—Paul Molitor   Milwaukee Brewers—October 12, 1982 vs. St. Louis.

18. A—Mickey Mantle

19. D—Duke Snider

20. C—Catfish Hunter

21. B—Casey Stengel—10 Times   7 Wins   3 Losses
    Joe McCarthy —9 Times   7 Wins   2 Losses
    Miller Huggins—6 Times   3 Wins   3 Losses
    Ralph Houk   —3 Times   2 Wins   1 Loss
    Billy Martin —2 Times   1 Win   1 Loss

22. D—Yogi Berra
All games with the New York Yankees

1947—6 Games	1953—6 Games	1960—7 Games
1949—4 Games	1955—7 Games	1961—4 Games
1950—4 Games	1956—7 Games	1962—2 Games
1951—6 Games	1957—7 Games	1963—1 Game
1952—7 Games	1958—7 Games	

23. E—Reggie Jackson

1971—3 Games—Oak.	1975—3 Games—Oak.	1981—2 Games—NYY
1972—5 Games—Oak.	1977—5 Games—NYY	1982—5 Games—Cal.
1973—5 Games—Oak.	1978—4 Games—NYY	1986—6 Games—Cal.
1974—4 Games—Oak.	1980—3 Games—NYY	

24. E   George Brett   Kansas City Royals

25. B   Dave Stewart   Oakland Athletics (6-0)—Toronto Blue Jays (2-0)

IIIb. Post-Season: Teams

1. Four times in the history of the National League there has been a first-place tie at the end of the regular season. To determine the NL champion, a best of three playoffs are used. Oddly enough, the Dodger franchise was involved each time: 1946, 1951, 1959 and 1962. Which one of the following teams was not an opponent of the Dodgers?
A. New York Giants   B. San Francisco Giants   C. St. Louis Cardinals
D. Pittsburgh Pirates   E. Milwaukee Braves

2. The Dodgers only won one of the four playoffs. Which team did they beat?
A. New York Giants   B. San Francisco Giants   C. St. Louis Cardinals
D. Pittsburgh Pirates   E. Milwaukee Braves

3. The 1948 season was the only year the American League needed a pennant playoff to determine its representative in the World Series. Unlike the National League, the American League used only a one game format. Which team did the Cleveland Indians defeat?
A. Boston Red Sox   B. Detroit Tigers   C. New York Yankees   D. Philadelphia Athletics   E. Washington Senators

4. Since 1922 the World Series has always been a best of seven. Prior to that it was, on occasion, a best of nine. How many times did this happen?
A. 1   B. 3   C. 4   D. 5   E. 8

5. Which franchise has gone the longest since winning the World Series?
A. Philadelphia Phillies   B. Chicago Cubs   C. Chicago White Sox
D. Cleveland Indians   E. Boston Red Sox

6. After winning the 2000 World Series, the New York Yankees upped their championship total to 26, the most titles for any professional franchise. Which National League franchise has the most World Series titles?
A. Pittsburgh Pirates   B. St. Louis Cardinals
C. Brooklyn—Los Angeles Dodgers
D. Cincinnati Reds   E. New York—San Francisco Giants

7. Which franchise have the Yankees victimized most in their 26 Series titles?
A. New York—San Francisco Giants
B. Brooklyn—Los Angeles Dodgers   C. St. Louis Cardinals
D. Cincinnati Reds   E. Boston—Milwaukee—Atlanta Braves

8. The Yanks have also lost the Series 11 times. Only one NL franchise can boast that it has a winning record against New York when it comes to the World Series. Which one?
A. New York—San Francisco Giants
B. Brooklyn—Los Angeles Dodgers   C. St. Louis Cardinals
D. Cincinnati Reds   E. Boston—Milwaukee—Atlanta Braves

9. With these 26 world championships how many different franchises have the Yanks bested?
A. 6   B. 8   C. 9   D. 10   E. 12

10. Winning the World Series is not an easy accomplishment. Winning consecutive titles is even harder. The New York Yankees have won the Series five straight times (1949-53). The Bronx Bombers have also put together a string of four consecutive championships (1936-39). Aside from the Yankees, only one franchise has ever won three titles in a row. Name the team and the years in which it won.
A. 1906-07-08 Chicago Cubs   B. 1929-30-31 Philadelphia Athletics
C. 1942-43-44 St. Louis Cardinals
D. 1969-70-71 Baltimore Orioles   E. 1972-73-74 Oakland Athletics

11. Previous to 2000, when was the last time that there was a "Subway Series" in New York?
A. 1950   B. 1952   C. 1954   D. 1956   E. 1958

12. Divisional playoffs were introduced in 1969. In what year was the Wild Card first used?
A. 1992   B. 1993   C. 1995   D. 1996   E. 1997

13. Who was the first Wild Card team in the National League?
A. Colorado Rockies   B. Chicago Cubs   C. San Francisco Giants   D. Pittsburgh Pirates   E. Houston Astros

14. Who was the first Wild Card team in the American League?
A. Seattle Mariners   B. Chicago White Sox   C. Baltimore Orioles   D. Toronto Blue Jays   E. New York Yankees

15. The League Championship Series began in 1969 with the winners going on to the World Series. Excluding recent expansion teams Tampa Bay, Colorado, and Arizona, only one team has never appeared in an LCS. Which team is it?
A. Houston Astros   B. Chicago Cubs   C. Seattle Mariners
D. Montreal Expos   E. Texas Rangers

16. Which team has appeared in the most ALCS?
A. Kansas City Royals   B. Oakland Athletics   C. New York Yankees
D. Cleveland Indians   E. Baltimore Orioles

17. Which team has won the most ALCS?
A. Kansas City Royals   B. Oakland Athletics   C. New York Yankees
D. Cleveland Indians   E. Baltimore Orioles

18. Which team has appeared in the most NLC.S.?
A. New York Mets   B. Atlanta Braves   C. Pittsburgh Pirates
D. Los Angeles Dodgers   E. Cincinnati Reds

19. There are three teams that have won the NLC.S. five times. Which team has lost the most NLC.S.?
A. New York Mets   B. Atlanta Braves   C. Pittsburgh Pirates
D. Los Angeles Dodgers   E. Cincinnati Reds

20. From all these questions you might have been able to deduce that one team has never qualified for post-season play. Who is that lonesome team?
A. Florida Marlins   B. Tampa Bay Devil Rays   C. New York Yankees
D. Arizona Diamondbacks   E. Colorado Rockies

IIIb. Post-Season: Teams—Answers

1.   D   Pittsburgh Pirates

2.   E   Milwaukee Braves   1946 St. Louis over Dodgers 2—0
                            1951 N.Y. Giants over Dodgers 2—1
                            1959 Dodgers over Milwaukee 2—0
                            1962 S.F. Giants over Dodgers 2—1
1980 Houston defeated the Dodgers in a one game playoff for the
Western Division title

3.   A   Boston Red Sox
     The playoff game in 1978, New York over Boston was for the Eastern
     Division title.
     The playoff game in 1995, Seattle over California was for the Western
     Division title.

4.   C   1903, 1919, 1920, 1921

5.   B   The Cubs last won the Series in 1908. The White Sox have the
         second-longest streak, as they have not been crowned champs
         since 1917, giving the Windy City a rather dubious distinction.
         Boston—1918   Cleveland—1948 Philadelphia—1980

6.   B   The Cardinals have won nine titles: 1926, 1931, 1934, 1942,
1944, 1946, 1964, 1967, 1982

7.   B   The Yanks beat the Dodgers in: 1941, 1947, 1949, 1952, 1953,
1956, 1977, 1978

8.   C   The Cardinals defeated the Yanks in 1926, 1942 and 1964. St. Louis has only lost to the Yankees twice, 1928 and 1943.

9.   D   Giants (5), Pirates (1), Cardinals (2), Cubs (2), Reds (2), Dodgers (8), Phillies (1), Braves (3), Padres (1) and Mets (1)

10. E   1972 Oakland 4   Cincinnati Reds 3
         1973 Oakland 4   New York Mets 3
         1974 Oakland 4   Los Angeles Dodgers 1
New York also has World Series titles in 1998, 1999 and 2000

11. D   1956   Yankees over the Dodgers

12. C   1995   The Wild Card was added for the 1994 season, but there were no playoffs that year.

13. A   Colorado Rockies

14. E   New York Yankees

15. E   Texas Rangers

16. B   Oakland Athletics—10 times: 1971, 1972, 1973, 1974, 1975, 1981, 1988, 1989, 1990, 1992

17. C   New York Yankees—8 times: 1976, 1977, 1978, 1981, 1996, 1998, 1999, 2000

18. B   Atlanta Braves—10 times: 1969, 1982, 1991, 1992, 1993, 1995, 1996, 1997, 1998, 1999

19. C   Pittsburgh Pirates—7 times: 1970, 1972, 1974, 1975, 1990, 1991, 1992

20. B   Tampa Bay Devil Rays

IV. Hall of Fame Gallery

1. The National Baseball Hall of Fame opened in Cooperstown, New York in 1935. Babe Ruth was one of the original five inductees and listed below are the other four members of the inaugural class. Which one of the following was not in that first class?
A. Cy Young   B. Walter Johnson   C. Ty Cobb
D. Christey Mathewson   E. Honus Wagner

2. Neither Josh Gibson nor Buck Leonard ever appeared in a Major League game, but both were inducted into the Hall of Fame. The two stars entered together, becoming the first inductees whose careers were spent entirely in the Negro Leagues. In what year did this historic event occur?
A. 1962   B. 1967   C. 1972   D. 1977   E. 1982

3. In his 21-year career pitcher Hoyt Wilhelm played on nine different teams and all nine appear on his Hall of Fame plaque (the most for any plaque). Which one of the following teams did Wilhelm never play for?
A. Cleveland Indians   B. New York Giants   C. New York Yankees
D. Chicago Cubs   E. Atlanta Braves

4. When a player is inducted into the Hall of Fame and he has played for more than one team, there is sometimes a question as to which team's cap he will be pictured wearing. One inductee in 1987 could not make up his mind, thus he is pictured with no insignia on his cap. Who is this indecisive inductee?
A. Ferguson Jenkins   B. Catfish Hunter   C. Rod Carew
D. Billy Williams   E. Joe Morgan

5. Nolan Ryan pitched for four franchises over his 27 seasons. Which of the following teams is not one of them?
A. Houston Astros   B. Los Angeles Dodgers   C. New York Mets
D. Texas Rangers   E. California Angeles

6. Nolan Ryan was inducted into the Hall of Fame in 1999. Which team's cap did he choose to be pictured in?
A. Houston Astros   B. Los Angeles Dodgers   C. New York Mets
D. Texas Rangers   E. California Angeles

7. Many greats of the game are remembered for their days with the Yankees. Which of these Hall of Famers did not play his entire career for the Yanks?
A. Bill Dickey   B. Whitey Ford   C. Phil Rizzuto
D. Lou Gehrig   E. Lefty Gomez

8. The Dodgers also have many greats that are remembered for their days with the team. Which of these Hall of Famers did not play his entire career for the Dodgers?
A. Roy Campanella   B. Duke Snider   C. Pee Wee Reese
D. Don Drysdale   E. Jackie Robinson

9-14. The next several questions list players who were contemporaries in their playing days and who were inducted in the Hall of Fame around the same time (same decade). In each group select the player who did not spend his entire career with one franchise.

9. 1990's: A. Jim Palmer   B. Rollie Fingers   C. Mike Schmidt
D. George Brett   E. Robin Yount

10. 1980's: A. Willie Stargell   B. Al Kaline   C. Lou Brock
D. Bob Gibson   E. Johnny Bench

11. 1970's: A. Early Wynn   B. Roberto Clemente   C. Ernie Banks
D. Sandy Koufax   E. Mickey Mantle

12. 1960's: A. Bob Feller   B. Luke Appling   C. Ted Williams
D. Joe Medwick   E. Stan Musial

13. 1950's: A. Mel Ott   B. Bill Terry   C. Joe DiMaggio
D. Bill Dickey   E. Joe Cronin

14. 1930's/1940's: A. Walter Johnson   B. Christy Mathewson
C. Lou Gehrig   D. Carl Hubbell   E. Charlie Gehringer

15. No player has ever received 100% of the votes cast for enshrinement
into the Hall of Fame. Votes are cast by the Baseball Writers' Association
of America and 75% of votes cast are needed for enshrinement. The top
percentage of votes received was 98.84% by a member of the Class of
1992. Who is this all-time vote getter?
A. Johnny Bench   B. Carl Yastrzemski   C. Reggie Jackson
D. Mike Schmidt   E. Tom Seaver

IV. Hall of Fame Gallery—Answers

1. A   Cy Young was not inducted until 1937

2. C   1972   Satchel Paige was inducted in 1971, but he played in the Major Leagues

3. C   Wilhelm played for the: Cleveland Indians, New York Giants, Chicago Cubs, Atlanta Braves, St. Louis Cardinals, Baltimore Orioles, Chicago White Sox, Los Angeles Dodgers and the Los Angeles Angeles. On his Hall of Fame plaque he is wearing a New York Giants cap.

4. B   Catfish Hunter

5. B   Los Angeles Dodgers

6. D   Texas Rangers

7. E   Lefty Gomez   Yankees 1930-1942   Washington Senators 1943

8. B   Duke Snider   Dodgers 1947-1962   New York Mets 1963   San Francisco Giants 1964

9. B   Rollie Fingers: Oakland 1968-76   San Diego 1977-80   Milwaukee (AL) 1981-85
Jim Palmer—Baltimore
Mike Schmidt—Philadelphia
George Brett—Kansas City
Robin Yount—Milwaukee (AL)

10. C Lou Brock: Chicago (NL) 1964-64 St. Louis 1965-79
Willie Stargell—Pittsburgh
Al Kaline—Detroit
Bob Gibson—St. Louis
Johnny Bench—Cincinnati

11. A Early Wynn: Washington 1939-48 Cleveland 1949-57, 63
Chicago (AL) 1958-62
Roberto Clemente—Pittsburgh
Ernie Banks—Chicago (NL)
Sandy Koufax—Brooklyn/L.A.
Mickey Mantle—New York (AL)

12. D Joe Medwick: St. Louis 1932-40, 47-48 Brooklyn 1940-43, 46
NY (NL) 1943-45 Boston (NL) 1945
Bob Feller—Cleveland Indians
Luke Appling—Chicago (AL)
Ted Williams—Boston (A. L.)
Stan Musial—St. Louis

13. E Joe Cronin: Pittsburgh 1926-27 Washington 1928-34 Boston
(AL) 1935-45
Mel Ott—New York (NL)
Bill Terry—New York (NL)
Joe DiMaggio—New York (AL)
Bill Dickey—New York (AL)

14. B   Christy Mathewson: New York (NL) 1900-16   Cincinnati 1916
Walter Johnson—Washington
Lou Gehrig—New York (AL)
Carl Hubbell—New York (NL)
Charlie Gehringer—Detroit

15. E   Tom Seaver

V. All in the Family

1. One baseball family can claim All-Star honors as the only family to have brothers be named MVP of the All-Star Classic. Who is this All-Star family?
A. Felipe & Matty Alou   B. Sandy, Jr. & Roberto Alomar
C. Joe & Vince DiMaggio   D. Ken & Cletis Boyer
E. Billy & Cal, Jr. Ripken

2. Another family can claim to be the only father-son tandem to win All-Star Game MVP honors. Who is this family?
A. Ken, Sr. & Ken, Jr. Griffey   B. Yogi & Dale Berra
C. Bob & Bret Boone   D. Felipe & Moises Alou
E. Bobby & Barry Bonds

3. All-Star heroics are nice, but these two brothers each claim a plaque in Cooperstown. Who are these Hall of Fame brothers?
A. Joe & Vince DiMaggio   B. Gaylord & Jim Perry
C. Phil & Joe Niekro   D. Paul & Lloyd Waner
E. Dizzy & Daffy Dean

4. It does not happen too often that a pair of brothers makes it to the Majors as pitchers, and this pair can boast of being the only brothers to each toss a no-hitter. Who are these no-hit brothers?
A. Dizzy & Daffy Dean   B. Joe & Phil Niekro   C. Bob & Ken Forsch
D. Greg & Mike Maddux   E. Jim & Gaylord Perry

5. Which of these pitching brothers have combined for the most career victories?
A. Dizzy & Daffy Dean   B. Joe & Phil Niekro   C. Bob & Ken Forsch
D. Greg & Mike Maddux   E. Jim & Gaylord Perry

6. Which two brothers each captured a Cy Young in their careers?
A. Pedro & Ramon Martinez   B. Joe & Phil Niekro
C. Bob & Ken Forsch   D. Greg & Mike Maddux
E. Jim & Gaylord Perry

7. Which brothers have combined to play in the most Major League games?
A. Hank & Tommie Aaron   B. Felipe, Jesus & Matty Alou
C. Ken, Cletis & Cloyd Boyer
D. Dom, Joe & Vince DiMaggio   E. Lloyd & Paul Waner

8. Which brothers have combined for the most career base hits?
A. Hank & Tommie Aaron   B. Felipe, Jesus & Matty Alou
C. Ken, Cletis & Cloyd Boyer
D. Dom, Joe & Vince DiMaggio   E. Lloyd & Paul Waner

9. Which brothers can boast of the highest combined batting average?
A. Hank & Tommie Aaron   B. Felipe, Jesus & Matty Alou
C. Ken, Cletis & Cloyd Boyer
D. Dom, Joe & Vince DiMaggio   E. Lloyd & Paul Waner

10. Which brothers have combined for the most career home runs?
A. Hank & Tommie Aaron   B. Felipe, Jesus & Matty Alou
C. Ken, Cletis & Cloyd Boyer
D. Dom, Joe & Vince DiMaggio   E. Lloyd & Paul Waner

V. All in the Family—Answers

1. B   Sandy Alomar, Jr.—1997   Roberto Alomar—1998

2. A   Ken Griffey, Sr.—1980   Ken Griffey, Jr.—1992

3. D   Paul & Lloyd Waner
The only other pair of brothers in the Hall of Fame are George and Harry Wright.

4. C
Bob Forsch—St. Louis Cardinals on April 16, 1978 vs. Philadelphia Phillies   5—0
                                                    Sept. 26, 1983 vs. Montreal Expos
                              3—0
Ken Forsch—Houston Astros on April 7, 1979 vs. Atlanta Braves
                              6—0

5. B   Niekro, Joe 221 & Phil 318=539 just edge out Perry, Jim 215 & Gaylord 314=529

6. E   Perry, Jim—1970 Minnesota Twins, Gaylord—1972 Cleveland Indians & 1978 San Diego Padres

7. B   Alou, Felipe—2082   Jesus—1380   Matty—1667 =5129 career games

8. E   Waner, Paul—3152   Lloyd—2459 =5611 career base hits

9. E   Lloyd & Paul Waner   .326 Combined BA

10. A   Aaron   Hank—755   Tommie—13=768 career home runs

VI. Franchises

1. In 1901 the American League began play with teams in eight cities. Which of the following cities was not represented in that inaugural season?
A. Boston   B. Chicago   C. New York   D. Cleveland   E. Detroit

2. Which of the following five current American League teams had exactly the same name at the start of the 2001 season as it had at the start of the 1901 season?
A. Toronto Blue Jays   B. Chicago White Sox   C. Kansas City Royals
D. Cleveland Indians   E. Detroit Tigers

3. What were the New York Yankees known as before they were called the Yankees?
A. Knickerbockers   B. Highlanders   C. Gothams
D. Metropolitians   E. Titans

4. The first World Series was played in 1903 between Pittsburgh and Boston. At the time, the Pittsburgh team was called the Pirates, just as it is today. But the Boston team was not known as the Red Sox. What was it called?
A. Pilgrims   B. Lobsters   C. Patriots   D. Beaneaters   E. Tea-Tossers

5. In what year did the beloved Dodgers play their last season at Ebbets Field and by moving, turn the world upside-down for the fans and residents of Brooklyn?
A. 1955   B. 1956   C. 1957   D. 1958   E. 1959

6. The Seattle Pilots only played for one season. What year was it?
A. 1966   B. 1968   C. 1969   D. 1971   E. 1973

7. The Pilots then moved to become what team?
A. Milwaukee Brewers   B. Los Angeles Angels   C. Toronto Blue Jays
D. Montreal Expos   E. Kansas City Royals

8. What team did the St. Louis Browns become when they moved in 1954?
A. San Diego Padres   B. Kansas City Royals   C. Houston Colt 45's
D. Baltimore Orioles   E. Minnesota Twins

9. The city of Washington, D.C. had an American League franchise from 1901-1960. In 1961 the Washington Senators moved to become what team?
A. Kansas City Royals   B. Baltimore Orioles   C. Texas Rangers
D. Houston Astros   E. Minnesota Twins

10. Despite the move, the Senators did not vanish from baseball until 11 years later, because the American League awarded Washington a new franchise upon the relocation of the first. But in 1972, the second incarnation of the Senators followed its predecessor by moving as well. Which team did they become?
A. Seattle Mariners   B. Colorado Rockies   C. Toronto Blue Jays
D. Texas Rangers   E. Minnesota Twins

11. Which team plays its home games in the oldest ball park at the start of the 2001 season?
A. Kansas City Royals—Kauffman Stadium
B. New York Yankees—Yankee Stadium
C. Boston Red Sox—Fenway Park
D. Los Angeles Dodgers—Dodger Stadium
E. Chicago Cubs—Wrigley Field

12. The record for losses in a single season is an astounding 120. Which franchise tops the loss chart?
A. 1905 Boston Braves   B. 1910 St. Louis Browns
C. 1956 Kansas City Athletics
D. 1962 New York Mets   E. 1969 San Diego Padres

13. Although, the record for one season is 120 losses, this franchise took losing to new (lows) with a record five consecutive 100 loss seasons. Name this franchise.
A. 1907—11 Boston Braves   B. 1926—30 St. Louis Browns
C. 1938—42 Philadelphia Phillies
D. 1962—66 New York Mets   E. 1977—81 Toronto Blue Jays

14. Which franchise has lost the most with a record sixteen 100-loss seasons?
A. St. Louis Browns—Baltimore Orioles
B. Philadelphia—Kansas City—Oakland Athletics
C. Chicago Cubs   D. Cleveland Indians   E. Boston Red Sox

15. What team is hoping that someday its Major League record of 23 consecutive losses will be broken?
A. 1955 Washington Senators   B. 1961 Philadelphia Phillies
C. 1964 New York Mets
D. 1977 Toronto Blue Jays   E. 1988 Baltimore Orioles

16—17. Only four teams, two from each league, have been able to have three consecutive seasons of 100 or more victories. The first to do so were the 1929—31 Philadelphia Athletics (AL) and the most recent were the 1997—99 Atlanta Braves (NL). Select the correct team in each question.

16. Who is the other American League team?
A. 1935—37 New York Yankees   B. 1954—56 Cleveland Indians
C. 1969—71 Baltimore Orioles
D. 1977—79 Kansas City Royals   E. 1991—93 Toronto Blue Jays

17. Who is the other National League team?
A. 1933—35 Chicago Cubs   B. 1942—44 St. Louis Cardinals
C. 1953—55 Brooklyn Dodgers
D. 1975—77 Cincinnati Reds   E. 1990—92 Pittsburgh Pirates

18. Which franchise has compiled the most 100 win seasons (15)?
A. Brooklyn/Los Angeles Dodgers
B. Philadelphia/Kansas City/Oakland Athletics
C. Detroit Tigers   D. New York/San Francisco Giants
E. New York Yankees

19. Which organization tops all others with 16 Rookie of the Year Award winners?
A. Chicago Cubs   B. Pittsburgh Pirates   C. New York Yankees
D. St. Louis Cardinals
E. Brooklyn/Los Angeles Dodgers

20. The Cy Young Award was first given in 1956. Which franchise has had the most number of pitchers claim at least one Cy Young?
A. Boston Red Sox   B. Brooklyn/Los Angeles Dodgers
C. Milwaukee/Atlanta Braves
D. New York Yankees   E. Baltimore Orioles

21. Which franchise has had their pitchers win the most Cy Young Awards?
A. Boston Red Sox   B. Brooklyn/Los Angeles Dodgers
C. Milwaukee/Atlanta Braves   D. New York Yankees
E. Baltimore Orioles

22. It is probably a safe assumption that a pitcher of the Colorado Rockies calling Coors Field his home park will not likely earn a Cy Young Award. Besides the Rockies, only four other franchises have not had a member of their staff win the Cy Young. They are listed below along with a fifth. Which one of these organizations is the only one to have a Cy Young pitcher?
A. Florida Marlins   B. Tampa Bay Devil Rays   C. Minnesota Twins
D. Texas Rangers   E. Cincinnati Reds

23. Since 1901 which National League franchise has pitched the most no-hit games (19)? All games must be at least nine innings
A. Chicago Cubs   B. New York/San Francisco Giants
C. Pittsburgh Pirates
D. Brooklyn/Los Angeles Dodgers   E. St. Louis Cardinals

24. Which American League franchise has pitched the most no-hit games (15)?
A. Chicago White Sox   B. St. Louis Browns/Baltimore Orioles
C. Cleveland Indians
D. Detroit Tigers   E. Los Angeles/California/Anaheim Angels

25. Which NL franchise has been the victim of the most no-hitters (16)?
A. New York Mets   B. Chicago Cubs   C. Philadelphia Phillies
D. Cincinnati Reds   E. Boston/Milwaukee/Atlanta Braves

26. Which franchise has been the victim of the most no-hitters in the AL (14)?
A. Toronto Blue Jays   B. Cleveland Indians   C. Boston Red Sox
D. Philadelphia/Kansas City/Oakland Athletics
E. St. Louis Browns/Baltimore Orioles

27. For a starting pitcher, the hallmark of a successful season is 20 victories. In 1920, the Chicago White Sox had such a dominant rotation that four pitchers reached this plateau. This astounding feat has only been matched by one other staff. Which one?
A. 1954 Cleveland Indians   B. 1966 Los Angeles Dodgers
C. 1971 Baltimore Orioles
D. 1973 Oakland Athletics   E. 1993 Atlanta Braves

28. Everyone knows that the Brooklyn Dodgers were the first to field a black player when Jackie Robinson suited up in 1947. But can you name the first American League franchise to follow the Dodgers' lead?
A. Chicago White Sox   B. Cleveland Indians   C. Washington Senators
D. Detroit Tigers   E. Kansas City Athletics

29. Who is the player referred to in the previous question?
A. Hector Lopez   B. Larry Doby   C. Luke Easter
D. Bob Boyd   E. Satchel Paige

30. Baseball purists cringed when the American League adopted the Designated Hitter rule. In what year did this heinous crime occur?
A. 1968   B. 1970   C. 1973   D. 1975   E. 1978

31. In 1999, this team established a single season Major League record for fielding excellence with a .989 percentage.
A. Cleveland Indians   B. Arizona Diamondbacks   C. New York Mets
D. Baltimore Orioles   E. Los Angeles Dodgers

32. How many errors did the above team commit?
A. 68   B. 78   C. 88   D. 98   E. 108

33. The League Championship Series began in 1969 and the New York Mets won that initial series and their first National League pennant. The "Miracle Mets" then went on to defeat the Baltimore Orioles in five games to claim thier first World Series title. Name the team the Mets defeated in that first NLC.S..
A. Los Angeles Dodgers   B. Cincinnati Reds   C. Houston Astros
D. San Francisco Giants   E. Atlanta Braves

34. The National League is the senior circuit and it began play in 1876. Only one franchise from that initial season is still in existence, that is, the franchise has not relocated to another city, nor folded at some point only to re-enter the NL in another season. Which franchise?
A. Philadelphia Phillies   B. Chicago Cubs   C. Pittsburgh Pirates
D. Cincinnati Reds   E. St. Louis Cardinals

35. Which National League franchise has played the most games (18,465)?
A. Philadelphia Phillies   B. Chicago Cubs   C. Pittsburgh Pirates
D. Cincinnati Reds   E. St. Louis Cardinals

36. Which National League franchise has won the most games (9,924)?
A. Philadelphia Phillies   B. Chicago Cubs   C. Pittsburgh Pirates
D. Cincinnati Reds   E. St. Louis Cardinals

37. Which National League franchise has lost the most games (9,496)?
A. Philadelphia Phillies   B. Chicago Cubs   C. Pittsburgh Pirates
D. Cincinnati Reds   E. St. Louis Cardinals

38. Which American League franchise has played the most games (15,556)?
A. Cleveland Indians   B. Detroit Tigers   C. New York Yankees
D. Boston Red Sox   E. Chicago White Sox

39. Which American League franchise has won the most games (8,579)?
A. Cleveland Indians   B. Detroit Tigers   C. New York Yankees
D. Boston Red Sox   E. Chicago White Sox

40. Which American League franchise has lost the most games (7,642)?
A. Claveland Indians   B. Detroit Tigers   C. New York Yankees
D. Boston Red Sox   E. Chicago White Sox

41. Which team holds the record for home runs in a season (264)?
A. Colorado Rockies   B. Texas Rangers   C. Baltimore Orioles
D. Chicago Cubs   E. Seattle Mariners

42. New ballparks are the rage, with many new parks opening since April of 1999. Which one of the following teams did not receive one of these new fields?
A. Houston Astros   B. Cleveland Indians   C. San Francisco Giants
D. Seattle Mariners   E. Detroit Tigers

43. It is so nice to see natural grass in these new parks. Still, at the start of the 2001 season six teams were playing on the "fake" stuff. Which one of the following plays on the "real" thing?
A. Cincinnati Reds   B. St. Louis Cardinals   C. Montreal Expos
D. Minnesota Twins   E. Philadelphia Phillies

44. Match the following stadiums of the past with the team that they housed.

Briggs Stadium	_____ Brooklyn Dodgers
Crosley Field	_____ Cincinnati Reds
Ebbets Field	_____ Detroit Tigers
Forbes Field	_____ Montreal Expos
Griffith Stadium	_____ New York Giants
Jarry Park	_____ Philadelphia
Athletics	
Polo Grounds	_____ Pittsburgh Pirates
Shibe Park	_____ St. Louis Browns
Sportman's Park	_____ Washington
Senators	

45. Match the following stadiums with the team that they currently house.

Bank One Ballpark	_____ Anaheim Angels
Cinergy Field	_____ Arizona
	Diamondbacks
Comerica Park	_____ Cincinnati Reds
Coors Field	_____ Cleveland Indians
Edison Field	_____ Colorado Rockies
Enron Field	_____ Detroit Tigers
Jacobs Field	_____ Houston Astros
Network Associates	
Coliseum	_____ Oakland Athletics
Pacific Bell Park	_____ San Diego Padres
Qualcomm Stadium	_____ San Francisco
	Giants
Safeco Field	_____ Seattle Mariners
Tropicana Field	_____ Tampa Bay Devil
	Rays

VI. Franchises—Answers

1. C   New York

2. E   Detroit

3. B   Highlanders

4. A   Pilgrims   Boston won the first World Series 5 games to 3 games.

5. C   1957

6. C   1969   The Pilots won 64 games in their first and only season.

7. A   Milwaukee Brewers   The team fared slightly better in their new city, winning 65 games.

8. D   Baltimore Orioles

9. E   Minnesota Twins

10. D   Texas Rangers

11. C   Boston Red Sox   Fenway Park—First game: April 20, 1912
      Chicago Cubs   Wrigley Field—First game: April 20, 1916
      New York Yankees   Yankee Stadium—First game: April 18, 1923

12. D   1962 New York Mets

13. C   Philadelphia Phillies   1938—105 Losses   1941—111 Losses
                                   1939—106 Losses   1942—109 Losses
                                   1940—103 Losses

14. B   Philadelphia—Kansas City—Oakland Athletics—16 Seasons
1915—109 Losses (Phil.)   1940—100 Losses (Phil.)   1956—102 Losses
                                                       (K.C.)
1916—117 Losses (Phil.)   1943—105 Losses (Phil.)   1961—100 Losses
                                                       (K.C.)
1919—104 Losses (Phil.)   1946—105 Losses (Phil.)   1964—105 Losses
                                                       (K.C.)
1920—106 Losses (Phil.)   1950—102 Losses (Phil.)   1965—103 Losses
                                                       (K.C.)
1921—100 Losses (Phil.)   1954—103 Losses (Phil.)   1979—108 Losses
                                                       (Oak.)
1936—100 Losses (Phil.)

15. B   1961 Philadelphia Phillies

16. C   Baltimore Orioles won 109, 108, and 101 games respectively.

17. B   St. Louis Cardinals won 106, 105, and 105 games respectively.

18. E   New York Yankees—15 Seasons
1927—110 Wins   1937—102 Wins   1954—103 Wins   1978—100 Wins
1928—101 Win   1939—106 Wins   1961—109 Wins   1980—103 Wins
1932—107 Wins   1941—101 Wins   1963—104 Wins   1998—114 Wins
1936—102 Wins   1942—103 Wins   1977—100 Wins

19. E   Brooklyn/Los Angeles Dodgers
1947—Jackie Robinson   1969—Ted Sizemore   1992—Eric Karros
1949—Don Newcombe   1979—Rick Sutcliffe   1993—Mike Piazza

1952—Joe Black   1980—Steve Howe   1994—Raul
                                                     Mondesi
1953—Junior Gilliam   1981—Fernando Valenzuela 1995—
                                                     Hideo
                                                     Nomo
1960—Frank Howard   1982—Steve Sax   1996—Todd
                                                     Hollandsworth
1965—Jim Lefebvre

20. B   Brooklyn/Los Angeles Dodgers—Six different pitchers
Don Newcombe—1956   Sandy Koufax—1963, 1965 & 1966
Fernando Valenzuela—1981
Don Drysdale—1962   Mike Marshall—1974
Orel Hershiser—1988

21. B   Brooklyn/Los Angeles Dodgers—Eight Awards (See previous answer)
Milwaukee/Atlanta Braves Baltimore Orioles   New York Yankees
Warren Spahn—1957   Mike Cuellar—1969   Bob Turley—1958
Tom Glavine—1991 & 1998 Jim Palmer—1973, 1975 & 1976
Whitey Ford—1961
Greg Maddux—1993, 1994 & 1995   Mike Flanagan—1979
Sparky Lyle—1977
Steve Stone—1980   Ron Guidry—1978

Boston Red Sox   Jim Lonborg—1967
                        Roger Clemens—1986, 1987 & 1991
                        Pedro Martinez—1999, 2000

22. C   Minnesota Twins—Frank Viola—1988

23. D   Brooklyn—Los Angeles Dodgers

24. A　Chicago White Sox

25. C　Philadelphia Phillies

26. D　Philadelphia/Kansas City/Oakland Athletics

27. C　1971 Baltimore Orioles:　　　1920 Chicago White Sox:

        Dave McNally　21—5　　Red Faber　　23—12

        Pat Dobson　　20—8　　Lefty Williams　　22—14

        Mike Cuellar　20—9　　Dickie Kerr　　　21—9

        Jim Palmer　　20—9　　Eddie Cicotte　21- 10

28. B　Cleveland Indians

29. B　Larry Doby

30. C　1973

31. C　New York Mets

32. A　68 Errors

33. E　Atlanta Braves　　The Mets swept the Braves in three games.

34. B　Chicago Cubs

35. B　Chicago Cubs

36. B　Chicago Cubs

37. A　Philadelphia Phillies

38. B Detroit Tigers

39. C New York Yankees

40. E Chicago White Sox

41. E Seattle Mariners

42. B Cleveland Indians—Jacobs Field: First game—April 4, 1994

43. B St. Louis Cardinals

44. Stadiums of the past:

Briggs Stadium	Detroit Tigers: 1938—60
Crosley Field	Cincinnati Reds: 1912—70
Ebbets Field	Brooklyn Dodgers: 1913—57
Forbes Field	Pittsburgh Pirates: 1909—70
Griffith Stadium	Washington Senators: 1903—60
Jarry Park	Montreal Expos: 1969—76
Polo Grounds	New York Giants: 1891—1957
Shibe Park	Philadelphia Athletics: 1909—54
Sportsman's Park	St. Louis Browns: 1902—53

45. Current stadiums:

Bank One Ballpark	Arizona Diamondbacks
Cincergy Field	Cincinnati Reds
Comerica Park	Detroit Tigers
Coors Field	Colorado Rockies
Edison Field	Anaheim Angels
Enron Field	Houston Astros
Jacobs Field	Cleveland Indians
Network Associates Coliseum	Oakland Athletics

Pacific Bell Park   San Francisco Giants
Qualcomm Stadium   San Diego Padres
Safeco Field   Seattle Mariners
Tropicana Field   Tampa Bay Devil Rays

VII. Trades

1. Roger Maris is best known for his playing days with the New York Yankees. The Yanks acquired Maris on December 11, 1959 in a trade. What team did they acquire him from?
A. Kansas City Athletics   B. St. Louis Cardinals   C. Detroit Tigers
D. Pittsburgh Pirates   E. Cleveland Indians

2. On March 30, 1992 the Chicago Cubs acquired Sammy Sosa. Which team let Slammin' Sammy go?
A. Philadelphia Phillies   B. Texas Rangers   C. Houston Astros
D. Chicago White Sox   E. Oakland Athletics

3. On November 18, 1954 the New York Yankees obtained pitchers Don Larsen and Bob Turley in one of Major League Baseball's biggest trades of all-time. This blockbuster trade would involve 18 players and not be finalized until December 1, 1954. What team did the Yanks trade with?
A. Boston Red Sox   B. Brooklyn Dodgers   C. New York Giants
D. Washington Senators   E. Baltimore Orioles

4. Throughout Major League history teams have occasionally traded their superstar players. On June 15, 1977 the New York Mets did just that, trading Tom Seaver. To what team?
A. Boston Red Sox   B. New York Yankees   C. Atlanta Braves
D. Cincinnati Reds   E. Philadelphia Phillies

5. For many Cleveland Indian fans, April 17, 1960 was a black day, for reigning home run champ and fan favorite Rocky Colavito was sent packing. To what team was Colavito traded?
A. Chicago White Sox   B. Kansas City Athletics
C. Washington Senators   D. Baltimore Orioles   E. Detroit Tigers

6. On December 13, 1956 the Brooklyn Dodgers did their part in making their fans cry. The Dodgers traded Jackie Robinson. However, Robinson then retired and the trade was cancelled. To what team did the Dodgers want to trade Robinson?
A. Chicago Cubs   B. New York Giants   C. St. Louis Cardinals
D. Pittsburgh Pirates   E. Milwaukee Braves

7. Reggie Jackson is known for his playing days with both the Oakland Athletics and the New York Yankees. Between his time with the A's and the Yanks, Jackson had a short stay in another city. What team received Jackson in this trade on April 2, 1976?
A. California Angels   B. Boston Red Sox   C. Baltimore Orioles
D. Chicago White Sox   E. Kansas City Royals

8. Fans associate future Hall of Fame shortstop Ozzie Smith's trademark back flip with the St. Louis Cardinals. On February 11, 1982 the Cardinals received Smith in a trade for Garry Templeton. With what team did the Cardinals trade?
A. Los Angeles Dodgers   B. San Diego Padres   C. San Francisco Giants
D. Houston Astros   E. Seattle Mariners

9. Believe it or not, legendary catcher Bob Uecker was obtained in a trade by the St. Louis Cardinals on April 9, 1964. What team let Uecker get away?
A. Milwaukee Braves   B. New York Mets   C. Chicago Cubs
D. Pittsburgh Pirates   E. Los Angeles Dodgers

10. For baseball fans Pete Rose will always be pictured as a Cincinnati Red. On December 5, 1978 Rose was not traded, but he signed with this team as a free agent. What team did Rose sign with?
A. Montreal Expos   B. St. Louis Cardinals   C. Chicago Cubs
D. Philadelphia Phillies   E. Atlanta Braves

VII. Trades—Answers

1. A—Kansas City Athletics Maris was traded with Joe De Maestri and Kent Hadley for Hank Bauer, Don Larsen, Norm Siebern and Marv Throneberry.

2. D—Chicago White Sox   Sosa was traded with Ken Patterson for George Bell

3. E—Baltimore Orioles   The first part of the trade was Larsen and Turley along with Billy Hunter were traded for Harry Byrd, Jim McDonald, Hal Smith, Gus Triandos, Gene Woodling and Willie Wiranda. The second part of the trade was Mike Blyzka, Darrell Johnson, Dick Kryhoski and Jim Fridley to the Yankees for Bill Miller, Kal Segrist, Don Leppert, minor league OF Ted Del Guercio, and a player to be named later.

4.   D—Cincinnati Reds   Seaver was traded for Pat Zachry, Doug Flynn, Steve Henderson and Dan Norman.

5.   E—Detroit Tigers   Colavito was traded for Harvey Kuenn

6.   B—New York Giants

7.   C—Baltimore Orioles   Jackson was traded with Ken Holtzman and minor leaguer Bill Van Bommell for Don Baylor, Mike Torez and Paul Mitchell.

8.   B—San Diego Padres

9. A—Milwaukee Braves Uecker was actually traded for two players: Jimmie Coker and Gary Kolb.

10. D—Philadelphia Phillies

VIII. Uniform Numbers

1. The New York Yankees have retired more uniform numbers (14) than any other Major League franchise. Match the Yankee great with his retired number. Please note that two players share the same retired number.

#1	#5	#8	#15	#32
#3	#7	#9	#16	#37
#4	#8	#10	#23	#44

____Yogi Berra   ____Elston Howard   ____Don Mattingly
____Bill Dickey   ____Reggie Jackson   ____Thurman Munson
____Joe DiMaggio   ____Mickey Mantle   ____Phil Rizzuto
____Whitey Ford   ____Roger Maris   ____Babe Ruth
____Lou Gehrig   ____Billy Martin   ____Casey Stengel

2. The #5 has graced the backs of some of the greatest players of all-time. In addition to the New York Yankees, five other franchises have retired #5. These five players are all inducted in to the Hall of Fame. Which of the following players did not wear #5?
A. Lou Boudreau   B. George Brett   C. Johnny Bench
D. Brooks Robinson   E. Joe Morgan

3. Match the following uniform numbers with the Hall of Fame players that wore them.

#1	#9	#24	#41
#3	#14	#29	#42
#4	#19	#32	#44
#6	#20	#34	#72
#8	#21		

____Hank Aaron   ____Harmon Killebrew   ____Jackie Robinson

____Ernie Banks   ____Sandy Koufax   ____Nolan Ryan

____Rod Carew   ____Willie Mays   ____Tom Seaver

____Roberto Clemente   ____Stan Musial   ____Duke Snider

____Bob Feller   ____Pee Wee Reese   ____Ted Williams

____Carlton Fisk   ____Frank Robinson   ____Carl Yastrzemski

4. Match the following uniform numbers with today's superstars (along with one recently retired player).

#1	#7	#21	#31
#2	#8	#22	#35
#3	#10	#25	#45
#5	#19	#30	#51

____Roger Clemens   ____Chipper Jones   ____Alex Rodriguez

____Nomar Garciaparra   ____Pedro Martinez   ____Ivan Rodriguez

____Ken Griffey, Jr.   ____Mark McGwire   ____Ozzie Smith

____Tony Gwynn   ____Mike Piazza   ____Sammy Sosa

____Derek Jeter   ____Cal Ripken, Jr.   ____Frank Thomas

____Randy Johnson

5. There have been five Hall of Fame players fortunate enough to have their numbers retired by more than one organization. Which of the following does not have his number retired by more than one team?
A. Frank Robinson   B. Nolan Ryan   C. Tom Seaver
D. Rod Carew   E. Hank Aaron

6. Taking it one step further, only one of above players has had his uniform retired by three different teams. Who is this player?
A. Frank Robinson   B. Nolan Ryan   C. Tom Seaver
D. Rod Carew   E. Hank Aaron

7. There is only one manager who had the distinction of having his number retired by two different teams. Who is this manager?
A. Casey Stengel   B. Earl Weaver   C. Danny Murtaugh
D. Al Lopez   E. Whitey Herzog

8. Major League Baseball has retired one number in honor of which truly remarkable player?
A. Babe Ruth   B. Cy Young   C. Willie Mays
D. Ted Williams   E. Jackie Robinson

VIII. Uniform Numbers—Answers

1. Retired New York Yankee uniform numbers:

#8—Yogi Berra	#32—Elston Howard	#23—Don Mattingly
#8—Bill Dickey	#44—Reggie Jackson	#15—Thurman Munson
#5—Joe DiMaggio	#7—Mickey Mantle	#10—Phil Rizzuto
#16—Whitey Ford	#9—Roger Maris	#3—Babe Ruth
#4—Lou Gehrig	#1—Billy Martin	#37—Casey Stengel

2. E—Joe Morgan   Cincinnati Reds retired #8 in honor of Joe Morgan Hank Greenberg—Detroit Tigers—also retired #5

3. Retired Hall of Fame uniform numbers:
#44—Hank Aaron—Atlanta Braves & Milwaukee Brewers
#14—Ernie Banks—Chicago Cubs
#29—Rod Carew—Anaheim Angels & Minnesota Twins
#21—Roberto Clemente—Pittsburgh Pirates
#19—Bob Feller—Cleveland Indians
#72—Carlton Fisk—Chicago White Sox
#3—Harmon Killebrew—Minnesota Twins
#32—Sandy Koufax—Los Angeles Dodgers
#24—Willie Mays—San Francisco Giants
#6—Stan Musial—St. Louis Cardinals
#1—Pee Wee Reese—Los Angeles Dodgers
#20—Frank Robinson—Cincinnati Reds & Baltimore Orioles
#42—Jackie Robinson—Los Angeles Dodgers
#34—Nolan Ryan—Texas Rangers & Houston Astros

#41—Tom Seaver—New York Mets
#4—Duke Snider—Los Angeles Dodgers
#9—Ted Williams—Boston Red Sox
#8—Carl Yastrzemski—Boston Red Sox

4. Today's superstars uniform numbers:

#22—Roger Clemens—Yankees   #25—Mark McGwire—Cardinals
#5—Nomar Garciaparra—Red Sox   #31—Mike Piazza—Mets
#30—Ken Griffey, Jr.—Reds   #8—Cal Ripken, Jr.—Orioles
#19—Tony Gwynn—Padres   #3—Alex Rodriguez—Rangers
#2—Derek Jeter—Yankees   #7—Ivan Rodriguez—Rangers
#51—Randy Johnson—Diamondbacks   #1—Ozzie   Smith—
Cardinals (Retired)
#10—Chipper Jones—Braves   #21—Sammy Sosa—Cubs
#45—Pedro Martinez—Red Sox   #35—Frank Thomas—White Sox

5. C—Tom Seaver—New York Mets Frank Robinson—Cincinnati Reds
                                 & Baltimore Orioles
                                 Rod Carew—Minnesota Twins &
                                 Anaheim Angels
                                 Hank Aaron—Atlanta Braves &
                                 Milwaukee Brewers
                                 Nolan Ryan—Anaheim Angels,
                                 Texas Rangers and
                                 Houston Astros

6. B—Nolan Ryan   Texas and Houston retired #34 and Anaheim
retired #30

7. A—Casey Stengel   New York Yankees & New York Mets

8. E—Jackie Robinson   #42 is permanently retired in honor of Jackie
Robinson

SECTION 2—PLAYER COMPARISONS

Baseball fans in any era love the home run. Fans have been thrilled by who hit the farthest; the most; how many for a career; how many for one season. Probably the three most well-known home run hitters of all-time are Babe Ruth, "The Sultan of Swat", the standard by which all other home run hitters are measured; Hank Aaron, "Hammerin' Hank", who measured up to the Babe and passed him on the all-time home run list; and Mark McGwire, "Big Mac", today's home run hero and the single season record holder with an incredible 70 home runs. These three players are from different eras but they all have one thing in common—the home run. One of the best things about baseball is that we can compare, at least on paper, the statistics of players from different eras. Have some fun and select the correct player for each question.

A. Hank Aaron   B. Mark McGwire   C. Babe Ruth

1. _____All three are members of the 500 Home Run Club, but who was the youngest when he hit his 500th home run?

2. _____With 11 seasons to his credit, which player holds the Major League record for seasons with 40 home runs?

3. _____Oddly enough, one of the three never had a 50 home run season. Who?

4. _____All three are in the top four all-time in multiple home run games. Surprisingly, none of these three home run kings ever hit four home runs in a game. However, they have all circled the bases three times in a game. Who leads the way with five three home run games?

5. _____Which player has the most two home run games? (He has 70 such games.)

6. _____All three have excelled with the bases loaded, as two of the three have 16 career grand slams. Who is the low man with **only** 13 career grand slams?

7. _____Who holds the Major League record for home run percentage for a single season?

8. _____Who holds the Major League record for home run percentage for his career?

9. _____We know all three are prolific home run hitters, but a player can't always hit a homer. Who is the only one of the three to lead his league in base hits?

10. _____Home run hitters have been known to occasionally strike out. Who has the lowest career strike out percentage?

11. _____Who has the highest career slugging percentage?

12. _____Who has the most seasons with 300 total bases? In fact, he is the career Major League leader in this category.

Answers to Aaron—McGwire—Ruth

1. A—Hank Aaron—34 yrs. 4 mos. 9 days   Babe Ruth 34 yrs. 6 mos. 5 days
    Mark McGwire 35 yrs. 10 mos. 4 days

2. C—Babe Ruth

1920—54	1924—46	1928—54	1931—46
1921—59	1926—47	1929—46	1932—41
1923—41	1927—60	1930—49	

Hank Aaron

1957—44	1966—44
1960—40	1969—44
1962—45	1971—47
1963—44	1973—40

Mark McGwire

1987—49	1997—58*
1992—42	1998—70
1996—52	1999—65

*2 Teams—Oakland—34   St. Louis—24

3. A—Hank Aaron

4. B—Mark McGwire

Mark McGwire	Babe Ruth	Hank Aaron
June 27, 1987	May 21, 1930	June 21, 1959
June 11, 1995	May 25, 1935	
April 14, 1998	October 6, 1926 (W.S.)	
May 19, 1998	October 9, 1928 (W.S.)	
May 18, 2000		

5. C—Babe Ruth   Hank Aaron   Mark McGwire
   70—2 HR Games   61—2 HR Games   59—2 HR Games
   72 Multi HR Games   62 Multi HR Games   64 Multi HR Games

6. B—Mark McGwire

7. B—Mark McGwire   13.8%

8. B—Mark McGwire—9.4%   Babe Ruth—8.5%   Hank
   Aaron—6.1%

9. A—Hank Aaron   1956—200 Hits
                       1959—223 Hits

10. A—Hank Aaron—11.2%
    Babe Ruth—15.8%   Mark McGwire—25.1%

11. C—Babe Ruth—.690   1st All-Time
    Mark McGwire—.593   6th All-Time
    Hank Aaron   —.555   20th All-Time

12. A—Hank Aaron—15   Babe Ruth   —11
                        Mark McGwire—2

The following questions concern three favorites of New York City base-ball fans in the mid 1950's: Mickey Mantle, Willie Mays and Duke Snider. The three played together (as regulars) in New York City for only four seasons: 1954, 55, 56 & 57, but New Yorkers had their favorite player and no one could convince these fans that their hero was not the best. Mantle, Mays and Snider all played centerfield and this only served to make the debate on who was best even more heated. During these glo-rious years, fans of all three teams celebrated a World Series Championship: Mays and the Giants in 1954, Snider and the Dodgers in 1955, and Mantle and the Yankees in 1956. Mantle, Mays and Snider all had stellar careers and were honored as such with induction into Baseball's Hall of Fame. However, since fans stand true to their favorite teams and players nothing is ever really settled as to who was the best.

The following questions are divided into two sections: the first section will only concern the years 1954, 55, 56 & 57—the years Mantle, Mays and Snider actually played together (as regulars) in New York. The second section will concern their entire careers. These questions are in no way intended to say who was the best, but only serve as a comparison of the three on paper.

A. Mickey Mantle   B. Willie Mays   C. Duke Snider

Section A: 1954—1955—1956—1957

1. _____Two of the three won MVP Awards in these years; who is the odd man out?

2. _____All three were home run hitters and the numbers are close: 165—163—150. Which one hit the most home runs during these four seasons?

3. _____All three were big run producers and each had over 400 RBI's for these four years. Which player led the way with 459 RBI's?

4. _____When it comes to the batting averages for these four seasons, all three hit over .300. Which one wins the batting title?

SECTION B: Career

5. _____His .365 avg. in 1957 was the top single season average.

6. _____His .302 avg. was the top career average.

7. _____His .286 avg. was the top World Series average.

8. _____Oddly enough, there was only one season in which any one of the three had a 200-hit season. Who did it with 208 hits in 1958?

9. _____Who was the only one of the three to hit for the cycle? It occurred on July 23, 1957.

10. ____ ____Which two led their league in runs scored for three consecutive seasons? This gives each a share of the Major League record.

11. _____All three had extra base power. The best mark for extra base hits in a single season was 90 in 1962. Which one?

12. ____Who was the center fielder on the first Gold Glove team in 1957?

Answers to Mantle—Mays—Snider

Section A

1. C—Duke Snider Willie Mays—1954 MVP   Mickey   Mantle—
                                                1956 & 1957 MVP

2. C—Duke Snider 40—42—43—40=165 HR   Mays   41—51—
                                            36—35=163 HR
                                            Mantle 27—37—
                                            52—34=150 HR

3. C—Duke Snider   130—136—101—92=459 RBI
      Mickey Mantle 102—99—130—94=425 RBI
      Willie Mays   110—127—84—97=418 RBI

4. A—Mickey Mantle   Willie Mays   Duke Snider
   1954 163 Hits 543 AB 1954 195 Hits 565 AB 1954 199 Hits 584 AB
   1955 158 Hits 517 AB 1955 185 Hits 580 AB 1955 166 Hits 538 AB
   1956 188 Hits 533 AB 1956 171 Hits 578 AB 1956 158 Hits 542 AB
   1957 173 Hits 474 AB 1957 195 Hits 585 AB 1957 139 Hits 508 AB
          682 Hits 2067 AB   746 Hits 2308 AB   662 Hits 2172 AB
          .330 AVG   .323 AVG   .305 AVG

Section B

5. A—Mickey Mantle   Willie Mays   1958—.347 Best
                        Duke Snider   1954—.341 Best

6. B—Willie Mays   Mickey Mantle   .298 Career BA
                        Duke Snider   .295 Career BA

7. C—Duke Snider   Mickey Mantle   .257 World Series BA
                        Willie Mays   .239 World Series BA

8. B—Willie Mays   Duke Snider   1950 & 1954   199 Hits
                                                          Best Season
                        Mickey Mantle   1956   188 Hits Best
                                                          Season

9. A—Mickey Mantle

10. A—Mickey Mantle   1956—57—58 Led AL in runs scored
    C—Duke Snider   1953—54—55 Led NL in runs scored

11. B—
Willie Mays   1962   36 Doubles 5 Triples 49 Home Runs =90   Extra
                                                                  Base Hits
Duke Snider   1954   39 Doubles 10 Triples 40 Home Runs =89   Extra
                                                                  Base Hits
Mickey Mantle 1956   22 Doubles 5 Triples 52 Home Runs =79   Extra
                                                                  Base Hits

12. B—Willie Mays

Three of the greatest ever to play the game were Joe DiMaggio, "The Yankee Clipper"; Stan Musial, "Stan the Man"; and Ted Williams, "The Splendid Splinter". Fans in the late 1930's, 1940's and 1950's got to see three of the greatest ballplayers ever to grace a baseball diamond. All three were legends even as they played, and after their playing days their baseball legacy still lives on. DiMaggio will forever be known for his 56 game hitting streak. Musial will be remembered for that classic stance that gave him so many hitting records. Williams was the last player to hit .400. The stature of each is fully entrenched in baseball history; their place marked in the ranks of the all-time greats. No visit to the Baseball Hall of Fame is complete without a look at the plaques of these baseball greats. The following questions only pertain to numbers; they can never fully measure the contributions of these three players. Select the correct great(s) for each question.

A. Joe DiMaggio   B. Stan Musial   C. Ted Williams

1. _____Each finished his career with a batting average well over .300. Who finished with the highest?

2. _____All three had a similar trait at the plate: they did not strike out often. In fact, in their careers, all three struck out in less than 10% of their total at bats. Based upon career percentages, who struck out the least?

3. _____When looking for league leaders in batting average, one does not have to look too far down the leader board to find one of these three names. Who captured the most batting titles with seven?

4. _____Two of these three had seasons with 400 total bases and in 1948, this player totaled 429 bases, the sixth best figure of all-time.

5. _____With men on base, all three were lethal to the opposition. The length of each career was not the same, so total career RBI's is not a fair comparison. But in terms of total games played and total RBI's, who produced the most runs per games played?

6. _____Who holds the Major League record for RBI's by a rookie with 145?

7. _____Who had the most 100 RBI seasons (10)?

8. _____Believe it or not, one of these players never had a 200 hit season. Which one?

9. _____On the career leader board for slugging average, you will find these three in the top twenty. (The totals are: .634, .579, and .559.) Who has the top slugging average?

10. _____None of the three ever had a 50 home run season; 46 home runs was the top single season total. Which one claims this mark?

11. _____None of the three were what one would call a prolific base stealer. In fact, the best single season total any of the trio had was nine. Who led the way with the most stolen bases in his career with 78?

12. _____ _____Two of the three have won three MVP's. Which two?

Answers to DiMaggio—Musial—Williams

1. C—Ted Williams—.344   Stan Musial—.331   Joe   DiMaggio—
                                                       .325

2. A—Joe DiMaggio—5.4% Stan Musial —6.3%   Ted   Williams—
                                                   9.2%

3. B—Stan Musial—7 Batting titles—
1943—.357   1948—.376   1951—.355   1957—.351
1946—.365   1950—.346   1952—.336
Ted Williams—6 Batting Titles
1941—.406   1948—.369   Joe   DiMaggio—2   Batting   Titles
                                  1939—.381
                 1942—.356   1957—.388   1940—.352
                 1947—.343   1958—.343

4. B—Stan Musial—1948   429 Total Bases 230 Hits
127 Singles   46 Doubles   18 Triples   39 Home runs

Joe DiMaggio—1937—418 Total Bases   215 Hits   119 Singles
                    35 Doubles   15 Triples   46 HR
Ted Williams —1949—365 Total Bases (Best) 194 Hits   109 Singles
                    39 Doubles   3 Triples   43 HR

5. A—Joe DiMaggio—.885 RBI/Game Ted Williams—.802 RBI/Game
Stan Musial—.645 RBI/Game

6. C—Ted Williams—1939

7. B—Stan Musial—Ten—100 RBI Seasons

1946—103 RBI	1953—113 RBI
1948—131 RBI 1st	1954—126 RBI
1949—123 RBI	1955—108 RBI
1950—109 RBI	1956—109 RBI 1st
1951—108 RBI	1957—102 RBI

8. C—Ted Williams   No 200 Hit Seasons

Stan Musial—Six—200 Hit Seasons   Joe   DiMaggio—Two—200   Hit
Seasons

1943—220 Hits	1949—207 Hits	1936—206 Hits
1946—228 Hits	1951—205 Hits	1937—215 Hits
1948—230 Hits	1953—200 Hits	

9. C—Ted Williams—.634 SA—2nd   Joe DiMaggio—.579 SA—7th
Stan Musial—.559 SA—16th Tie

10. A—Joe DiMaggio—1937—46 HR Only 40+ Season Ted Williams—
1949—43 HR Only 40+ Season
        Stan Musial—1948—39 HR Best Season

11. B—Stan Musial—78 Stolen Bases 1943—9 SB Best
                Joe DiMaggio—30 Stolen Bases
                Ted Williams —24 Stolen Bases

12. A—Joe DiMaggio—1939, 41 & 47   Ted Williams—1946 & 49
    B—Stan Musial   —1943, 46 & 48

Ty Cobb, "The Georgia Peach," and Pete Rose, "Charlie Hustle," are the only two players in Major League Baseball history to amass over 4,000 base hits for their careers. Cobb is the American League's record holder for base hits with 4,191 and Rose holds the National League's mark with 4,256. The two were very similar in their desire and demeanor on the playing field. Neither gave nor asked for quarter. Both players were driven in a quest for excellence and would let no opposing player stand in their way. Yet, they played in times and eras that were very different, Cobb from 1905 to 1928 and Rose from 1963 to 1986: Cobb played 24 seasons in the American League and Rose played 24 seasons in the National League, yet it is a testament to baseball's ability to transcend time that we are able to compare these two players.

A. Ty Cobb   B. Pete Rose

1. _____Which one had the higher career batting average?

2. _____These players are the only two in Major League history to have over 3,000 singles for their careers. The lesser of the two had **only** 3,053. Which one is number one all-time with 3,215 singles?

3. _____Neither one of these players was considered a home run threat, but one of the two can lay claim to one league home run title. Which one?

4. _____Which one had more home runs for his career?

5. _____On the all-time career doubles list, both finished in the top four. Which one was closer to the top?

6. _____Both players were also their respective leagues' leader in games of five hits or more. One player had 14 such games and the other 10. Who had the higher total?

7. _____With all those base hits, it follows that each scored a lot of runs, and again, each is their respective leagues' all-time leader in runs scored. Who won this battle (2,246 to 2,165)?

8. _____Both players can lay claim to hitting streaks of 40 games or more. Which one topped the other with a 44 game streak to the other's 40 games?

9. _____Both collected over 1,000 extra-base hits in their careers. Which one topped the other, 1,136 to 1,041?

10. _____It is amazing that when you look at Major League Baseball's all-time lists, these two players are either at the top or very near the top on so many of them. One such list is 200-hit seasons, where they are one and two. Who is number one?

11. _____One of them led his league in base hits for a season eight times and the other seven. Who outdid who in this category?

12. _____In this last category, RBI's, one greatly outdistances the other. He is number five on the all-time list with 1,938 RBI's. (The other has 1,314) Who was the better run-producer?

Answers to Cobb—Rose

1. A—Ty Cobb   Number one all-time with a .367 BA   Pete
                                                          Rose—.303 BA

2. B—Pete Rose

3. A—Ty Cobb
Led the AL in 1909 with 9HR's   Best Season—1921 & 1925—12 HR's
Pete Rose   Best Season—1966 & 1969—16 HR's

4. B—Pete Rose—160 HR's   Ty Cobb—117 HR's

5. B—Pete Rose—746 Doubles—2nd all-time   Ty Cobb—724
                                                    Doubles—4th
                                                      all-time

6. A—Ty Cobb

7. A—Ty Cobb

8. B—Pete Rose—44 Game Hitting Streak in 1978 2nd All-Time
        Ty Cobb—40 Game Hitting Streak in 1911 4th All-Time

9. A—
Ty Cobb   1,136 Extra base-hits: 724 Doubles
295 Triples   117 Home Runs
Pete Rose   1,041 Extra base-hits: 746 Doubles
135 Triples   160 Home Runs

10. B—

Pete Rose	1965—209 Hits	1970—205 Hits	1976—215 Hits
	1966—205 Hits	1973—230 Hits	1977—204 Hits
	1968—210 Hits	1975—210 Hits	1979—208 Hits
	1969—218 Hits		
Ty Cobb	1907—212 Hits	1912—227 Hits	1917—225 Hits
	1909—216 Hits	1915—208 Hits	1922—211 Hits
	1911—248 Hits	1916—201 Hits	1924—211 Hits

11. A—

Ty Cobb	1907—212 Hits	1911—248 Hits	1917—225 Hits
	1908—188 Hits	1912—227 Hits	1919—191 Hits
	1909—216 Hits	1915—208 Hits	
Pete Rose	1965—209 Hits	1972—198 Hits	1981—140 Hits
	1968—210 Hits	1973—230 Hits	
	1970—205 Hits	1976—215 Hits	

12. A—Ty Cobb—1,938 RBI's—5th All-Time   Pete Rose 1,314 RBI's

This player comparison involves three of the finest batsmen from the last third of the 20th century: George Brett, Rod Carew, and Tony Gwynn. All three took aim at becoming the next .400-hitter but fell just short; proving once again how difficult it is to reach that lofty plateau. Each of these left-handers is considered to be one of the finest hitters ever to play the game. All three are members of the 3000 hit club and each had a career batting average over .300. Brett and Carew are both in the Hall of Fame and when Gwynn becomes eligible, he will certainly join them in Cooperstown. Select the appropriate player for each question.

A. George Brett   B. Rod Carew   C. Tony Gwynn

1. _____Of the three, who had the highest career batting average?

2. _____Who came the closest to hitting .400?

3. _____Two hundred hits in one season is the magic number for a hitter. Who had the most such years (5)?

4. _____One of these three once belted out 239 hits, which is the 12th best single season mark of all-time. Who?

5. _____With 3,000 career hits, each has proven to be a prolific batsman, but one demonstrated more extra-base power and ranks in the top ten of all-time for extra base hits. Who?

6. _____All three were dangerous base stealers, with each having at least 200 stolen bases for his career. Who swiped the most bases (353)?

7. _____It wasn't 56 consecutive games, but his 30-game hitting streak was still an amazing feat.

8. _____All three were tough strikeout victims, but with a strike percentage of only 4.6%, who was the toughest?

9. _____Each scored over 1,350 runs in his career. Who had the most?

10. _____It is sometimes astounding to know that a player has never won a Most Valuable Player Award. Such is the case here; which one was never named League MVP?

11. _____Each had a career batting average over .300, but who had the most .300 seasons (17)?

12. _____All three have tasted post-season play in the form of the League Championship Series, but one had the Ernie Banks syndrome; he never played in a World Series. Who is this unfortunate player?

Answers to Brett—Carew—Gwynn

1. C—Tony Gwynn—.338 BA   Rod Carew —.328 BA
                               George Brett—.305 BA

2. C—Tony Gywnn—1994—.394 BA   George Brett—1980—
                                                 .390 BA
                                    Rod Carew —1977—
                                                 .388 BA

3. C—Tony Gwynn—Five—200 Hit Seasons
1984—213 Hits 1st   1989—203 Hits 1st
1986—211 Hits 1st   1997—220 Hits 1st
1987—218 Hits 1st

Rod Carew—Four—200 Hit Seasons
1973—203 Hits 1st   1976—200 Hits
1974—218 Hits 1st   1977—239 Hits 1st
George Brett—Two—200 Hit Seasons
1976—215 Hits 1st
1979—212 Hits 1st

4. B—Rod Carew

5. A—George Brett—1,119 Extra Base Hits—10th All-Time
665 Doubles   137 Triples   317 HR

Tony Gwynn—752 Extra Base Hits: 534 Doubles   84 Triples 134 HR
Rod Carew   —649 Extra Base Hits: 445 Doubles 112 Triples   92 HR

6. B—Rod Carew—353 Stolen Bases Tony Gwynn—318 SB
George Brett—201 SB

7. A—George Brett—1980—30 Games

8. C—Tony Gwynn—4.6% Strikeouts
George Brett— 8.8% Strikeouts
Rod Carew —11.0% Strikeouts

9. A—George Brett 1583 Runs
Rod Carew—1424 Runs   Tony Gwynn—1378 Runs

10. C—Tony Gwynn   Rod Carew—1977 MVP   George Brett—
1980 MVP

11. C—Tony Gwynn—17—.300 Seasons

1983—.309	1989—.336 1st	1995—.368 1st
1984—.351 1st	1990—.309	1996—.353 1st
1985—.317 4th	1991—.317 3rd	1997—.372 1st
1986—.329 3rd	1992—.317 5th	1998—.321
1987—.370 1st	1993—.358 2nd	1999—.338
1988—.313 1st	1994—.394 1st	

12. B—Rod Carew   (George Brett was the only one to win a World Series)

Entering the 21st century, the American League is fortunate to have three of the best shortstops not only of this era, but of any era of baseball. These three are all leaders on their teams and quite possibly all have a plaque waiting for them in Cooperstown. They are Nomar Garciaparra of Boston, the Yankees' Derek Jeter, and Texas's Alex Rodriguez While Jeter and the Yankees have had more team success, all three have excelled in post-season play. The questions are not intended to imply which is the best, for as fans we choose our favorites. They serve only as a statistical comparison. Mere numbers cannot measure the leadership qualities of these three, both on and off the field. Select the correct player for each question.

A. Nomar Garciaparra   B. Derek Jeter   C. Alex Rodriguez

1. _____Two of the three were named Rookie of the Year. Which one was not?

2. _____In 1997, this shortstop got better than half-way to Joe DiMaggio's record with a 30 game hitting streak.

3. _____Entering the 2001 season, all three have career batting averages over .300. Which one has the highest at .333?

4. _____Which one has been named MVP of the All-Star Game?

5. _____Which one is a member of the 40-40 club (40 home runs and 40 stolen bases)?

6. _____Only one of the three has hit for the cycle, and he accomplished this hitting gem on June 5, 1997. Who has this accomplishment on his resume?

7. _____All three have led the American League in hits. Which player has the highest single-season total with 219?

8. _____On May 10, 1999, this player became only the ninth player in American League history to hit two grand slams in the same game.

9. _____In the 1999 season, this player reached base, via a hit or a walk, in an incredible 53 consecutive games. Who?

10. _____Two of the three have won American League batting titles with .372 and .358 averages respectively. The third has a season best average of .349, but no title to show for it. Who?

11. _____In their short Major League careers, all three have established themselves as top-flight hitters. But which one is the toughest to strike out?

12. _____Since all three play the same position, only one can win the Silver Slugger Award. Which one has not done so?

Answers to Garciaparra—Jeter—Rodriguez

1. C—Alex Rodriguez   1996—Derek Jeter
                          1997—Nomar Garciaparra

2. A—Nomar Garciaparra

3. A—Nomar Garciaparra .333   Derek Jeter .322   Alex
                                                        Rodriguex .309

4. B—Derek Jeter (2000)

5. C—Alex Rodriguez   1998   42 HR   46 SB

6. C—Alex Rodriguez

7. B—Derek Jeter
1999—219 Hits   Alex Rodriguez   1998—213 Hits
                       Nomar Garciaparra   1997—209 Hits

8. A—Nomar Garciaparra

9. B—Derek Jeter

10. B—Derek Jeter   1999—.349 BA 2nd
Nomar Garciaparra   1999—.357 BA
                        2000—.372 BA
Alex Rodriguex   1996—.358 BA

11. A—Nomar Garciaparra—10.6% Derek Jeter   —18.3%
Alex Rodriguez—19.7%

12. B—Derek Jeter   Alex Rodriguez—1996, 1998, 1999
Nomar Garciaparra—1997

Baseball fans love the home run, and the decade of the 90's provided a lot of love. Home runs were hit in record numbers, leaving pitchers shaking their heads. New league standards were set for both the National and American Leagues. The NL (14 teams) hit a record 2,220 home runs in 1996, and in 1999 (16 teams), set a new standard of 2,893 home runs. In the AL, a new mark of 2,742 home runs was established in 1996 (14 teams). The Seattle Mariners set a new record in 1997 when they hit 264 home runs. That same season; the Colorado Rockies set a new National League team record with 239 round trippers. On May 28, 1995, the Detroit Tigers (7) and the Chicago White Sox (5) combined for 12 home runs, which established a new record for home runs in a single game by both clubs. The Detroit Tigers (1994) and the Atlanta Braves (1998) hit home runs in 25 consecutive games; tying the mark set by the 1941 New York Yankees. The list of records set or tied in the 90's goes on and on, capped off by the home run battle of the century in 1998 between Mark McGwire and Sammy Sosa. Big Mac topped out with 70 round-trippers and Slammin' Sammy finished second with a modest 66 homers. There is also a third home run hitter the fans are intrigued by: Ken Griffey, Jr.. Most fans consider Junior the one with the best chance of breaking Hank Aaron's career record. This section will deal with these three, so put your glove on and see if you can catch a home run souvenir and select one of these three players for each question.

A. Ken Griffey, Jr.   B. Mark McGwire   C. Sammy Sosa

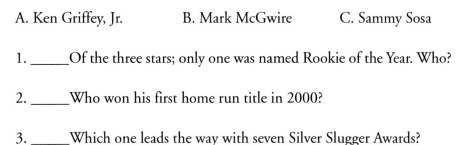

1. _____Of the three stars; only one was named Rookie of the Year. Who?

2. _____Who won his first home run title in 2000?

3. _____Which one leads the way with seven Silver Slugger Awards?

4. _____All three have one RBI title to their credit, but which one has the best single season mark of 158?

5. _____These three long ball bashers all know how to circle the bases with ease, but who has the most career base hits?

6. _____Each holds the Major League record for home runs in a particular month and one is the title holder for two different months. Who?

7. _____Who holds the Major League record for home runs in any calendar month with 20?

8. _____Which slugger hit a homer in eight consecutive games, giving him a share of the Major League record?

9. _____On July 2, 1993, this player had one of those games very few players have: six hits in six at bats in a nine-inning game.

10. _____Despite his longball heroics, one of the three has not been named MVP of his league. Which player is still waiting to add this honor to his resume?

11. _____Rather than give up a home run, a pitcher might decide that surrendering a base on balls is not such a bad idea. Who leads the way with 1261 career walks?

12. _____Who has made the most use of the stolen base with 231 in his career?

Answers to Griffey, Jr.—McGwire—Sosa

1.　B—Mark McGwire—1987

2.　C—Sammy Sosa—2000—50 HR's
Ken Griffey, Jr.　　　1994—40 HR's
　　　　　　　　　　1997—56 HR's
　　　　　　　　　　1998—56 HR's
　　　　　　　　　　1999—48 HR's
Mark McGwire　　　1987—49 HR's
　　　　　　　　　　1996—52 HR's
　　　　　　　　　　1998—70 HR's
　　　　　　　　　　1999—65 HR's

3.　A—Ken Griffey, Jr.　1991, 1993, 1994, 1996, 1997, 1998, 1999
　　　Sammy Sosa　　1995, 1998, 1999, 2000
　　　Mark McGwire　1992, 1996, 1998

4.　C—Sammy Sosa　　1998

5.　A—Ken Griffey, Jr.—1883 Hits
Sammy Sosa　　　　—1606 Hits
Mark McGwire　　　—1570 Hits

6.　B—Mark McGwire— May—16 Home Runs in 1998 (NL)
　　　　　　　　　　July—16 Home Runs in 1999 (NL)

Ken Griffey, Jr.　　　April—13 Home Runs in 1997 (AL)
Sammy Sosa　　　　June—20 Home Runs in 1998 (NL)

7. C—Sammy Sosa—June, 1998

8. A—Ken Griffey, Jr.　　July 20—28, 1993

9. C—Sammy Sosa　　July 2, 1993—5 Singles and 1 Double

10. B—Mark McGwire　　Ken Griffey, Jr.—1997
　　　　　　　　　　　　Sammy Sosa　—1998

11. B—Mark McGwire—1261 Walks
Ken Griffey, Jr.—841 Walks
Sammy Sosa　—519 Walks

12. C—Sammy Sosa—231 SB　　Ken Griffey, Jr.—173 SB
　　　　　　　　　　　　　　Mark McGwire— 12 SB　(Were
　　　　　　　　　　　　　　you expecting more?)

Fans love to see the home run, but they also love to see a dominating pitcher. The more strikeouts, the better, and three pitchers stand out as dominating strikeout artists: Walter Johnson, Bob Feller and Nolan Ryan. Johnson was the first pitcher to reach 3,000 strikeouts. Ryan is now number one on the all-time strikeout list. Feller did not reach 3,000 strikeouts because World War II interrupted his career. He enlisted in the Navy on January 6, 1942 and served his country until his discharge in the summer of 1945. All three commanded respect and awe with the 'ole #1: the fastball. Whenever one of the three took the mound fans were on the edge of their seats hoping for another command performance (or possibly a no-hitter). True, they all pitched in different eras, but the mound was still 60'6" from home plate, a swing and a miss a strike and three strikes an out. Each truly dominated and all are enshrined in Cooperstown. If you talked to a fan who saw each pitch in his prime, that fan would likely say, "There goes the best". See if you can select the correct Hall of Fame strikeout pitcher(s) for each question.

A. Bob Feller   B. Walter Johnson   C. Nolan Ryan

1. _____When the final score of a baseball game is 1 to 0, it is said to be a pitchers' duel. Who is the Major League record holder with 38 victories in these 1 to 0 battles?

2. _____Who holds the Major League record with seven career no-hitters?

3. _____ _____A one-hitter is oh so close, and two of these strikeout artists top the all-time list with twelve one-hitters in their careers. Which two?

4. _____Who is the only one to win a World Series game?

5. _____Who lays claim to the most league strikeout titles with twelve?

6. _____A magic number for a strikeout pitcher is 300 in a season. Which fireballer reached this figure six times in his career?

7. _____Bob Feller had his career interrupted by World War II. Consequently, career totals are not a fair comparison. However, we can compare averages. Who had the most strikeouts per nine innings with 9.546?

8. _____Who had the best control, surrendering only 2.058 BB/9 innings?

9. _____A pitcher may be dominating, but batters won't always strike out. Who gave up the fewest hits per nine innings 6.554?

10. _____Who had the highest career winning percentage at .621?

11. _____It doesn't happen often, but sometimes a pitcher has to strike out four batters to get three outs in an inning (due to a dropped third strike). Which one of these pitchers had to get that fourth strikeout?

12. _____A pitcher's dream inning is three K's in nine pitches. Which one accomplished this feat twice during his career?

Answers to Feller—Johnson—Ryan

1. B—Walter Johnson

2. C—Nolan Ryan

3. A—Bob Feller
    C—Nolan Ryan

4. B—Walter Johnson   3 Wins—3 Losses
    Bob Feller   0 Wins—2 Losses
    Nolan Ryan 0 Wins—0 Losses

5. B—Walter Johnson—12 Titles

1910—313 K's	1915—203 K's	1919—147 K's
1912—303 K's	1916—228 K's	1921—143 K's
1913—243 K's	1917—188 K's	1923—130 K's
1914—225 K's	1918—162 K's	1924—158 K's

Bob Feller—7 Titles

1938—240 K's	1946—348 K's
1939—246 K's	1947—196 K's
1940—261 K's	1948—164 K's
1941—260 K's	

Nolan Ryan—11 Titles

1972—329 K's	1977—341 K's	1988—228 K's
1973—383 K's	1978—260 K's	1989—301 K's
1974—367 K's	1979—223 K's	1990—232 K's
1976—327 K's	1987—270 K's	

6. C—Nolan Ryan

7. C—Nolan Ryan   9.546 K's/ 9 inn.   Bob Feller   6.070 K's/
                                                        9 inn.
                                    Walter Johnson 5.330 K's/
                                                        9 inn.

8. B—Walter Johnson   2.058 BB/ 9 inn. Bob Feller   4.148 BB/
                                                        9 inn.
                                        Nolan Ryan   4.669 BB/
                                                        9 inn.

9. C—Nolan Ryan   6.554 Hits/ 9 inn. Walter Johnson   7.476
                                                    Hits/ 9 inn.
                                        Bob Feller   7.692
                                                    Hits/ 9 inn.

10. A—Bob Feller—.621 Pct.   Walter Johnson.   599 Pct.
                                    Nolan Ryan   .526 Pct.

11. B—Walter Johnson   April 15, 1911 (5th inn.)

12. C—Nolan Ryan   April 19, 1968 (2nd inn.)
                    July 9, 1972 (3rd inn.)

Bob Gibson, Sandy Koufax and Juan Marichal were three of the greatest pitchers to ever take the mound. Fans were in for a real treat when one of these aces pitched and American League batters could be extremely grateful that interleague play was still some 35 years away. These three were so over-powering, so intimidating, that batters were virtually helpless at the plate. Today's hitters can thank this trio because their dominance led the way to the lowering of the mound in 1968. Select the correct legend for each question.

A. Bob Gibson   B. Sandy Koufax   C. Juan Marichal

1. _____All three have no-hitters on their resume, but only one has known perfection. Who pitched a perfect game on September 9, 1965?

2. _____A good fielding pitcher is always a plus, and one of these hurlers was so good, he won nine consecutive Gold Glove Awards. Who was this expert fielder?

3. _____Surprisingly, one of these greats won neither a Cy Young Award nor League MVP during his career. Whose trophy case is sparser than the others?

4. _____All three could boast of a career ERA under 3.00 (2.76, 2.89, 2.91). All were very close, but who finished with the lowest ERA?

5. _____Another category in which the three had similar statistics was career shutouts. Who led the way with 56?

6. _____All three also excelled in career winning percentage. Who had the highest?

7. _____To have a high winning percentage, a pitcher has to have some 20-win seasons along the way. Who had the most with 6?

8. _____A good pitcher does not give up too many bases on balls, and this pitcher's control was so good that he finished his career with a mere 1.82 walks/ 9 innings.

9. _____Opposing batters did not fare too well against any of the three; each gave up less than a hit per inning. However, one was extremely stingy, allowing only 6.79 hits/ 9 innings. Who was this nightmare for hitters?

10. _____A team always wants its best pitcher to start the first game of the year, and one of these three affirmed his status as ace by posting six opening day victories. Who?

11. _____One of these hurlers shone the brightest in All-Star games. He is tied with three others for the most appearances (8) and has the lowest ERA at 0.50 (min. nine innings). Who?

12. _____It is difficult enough to strike out the side, but when the side is four batters, that's almost too much. But on June 7, 1966, a dropped third strike forced one pitcher to do just that. Who had to work a little harder that inning?

Answers to Gibson—Koufax—Marichal

1. B—Sandy Koufax vs. Chicago Cubs 1 to 0

2. A—Bob Gibson—1965 to 1973 Koufax and Marichal never won a Gold Glove

3. C—Juan Marichal
Sandy Koufax   Cy Young: 1963, 1965, 1966   MVP: 1963

Bob Gibson   Cy Young: 1968, 1970   MVP: 1968

4. B—Sandy Koufax—2.76 ERA   Juan Marichal—2.89 ERA
                               Bob Gibson   —2.91 ERA

5. A—Bob Gibson—56 Shutouts   Juan Marichal—52 Shutouts
                               Sandy Koufax—40 Shutouts

6. B—Sandy Koufax—.655 Pct.   Juan Marichal—.631 Pct.
                               Bob Gibson   —.591 Pct.

7. C—Juan Marichal—6 Seasons   1963 (25), 1964 (21), 1965 (22), 1966 (25), 1968 (26), 1969 (21)

Bob Gibson—5 Seasons   1965 (20), 1966 (21), 1968 (22), 1969 (20), 1970 (23)

Sandy Koufax—3 Seasons   1963 (25), 1965 (26), 1966 (27)

8. C—Juan Marichal—1.82 Walks/ 9 inn.   Bob Gibson   —3.09
                                             Walks/ 9 inn.
                                        Sandy Koufax—3.16
                                             Walks/ 9 inn.

9. B—Sandy Koufax—6.79 Hits/ 9 inn.   Bob Gibson   —7.60
                                             Hits/ 9 inn.
                                        Juan Marichal—8.09
                                             Hits/ 9 inn.

10. C—Juan Marichal

11. C—Juan Marichal
The other pitchers with eight All-Star appearances are Jim Bunning, Don Drysdale, and Tom Seaver.

12. A—Bob Gibson   June 7, 1996   4th inning vs. Pittsburgh
                                                        Pirates

In the late 1960's and 1970's, a new trio of pitchers dominated baseball: future Hall of Famers Steve Carlton, Jim Palmer and Tom Seaver. These three proved once again that good pitching beats good hitting. Each left his mark on the game and their career stats validate their enshrinement at Cooperstown. Select the correct great(s) for the following questions.

A. Steve Carlton   B. Jim Palmer   C. Tom Seaver

1. _____None of the three were strangers to the Cy Young Award; each won three. But only one captured a fourth. Who?

2. _____All three were consistent winners as evidenced by their career winning percentages. Who bested the other two with a .638 career winning pct.?

3. _____Who had the highest single season winning percentage at .875 (min. 15 decisions)?

4. _____ _____All three claimed single season ERA titles and amazingly, two of the three finished their careers with identical 2.86 ERA's. Which two?

5. _____Believe it or not, one of the three actually led his league in losses for a single season. Who has this dubious distinction?

6. _____Winning 20 games was nothing special for these three, as they combined for 19 such seasons. Who led the way with eight?

7. _____It is uncanny how similar the statistics of Carlton, Palmer and Seaver are. They posted comparable numbers in several categories, including victories. One led his league in wins four times while the other two claimed three titles each. Who was the four-time league leader?

8. ____Post-season play was not foreign to this group. Based upon winning percentage, who had the best post-season record (divisional and World Series play)?

9. ____On the all-time shutout list, all three appear in the top twenty. Who has the most with 61?

10. ____Both Carlton and Seaver have over 3,000 strikeouts for their careers and, in fact, Carlton has over 4,000 strikeouts. But which of the three has the highest strikeout total per nine innings?

11. ____All pitchers know they are going to give up their share of hits, but who allowed the fewest per nine innings?

12. ____A good fielding pitcher always helps his team (and himself). Which one can claim four Gold Glove Awards?

Answers to Carlton—Palmer—Seaver

1. A—Steve Carlton—1972, 77, 80 & 82   Jim Palmer —1973, 75 &
                                                              76
                                            Tom Seaver—1969, 73 &
                                                              75

2. B—Jim Palmer—638 Pct.   Tom Seaver —.603 Pct.
                              Steve Carlton—.574 Pct.

3. C—Tom Seaver—1981—14 Wins 2 Losses .875 Pct.
Jim Palmer   —1969—16 Wins 4 Losses .800 Pct.
Steve Carlton—1981—13 Wins 4 Losses .765 Pct.

4. B—Jim Palmer   Steve Carlton—3.22
   C—Tom Seaver

5. A—Steve Carlton—1970—19 Losses & 1973—20 Losses

6. B—Jim Palmer—8 Seasons
   1970—20 Wins   1975—23 Wins 1st
   1971—20 Wins   1976—22 Wins 1st
   1972—21 Wins   1977—20 Wins 1st
   1973—22 Wins   1978—21 Wins

7. A—Steve Carlton

8. B—Jim Palmer   4 Wins 1 Loss (L.C.S.)
                          4 Wins 2 Losses (W.S.)
                          8 Wins 3 Losses   .727 Pct.

Steve Carlton   4 Wins 2 Losses (L.C.S.)
                          2 Wins 2 Losses (W.S.)
                            6 Wins 4 Losses   .600 Pct.
Tom Seaver   2 Wins 1 Loss (L.C.S.)
                          1 Win   2 Losses (W.S.)
                          3 Wins 3 Losses   .500 Pct.

9. C—Tom Seaver—61 Shutouts   Steve Carlton—55 Shutouts
                                Jim Palmer   —53 Shutouts

10. A—Steve Carlton—7.14 K's/ 9 inn.   Tom Seaver—6.85 K's/ 9 inn.
                                        Jim Palmer —5.04 K'/ 9 inn.

11. C—Tom Seaver—7.47 Hits/ 9 inn.   Jim Palmer—7.63 Hits/ 9 inn.
                                      Steve Carlton—8.06 Hits/ 9
                                                         inn.

12. B—Jim Palmer—4 Gold Gloves—1976, 77, 78 & 79
    Steve Carlton—1 Gold Glove—1981
    Tom Seaver   —0 Gold Gloves

In recent years, the adage that states, "good pitching beats good hitting" has been sorely tested. Offensive statistics are up and it is not uncommon for a team to score ten runs in a game. However, three pitchers have managed to perform well, posting statistics that not only dominate this era, but compare favorably with other eras as well. These aces, Roger Clemens, Greg Maddux, and Pedro Martinez, still excite fans, proving that the art of pitching is not a lost one. Select the correct ace for each question.

A. Roger Clemens   B. Greg Maddux   C. Pedro Martinez

1. _____None of the three are strangers to the Cy Young Award, and in 11 of the last 15 seasons, one of the three has captured one. Who tops the list with five Cy Young Awards?

2. _____All three have won the Cy Young Award with two different franchises, but only one has claimed the award in both leagues. Who?

3. _____Opposing teams know they are not going to score too many runs off these aces and that whenever one steps on the mound they might get shutout. Which one of the three has the most career shutouts?

4. _____All three have dominated as shown by their Cy Young Awards. But one exerted such dominance that he was selected League MVP. Who claims this honor?

5. _____All three have ERA titles on their resumes and all have single-season bests of under 2.00. Who comes in with the lowest single season ERA at 1.56?

6. _____Career ERA's for the three are very close (2.68, 2.83, 3.07). Who has the lowest?

7. _____These three are used to winning and each has a career winning percentage of over .600. Who tops the list at .691?

8. _____One of the three had a winning percentage of over .900 for a single season. Who can boast of this rare feat?

9. _____These three hurlers have all been league leaders in victories for a single season. Who has the best total with 24?

10. ____All three have demonstrated that they have command of the strike zone. They do not hurt themselves by surrendering bases on balls, as evidenced by each having less than three per nine innings. Who leads the three with only 1.99 walks per nine innings?

11. ____One strikeout per inning is excellent and to average more than one is phenomenal. In his career, who has an average of 10.38 K's per nine innings?

12. ____Oddly enough, none of the three has ever pitched a no-hitter. On June 3, 1995, this pitcher had a perfect game for nine innings, but his team failed to score, forcing extra innings. His team scored a run in the top of the 10th but he gave up a double in the bottom of the inning, losing not only the perfect game but the no-hitter as well. He was relieved, but was credited with a 1-0 victory. Who is this pitcher?

BONUS QUESTION

13. ____While all three have dominated Major League Baseball, only one was good enough to make it onto the Springfield Nuclear Power Plant softball team. Unfortunately, he was hypnotized into thinking that he was a chicken before the big game. Who made this memorable appearance on *The Simpsons*?

Answers to Clemens—Maddux—Martinez

1. A—Roger Clemens   1986, 87 & 91—Boston Red Sox
                        1997 & 98—Toronto Blue Jays

Greg Maddux—   1992—Chicago Cubs
                        1993, 94 & 95—Atlanta Braves
Pedro Martinez   1997—Montreal Expos
                        1999 & 2000—Boston Red Sox

2. C—Pedro Martinez

3. A—Roger Clemens—45 Shutouts   Greg Maddux —31 Shutouts
                                   Pedro Martinez—15 Shutouts

4. A—Roger Clemens—1986

5. B—Greg Maddux—1994—1.56   Pedro Martinez—2000—1.74
                               Roger Clemens—1990—1.93

6. C—Pedro Martinez—2.68 ERA Greg Maddux—2.83 ERA
                               Roger Clemens—3.07 ERA

7. C—Pedro Martinez—.691 Pct. Roger Clemens—.647 Pct.
                                Greg Maddux —.640 Pct.

8. B—Greg Maddux—1995—19 Wins & 2 Losses—.905 Pct.
Roger Clemens—1986—24 Wins & 4 Losses—.857 Pct.
Pedro Martinez—1999—23 Wins & 4 Losses—.852 Pct.

9. A—Roger Clemens—1986—24 Wins   Pedro Martinex—1999—
23 Wins
Greg Maddux—1992 &
93—20 Wins

10. B—Greg Maddux—1.99 BB/ 9 innings   Pedro   Martinez—2.52
BB/ 9 innings
Roger   Clemens—2.91
BB/ 9 innings

11. C—Pedro Martinez   10.38 K's/ 9 innings   Roger   Clemens—
8.60 K's/ 9 innings
Greg   Maddux—
6.37 K's/ 9 innings

12. C—Pedro Martinez—Montreal Expos. Bip Roberts of the San Diego
Padres hit a double.

13. A—Roger Clemens

Section 3—Decades

Listed below are 12 players who starred in the 1990's. They have led their league in statistical categories, won awards or accomplished some other noteworthy feat. The questions and answers will only concern statistics, awards and accomplishment from the years 1990—1999. Select the correct player for each question.

A. Jeff Bagwell   E. Tony Gwynn   I. Cal Ripken, Jr.
B. Ken Caminiti   F. Todd Hundley   J. Ivan Rodriguez
C. Cecil Fielder   G. Mark McGwire   K. Sammy Sosa
D. Ken Griffey, Jr.   H. Manny Ramirez   L. Frank Thomas

1. _____I was the only player in the 90's to win both a Rookie of the Year Award (1991) and be named my league's MVP (1994).

2. _____In the 90's, I had the most batting titles (4) and they happen to be in successive seasons: 1994-97.

3. _____In 1996, I hit 41 home runs, setting a Major League record for home runs by a catcher in a single season.

4. _____My career has been one of consistency and durability, as I had at least 100 RBI's and scored at least 100 runs for eight consecutive seasons (1991-98).

5. _____I became just the seventh player in ML history to win three consecutive RBI titles (1990-92).

6. _____My 165 RBI's in 1999 put me eighth on the all-time list for a single season.

7. _____My total of 162 walks in 1998 is second only to Babe Ruth's 170 in 1923.

8. _____In the 90's, I won the most home run titles with four, including three consecutive crowns (1994, 1997—99).

9. _____In 1999, I became the first catcher to have at least 20 home runs and 20 stolen bases in the same season.

10. _____My 416 total bases in 1998 was the 12th best total of all-time and the best mark of the decade.

11. _____I was named MVP in 1996 and in that season, I tied Mickey Mantle for the single season record for RBI's by a switch hitter with 130.

12. _____I played the most games in the 1990's.

Answers to Players of the 1990's

1. A—Jeff Bagwell   Houston Astros 1991—Rookie of the Year
                        Houston Astros 1994—MVP

2. E—Tony Gwynn   San Diego Padres   1994—.394
                                       1995—.368
                                       1996—.353
                                       1997—.372

3. F—Todd Hundley   New York Mets

4. L—Frank Thomas   Chicago White Sox

1991	104 Runs	109 RBI	1995	102 Runs	111 RBI
1992	108 Runs	115 RBI	1996	110 Runs	134 RBI
1993	106 Runs	128 RBI	1997	110 Runs	125 RBI
1994	106 Runs	101 RBI	1998	109 Runs	109 RBI

5. C—Cecil Fielder—Detroit Tigers 1990—132 RBI's
                                    1991—133 RBI's
                                    1992—124 RBI's

The other six players are:

Ty Cobb—1907, 08 & 09   Rogers Hornsby—1920 (tied), 21
                                  & 22

Honus Wagner—1907, 08 & 09   Joe Medwick—1936, 37 & 38
Babe Ruth—1919, 20 & 21   George Foster—1976, 77 & 78

6. H—Manny Ramirez   Cleveland Indians

7. G—Mark McGwire   St. Louis Cardinals

8. D—Ken Griffey, Jr.   Seattle Mariners   1994—40 HR
                                              1997—56 HR
                                              1998—56 HR
                                              1999—48 HR

9. J—Ivan Rodriguez   Texas Rangers   35 Home Runs   25 Stolen Bases

10. K—Sammy Sosa   Chicago Cubs   112 Singles   20 Doubles   0 Triples
66 Home Runs

11. B—Ken Caminiti—San Diego Padres

12. I—Cal Ripken, Jr.   Baltimore Orioles   1475 Games

Listed below are 12 pitchers who starred in the 1990's. They have led their league in statistical categories, won awards or accomplished some other noteworthy feat. The questions and answers will only concern statistics, awards and accomplishment from the years 1990—1999. Select the correct player for each question.

A. Roger Clemens   E. Andy Hawkins   I. Mike Mussina
B. David Cone   F. Randy Johnson   J. Bob Welch
C. Dennis Eckersley   G. Greg Maddux   K. Kerry Wood
D. Tom Glavine   H. Pedro Martinez   L. Anthony Young

1. _____I was the Major League leader in victories for the decade with 176. Included in this win total is my 19-2 record in 1995, which was the best win percentage (.905) of the 1990's (minimum of 15 victories).

2. _____From May 29, 1998 to June 1, 1999, no one could beat me as I won an American League record 20 consecutive decisions.

3. _____My combined strikeout total (33) set the Major League record for K's in two consecutive games (May 6 & May 11, 1998).

4. _____I led my league in victories in four seasons, three of which were consecutive (1991-93, 1998).

5. _____From May 6, 1992 to July 24, 1993, I established a Major League record that might not ever be broken: I lost 27 consecutive decisions.

6. _____On October 11, 1997, I established a League Championship Series record of 15 strikeouts in one game.

7. _____I have led my league in strikeouts five times, with four of those titles coming in successive years (1992-95, 1999).

8. _____For one game I was just perfect, as on July 18, 1999, I hurled the 14th perfect game in Major League history.

9. _____My victory total of 27 in 1990 was not only the Major's best total of the 90's, but also the best total of any year since Denny McLain's 31 victories in 1968.

10. _____I was the only pitcher in the 90's to win both the Cy Young Award and League MVP in the same season (1992).

11. _____In 1999, I became the first pitcher since Nolan Ryan in 1977 to reach double digits in strikeouts for seven consecutive games.

12. _____Talk about bad luck. On July 1, 1990, I became the second pitcher in Major League history to throw a no-hitter and lose the game (4—0).

Answers to Pitchers of the 1990's

1. G—Greg Maddux   Overall record 176 wins and 88 losses good for a .667 pct.

2. A—Roger Clemens—New York Yankees

3. K—Kerry Wood—Chicago Cubs May 6 —20 K's vs. Houston (9 innings)
   May 11—13 K's at Arizonz (7 innings)
Wood won both games but what is more amazing is that he issued no walks to Houston and only one to Arizona.

4. D—Tom Glavine—Atlanta Braves   1991—20 Wins
   1992—20 Wins
   1993—22 Wins
   1998—20 Wins

5. L—Anthony Young—New York Mets 14 Games in 1992 and 13 games in 1993. He finally won on July 28 against the Florida Marlins

6. I—Mike Mussina—October 11, 1997 at Cleveland. Mussina was relieved by Armando Benitez in the 8th inning with Baltimore trailing 1 to 0. The Orioles tied the game with a run in the top of the 9th but the Indians scored in the bottom of the 12th to win 2-1.

7. F—Randy Johnson—Seattle Mariners   1992—241 K's
   1993—308 K's

1994—204 K's
1995—294 K's
Arizona Diamondbacks   1999—364 K's

8. B—David Cone—New York Yankees over the Montreal Expos 6-0.

9. J—Bob Welch—Oakland Athletics had a 27-6 record

10. C—Dennis Eckersley—Oakland Athletics

11. H—Pedro Martinez—Boston Red Sox

12. E—Andy Hawkins—New York Yankees lost to the Chicago White Sox 4-0

Listed below are 12 players who starred in the 1980's. They have led their league in statistical categories, won awards or accomplished some other noteworthy feat. The questions and answers will only concern statistics, awards and accomplishment from the years 1980—1989. Select the correct player for each question.

A. Wade Boggs	E. Bob Horner	I. Eddie Murray
B. Jose Canseco	F. Don Mattingly	J. Kirby Puckett
C. Rickey Henderson	G. Paul Molitor	K. Mike Schmidt
D. Keith Hernandez	H. Dale Murphy	L. Willie Wilson

1. _____I was the whiff king of the 80's. I struck out 1,268 times, more than any other Major League player in the decade.

2. _____I loved to see the bases loaded. In 1987, I set a Major League record by hitting six grand slam home runs in one season.

3. _____My 39-game hitting streak in 1987 was the fifth-longest in baseball history.

4. _____With men on base, I was the decade's best with a Major League leading 996 RBI's.

5. _____I am the Major League record holder for game-winning RBI's in a career (129). No one will be able to break my record because this statistic was only kept for nine seasons (1980-88).

6. _____Only five players in the history of baseball had more consecutive 200-hit seasons than my run of seven (1983-89).

7. _____I collected 115 triples, the most of anyone for the decade. I also led my league five times (no other player in M.L. history has led either league in triples more times) and in 1985, my 21 triples were the best total of the decade.

8. _____I scored over 100 runs eight times during the eighties. In 1988, my 146 runs scored was the highest total of the decade and the best mark since Ted Williams crossed the plate 150 times in 1949.

9. _____In 1988, I became the first player in Major League history to steal at least 40 bases and hit 40 home runs in the same season.

10. _____I was the only player in the decade to lead my league in hits for three consecutive seasons (1987-89), tying the Major League record.

11. _____My 313 home runs were the most for the decade.

12. _____On July 6, 1986 I joined an exclusive group of players who have hit four home runs in a nine-inning game. It was little comfort, though. My team lost the game.

Answers to Players of the 1980's

1. H—Dale Murphy—Atlanta Braves

2. F—Don Mattingly—New York Yankees

3. G—Paul Molitor—Milwaukee Brewers

4. I—Eddie Murray—Baltimore Orioles 1980-88, Los Angeles Dodgers 1989

1980—116 RBI	1985—124 RBI
1981—78 RBI	1986—84 RBI
1982—110 RBI	1987—91 RBI
1983—111 RBI	1988—84 RBI
1984—110 RBI	1989—88 RBI

5. D—Keith Hernandez—St. Louis Cardinals 1980-83, New York Mets 1983-88

6. A—Wade Boggs—Boston Red Sox

1983—210 Hits 2nd	1987—200 Hits 4th
1984—203 Hits 2nd	1988—214 Hits 2nd
1985—240 Hits 1st	1989—205 Hits 2nd
1986—207 Hits 4th	

7. L—Willie Wilson—Kansas City Royals

1980—15 Triples	1987—15 Triples
1982—15 Triples	1988—11 Triples
1985—21 Triples	

8.　C—Rickey Henderson—Oakland Athletics 1980-84, 1989, New York Yankees 1985-1989

1980—111 Runs	1985—146 Runs
1982—119 Runs	1986—130 Runs
1983—105 Runs	1988—118 Runs
1984—113 Runs	1989—113 Runs

9.　B—Jose Canseco—Oakland Athletics　40 SB　42 HR

10.　J—Kirby Puckett—Minnesota Twins
1987—207 Hits
1988—234 Hits
1989—215 Hits

11.　K—Mike Schmidt—Philadelphia Phillies

12.　E—Bob Horner—Atlanta Braves　His four home runs weren't enough as the Braves lost to Montreal Expos 11—8

Listed below are 12 pitchers who starred in the 1980's. They have led their league in statistical categories, won awards or accomplished some other noteworthy feat. The questions and answers will only concern statistics, awards and accomplishment from the years 1980—1989. Select the correct player for each question.

A. Bert Blyleven   E. Orel Hershiser   I. Rick Sutcliffe
B. Roger Clemens   F. Nolan Ryan   J. John Tudor
C. Rollie Fingers   G. Bret Saberhagen   K. Fernando Valenzuela
D. Dwight Gooden   H. Steve Stone   L. Mike Witt

1. _____In 1980, I was a Cy Young Award winner with a 25-7 record, good for a .781 winning percentage (the top percentage in baseball that year). My 25 wins were the most for any pitcher in the 80's.

2. _____In 1981, I accomplished something that no other pitcher had ever done. I won both the Rookie of the Year and Cy Young Awards.

3. _____In 1981 I wasn't a rookie but I did win my league's MVP and Cy Young.

4. _____In 1987 and 1988 I won strikeout titles. The next year, I switched teams (and leagues) and won my third consecutive strikeout title.

5. _____On September 30, 1984, I brought the regular season to a dramatic close when I fired the 11th perfect game in Major League history.

6. _____My resume includes a 1.53 ERA in 1985, the Majors' best of the decade. Oh! I also forgot to mention that I won my league's Cy Young that year.

7. _____My ERA in 1985 was not too shabby at 1.93 (third best of the decade). Also, I was the only pitcher of the decade to hit double digits in shutouts (season) with 10. This figure put me in the top 20 all-time.

8. _____1985 was a good year for pitchers. However, I topped them all with a World Series MVP and a Cy Young Award.

9. _____From August 30 to September 28, 1988, no one scored a run off me. This was a Major League record 59 consecutive scoreless innings.

10. _____On April 29, 1986, I became the first pitcher in Major League history to strike out 20 batters in a nine-inning game.

11. _____I started 1984 in one league but finished the year in the other. The change was good for me; I won the Cy Young and my 16-1 record helped my new team win a division title.

12. _____In 1986, I set a single season Major League record (one I hope gets broken): 50 home runs were hit off me.

Answers to Pitchers of the 1980's

1. H—Steve Stone—Baltimore Orioles
Stone's following season, 1981, would see him win only four games and be his last Major League season. He finished his eleven-year career with a record of 107 wins and 93 losses. Due to these lackluster numbers, Stone's 1980 season led some to believe that his short-lived success was not without some other form of pitching aid.

2. K—Fernando Valenzuela—Los Angeles Dodgers

3. C—Rollie Fingers—Oakland A's

4. F—Nolan Ryan—Houston Astros   1987—270 Strikeouts
                                          1988—228 Strikeouts
                Texas Rangers   1989—301 Strikeouts
Ryan also won the title in 1990 with Texas—232 Strikeouts

5. L—Mike Witt—California Angels over the Texas Rangers 1—0

6. D—Dwight Gooden—New York Mets

7. J—John Tudor—St. Louis Cardinals

8. G—Bret Saberhagen—Kansas City Royals

9. E—Orel Hershiser—Los Angels Dodgers

10. B—Roger Clemens—Boston Red Sox   Allowed only 3 hits and struck out 20 Seattle Mariners in a 3-1 victory. Amazingly, Clemens issued no walks.

11. I—Rick Sutcliffe—He was traded from the Cleveland Indians on June 13, and at the time he had a 4-5 record.

12. A—Bert Blyleven—Minnesota Twins   50 Home Runs in 36 games and 271.2 innings

Listed below are 12 players who starred in the 1970's. They have led their league in statistical categories, won awards or accomplished some other noteworthy feat. The questions and answers will only concern statistics, awards and accomplishment from the years 1970—1979. Select the correct player for each question.

A. Johnny Bench   E. George Foster   I. Jim Rice
B. Bobby Bonds   F. Reggie Jackson   J. Pete Rose
C. Rod Carew   G. Fred Lynn   K. Mike Schmidt
D. Nate Colbert   H. Joe Morgan   L. Willie Stargell

1. _____In 1975, I won Rookie of the Year honors and was also named League MVP. I am the only player ever to capture both awards in the same season.

2. _____It may have taken 10 innings, but I hit four home runs on April 17, 1976.

3. _____On August 1, 1972, I put my name all over the record books. I tied the Major League record for home runs in a doubleheader with five, and set new M.L. records for RBI's (13) and total bases (22).

4. _____I collected a decade-best six batting titles, including four in a row (1972-75, 1977, 1978).

5. _____I led my league in doubles four times (1974-76, 1978) and my total of 394 was the most for the decade.

6. _____My game was a combination of power and speed. I led the Major Leagues with four seasons of 30 stolen bases and 30 home runs (1973, 1975, 1977-78).

7. _____In 1978, I had 406 total bases, the Majors' most since Hank Aaron in 1959. My total put me in the top twenty of all-time.

8. _____My 52 home runs in 1977 was the decade's best and highest total since Willie Mays hit 49 in 1962.

9. _____My trophy case expanded in 1979 as I was named MVP in the regular season, MVP in the league championship series, and MVP in the World Series.

10. _____In the 1970's, I was the only player to be named MVP in consecutive seasons (1975-76).

11. _____Nobody won more Gold Gloves in the decade than me. I captured eight (1970-77).

12. _____I collected four World Series rings in the 1970's, tops for any player.

Answers to Players of the 1970's

1. G—Fred Lynn—Boston Red Sox

2. K—Mike Schmidt—Philadelphia Phillies   His 4th home run in the 10th defeated the Cubs at Wrigley 18 to 16.

3. D—Nate Colbert—San Diego Padres   The Padres swept the Braves 9 to 0 and 11 to 7

4. C—Rod Carew—Minnesota Twins

1972—.318	1977—.388
1973—.350	1978—.333
1974—.364	
1975—.359	

Carew also won the batting title in 1969 with a .332 average, giving him seven batting titles and placing him fourth all-time.

5. J—Pete Rose—Cincinnati Reds   1974—45 doubles
1975—47 doubles
1976—42 doubles
1978—51 doubles (M.L. record for switch hitters)
Rose's career total of 746 doubles is second only to Tris Speaker's 792.

6. B—Bobby Bonds   1973 San Francisco   43 SB   39 HR
1975 New York Yankees   30 SB   32 HR
1977 California   41 SB   37 HR
1978 Chi. White Sox/Texas 43 SB   31 HR
Also   1969 San Francisco   45 SB   32 HR
Major League leader with five seasons

7. I—Jim Rice—Boston Red Sox

8. E—George Foster—Cincinnati Reds

9. L—Willie Stargell—Pittsburgh Pirates

10. H—Joe Morgan—Cincinnati Reds

11. A—Johnny Bench—Cincinnati Reds   Catcher

12. F—Reggie Jackson   Oakland A's—1973, 1974
N.Y. Yankees—1977, 1978

Listed below are 12 pitchers who starred in the 1970's. They have led their league in statistical categories, won awards or accomplished some other noteworthy feat. The questions and answers will only concern statistics, awards and accomplishment from the years 1970—1979. Select the correct player for each question.

A. Vida Blue   E. Catfish Hunter   I. Gaylord Perry
B. Steve Carlton   F. Dave McNally   J. J. R. Richard
C. Bob Gibson   G. Phil Niekro   K. Nolan Ryan
D. Ron Guidry   H. Jim Palmer   L. Tom Seaver

1. _____I had eight 20-win seasons in the 1970's, more than any other pitcher (1970-73, 1975-78).

2. _____I certainly traveled a lot. In the 1970's, I pitched for four different teams. Oh, did I mention that I had 20-win seasons for three of them?

3. _____My 25 victories in 1978 (.893 winning percentage) set the all-time record for winning percentage in a 20 win season.

4. _____On October 13, 1970, I hit a grand slam home run. What's special about that, you say? Well, it was the only time that a pitcher ever did so in a World Series game.

5. _____I did not hit a grand slam, but in the decade I appeared in World Series six times, compiling a pitching record of 5 wins and 3 losses.

6. _____In 1978, I became the first righthander in National League history to strikeout 300 or more batters in a single season, and the following year I bettered that total.

7. _____When my turn came in the pitching rotation, my team could count on me to take the mound as evidenced by my 376 game starts (most in the 1970's).

8. _____I'd walk 'em, then I'd strike 'em out. In six different seasons I led my league in both strikeouts and walks (1972-74, 1976-78).

9. _____Some fans think that a pitcher should not be eligible to be named Most Valuable Player. I'm glad we are, since I won the award in 1971 to go along with my Cy Young.

10. _____In 1972, I led my league with 27 victories (most in the decade) and the next season I led my league with 20 losses.

11. _____I led the National League in strikeouts five times (1970, 1971, 1973, 1975, 1976).

12. _____On July 17, 1974, I became just the second pitcher in Major League history to strike out 3000 batters.

Answers to Pitchers of the 1970's

1. H—Jim Palmer—Baltimore Orioles:

1970—20 Wins	1975—23 Wins
1971—20 Wins	1976—22 Wins
1972—21 Wins	1977—20 Wins
1973—22 Wins	1978—21 Wins

2. I—Gaylord Perry

San Francisco Giants (1970—71):	1970—23 Wins
Cleveland Indians (1972—75):	1972—24 Wins & 74—21 Wins
Texas Rangers (1975—77)	
San Diego Padres (1978—79):	1978—21 Wins

3. D—Ron Guidry—New York Yankees 25 Wins and 3 Losses

4. F—Dave McNally—Baltimore Orioles In game 3 in a 9—3 victory vs. Cincinnati Reds

5. E—Catfish Hunter

Oakland A's (1972—74)	4 Wins	0 Losses
N.Y. Yankees (1976—78)	1 Win	3 Losses

6. J—J.R. Richard—Houston Astros

1978—303 Strikeouts
1979—313 Strikeouts

7. G—Phil Niekro—Atlanta Braves

8. K—Nolan Ryan—California Angels

Year	Walks	K's

1972	157	329
1973	162	383
1974	202	367
1976	183	327
1977	204	341
1978	148	260

Ryan also led the American League in K's in 1979 with 223

9. A—Vida Blue—Oakland A's

10. B—Steve Carlton—Philadelphia Phillies

11. L—Tom Seaver—New York Mets 1970—283 K's 1975—243 K's
1971—289 K's 1976—235 K's
1973—251 K's

12. C—Bob Gibson—St. Louis Cardinals on July 17, 1974

Listed below are 12 players who starred in the 1960's. They have led their league in statistical categories, won awards or accomplished some other noteworthy feat. The questions and answers will only concern statistics, awards and accomplishment from the years 1960—1969. Select the correct player for each question.

A. Hank Aaron	E. Norm Cash	I. Roger Maris
B. Matty Alou	F. Roberto Clemente	J. Willie Mays
C. Bobby Bonds	G. Harmon Killebrew	K. Willie McCovey
D. Lou Brock	H. Mickey Mantle	L. Tony Oliva

1. _____I was the top slugger of the decade, with the most home runs (393), the most 40-home run seasons (6), and the most home run titles (5).

2. _____In 1969, I was issued 45 intentional walks, a Major League record for a single season.

3. _____Included in my decade best 231 hits in 1969 were 183 singles, the fourth highest singles total of all-time.

4. _____My .361 batting average in 1961 was the best of the decade. But, this was the only season in my 17-year career that I hit over .300, and I later admitted to using an illegal bat.

5. _____I had seven consecutive seasons with 100 RBI's (1960-66), the most of the decade. However, I never led my league in any season.

6. _____In 1967, I was the charter member of a new club: 50 stolen bases and 20 home runs in a single season.

7. _____In 1964, I set the American League record for hits by a rookie with 217.

8. _____My 187 strikeouts in 1969 was the second highest single season total of all-time and in the following season I broke my own record with 189 K's.

9. _____My slugging percentage of .687 and my home run percentage of 10.5 in 1961 were both the top marks of the decade.

10. _____I was the best of the decade with men on base, as I amassed 1107 RBI's, including three RBI titles (1960, 1963, 1966).

11. _____In the 1960's, I had the most seasons batting over .300 (9) and collected the most batting titles (4). Also, my batting average for the decade was .328.

12. _____I was the only player of the decade to hit 100 or more home runs in two consecutive seasons combined.

Answers to Players of the 1960's

1. G—Harmon Killebrew—Minnesota Twins
    1961—46 HR's   1964—49 HR's—Title
    1962—48 HR's—Title   1967—44 HR's—Title
    1963—45 HR's—Title   1969—49 HR's—Title

2. K—Willie McCovey—San Francisco Giants

3. B—Matty Alou—Pittsburgh Pirates

4. E—Norm Cash—Detroit Tigers

5. J—Willie Mays—San Francisco Giants
    1960—103 RBI's—4th   1964—111 RBI's—3rd
    1961—123 RBI's—3rd   1965—112 RBI's—3rd
    1962—141 RBI's—2nd   1966—103 RBI's—3rd (Tie)
    1963—103 RBI's—5th

6. D—Lou Brock—St. Louis Cardinals   52 SB & 21 HR

7. L—Tony Oliva—Minnesota Twins   Also won the batting title with a .323 avg.

8. C—Bobby Bonds—San Francisco Giants

9. H—Mickey Mantle—New York Yankees

10. A—Hank Aaron—Milwaukee Braves   1960—126 RBI's
                                    1963—130 RBI's

Atlanta Braves 1966—127 RBI's

11. F—Roberto Clemente—Pittsburgh Pirates
    1960—.314 BA   1965—.329 BA—Title
    1961—.351 BA—Title 1966—.317 BA
    1962—.312 BA   1967—.357 BA—Title
    1963—.320 BA   1969—.345 BA
    1964—.339 BA—Title
    Clemente's BA in 1968 was .291

12. I—Roger Maris—New York Yankees   1960—39 HR's
                                          1961—61 HR's
                                          Total—100 HR's
Willie Mays had 47 HR's in 1963 and 52 HR's in 1964 for a total of 99
Mickey Mantle had 40 HR's in 1960 and 54 HR's in 1961 for a total of
94
Harmon Killebrew also came close. See answer #1 for statistics.

Listed below are 12 pitchers who starred in the 1960's. They have led their league in statistical categories, won awards or accomplished some other noteworthy feat. The questions and answers will only concern statistics, awards and accomplishment from the years 1960—1969. Select the correct player for each question.

A. Steve Carlton	E. Don Drysdale	I. Sandy Koufax
B. Dean Chance	F. Whitey Ford	J. Juan Marichal
C. Tom Cheney	G. Bob Gibson	K. Jim Palmer
D. Tony Cloninger	H. Ferguson Jenkins	L. Jack Sanford

1. _____In 1968, I pitched 13 shutouts, which is tied for the second best in Major League history and the most since 1916.

2. _____My 16 consecutive wins in 1962 was the best streak of the decade and is tied for the third longest in Major League history.

3. _____On July 3, 1966, I became the fifth player and first pitcher to hit two grand slams in one game.

4. _____Talk about not getting any run support. In 1968, I tied the Major League record by losing five 1-0 games.

5. _____My name went into the record books in 1964 when I pitched five complete game 1-0 victories.
I was the first to do so since Carl Hubbell in 1933.

6. _____I am the only pitcher in Major League history to lead my league in ERA for five consecutive seasons (1962-66).

7. _____My 33 consecutive scoreless innings in World Series play (1960-62) is a record that still stands at the conclusion of the 2000 World Series.

8. _____On September 12, 1962, I struck out 21 batters in a 16-inning game. No pitcher has ever thrown more strikeouts in any game in Major League history.

9. _____In the 1960's I led the way with six 20 win seasons (1963-66, 1968, 1969) on the way to a decade-best 191 wins and 88 losses.

10. ____On October 6, 1966, I became the youngest pitcher to toss a complete game shutout in the World Series.

11. ____In 1968, I held the opposition scoreless for a then-record 58 consecutive innings. Included in those 58 innings are a record six consecutive shutouts.

12. ____On September 15, 1969, I became the first pitcher to strike out 19 batters in a nine-inning game and believe it or not, I lost the darn game 4-3. So I hold the Major League record for most strikeouts in a losing effort.

Answers to Pitchers of the 1960's

1. G—Bob Gibson—St. Louis Cardinals

2. L—Jack Sanford—San Francisco Giants   Had 24 Wins and 7 losses

3. D—Tony Cloninger—Atlanta Braves vs. San Francisco Giants
Cloninger had nine RBI's, a Major League record for pitchers. Also, he is
the only pitcher to ever hit two grand slams in one game.

4. H—Ferguson Jenkins—Chicago Cubs   Jenkins did not win any 1-
0 games that year.

5. B—Dean Chance—Los Angeles Angels

6. I—Sandy Koufax—Los Angeles Dodgers
1962—2.54 ERA
1963—1.88 ERA— Led Majors
1964—1.74 ERA
1965—2.04 ERA—Led Majors
1966—1.73 ERA—Led Majors

7. F—Whitey Ford—New York Yankees
October 8, 1960—9 Innings
October 12, 1960—9 Innings
October 4, 1961—9 Innings
October 8, 1961—5 Innings
October 4, 1962—1 Inning

8. C—Tom Cheney—Washington Senators—Struck out 21 Baltimore Orioles in a 2—1 victory

9. J—Juan Marichal—San Francisco Giants

	W	L		W	L
1960	6	2	1965	22	13
1961	13	10	1966	25	6
1962	18	11	1967	14	10
1963	25	8	1968	26	9
1964	21	8	1969	21	11

Led NL in wins: 1963, 1968

10. K- Jim Palmer—Baltimore Orioles   6—0 over the Los Angeles Dodgers and Sandy Koufax.
Palmer was 20 years, 11 months, and 21 days old.

11. E—Don Drysdale—Los Angeles Dodgers
Orel Hershiser broke the consecutive scoreless innings record in 1988. The shutout record still stands.

12. A—Steve Carlton—St. Louis Cardinals
Carlton lost the game to the New York Mets 4-3 as Ron Swoboda hit two two run homers.

Listed below are 12 players who starred in the 1950's. They have led their league in statistical categories, won awards or accomplished some other noteworthy feat. The questions and answers will only concern statistics, awards and accomplishment from the years 1950—1959. Select the correct player for each question.

A. Hank Aaron	E. Nellie Fox	I. Willie Mays
B. Joe Adcock	F. Gil Hodges	J. Stan Musial
C. Ernie Banks	G. Al Kaline	K. Duke Snider
D. Walt Dropo	H. Mickey Mantle	L. Ted Williams

1. _____I was the batter that pitchers hated to see when the bases were loaded. In 1955, I hit a National League record five grand slams.

2. _____My 52 home runs in 1956 was the decade's best total and helped me capture the Triple Crown.

3. _____In 1957, my .731 slugging percentage put me in the top 15 of all-time and my .388 batting average was the highest of the decade.

4. _____On July 31, 1954, I established a Major League record with 18 total bases (four home runs and a double) in a nine-inning game.

5. _____In 1955, I hit .340 and became the youngest player ever to win a league batting title.

6. _____I won the most batting titles in the 1950's (four: 1950-52, 1957) and the only year in which I failed to hit .300 was 1959.

7. _____I led my league in hits four times (1952, 1954, 1957-58) and my total of 1837 base hits was the decade's top mark.

8. _____I certainly was consistent. For five consecutive seasons I hit 40 home runs (1953-57) and my total of 326 homers was the highest of the decade.

9. _____In 1952, I tied Pinky Higgins's Major League record of 12 consecutive hits and my streak included no walks.

10. _____In 1959, I collected 400 total bases. This was the only time that anyone reached this plateau in the 1950's.

11. _____I was considered an all-around ballplayer. In the 1950's, I won three Gold Glove Awards (1957-59) and led my league in stolen bases four times (1956-59). My 179 steals were more than anyone else in the decade and I was the only player to hit 20 triples in one season (1957).

12. _____I was the only player in the decade to have more than 1,000 RBI's.

Answers to Players of the 1950's

1. C—Ernie Banks—Chicago Cubs

2. H—Mickey Mantle—New York Yankees .353 BA 52 HR 30 RBI

3. L—Ted Williams—Boston Red Sox

4. B—Joe Adcock—Milwaukee Braves

5. G—Al Kaline—Detroit Tigers Kaline was born on December 19, 1934, so when the season ended he was only 20 years old.

6. J—Stan Musial—St. Louis Cardinals

1950—.346	1st	1955—.319	2nd (Tie)
1951—.355	1st	1956—.310	4th
1952—.336	1st	1957—.351	1st
1953—.337	3rd	1958—.337	3rd
1954—.330	4th	1959—.255	

7. E—Nellie Fox—Chicago White Sox Fox was one of the great singles hitters of any era, of his 1,837 hits 1,474 were singles and he led the American League in singles seven times.

1950—113 Hits	94 Singles
1951—189 Hits 2nd	141 Singles
1952—192 Hits 1st	157 Singles 1st
1953—178 Hits	136 Singles
1954—201 Hits 1st	167 Singles 1st
1955—198 Hits 2nd	157 Singles 1st

1956—192 Hits 2nd   158 Singles 1st
1957—196 Hits 1st   155 Singles 1st
1958—187 Hits 1st   160 Singles 1st
1959—191 Hits 2nd   149 Singles 1st
Fox also lead the American League in 1960 with 139 singles

8. K—Duke Snider—Brooklyn/Los Angeles Dodgers

1950—31 HR	1955—42 HR 4th
1951—29 HR	1956—43 HR 1st
1952—21 HR	1957—40 HR 3rd
1953—42 HR 2nd	1958—15 HR
1954—40 HR 5th (Tie)	1959—23 HR

9. D—Walt Dropo—Detroit Tigers

10. A—Hank Aaron—Milwaukee Braves   131 Singles 46 Doubles 7 Triples 39 Home Runs

11. I—Willie Mays—New York/ San Francisco Giants

1956—40 SB	1958—31 SB
1957—38 SB	1959—27 SB

12. F—Gil Hodges—Brooklyn/Los Angeles Dodgers

1950—113 RBI 3rd	1955—102 RBI
1951—103 RBI 6th	1956— 87 RBI
1952—102 RBI 4th	1957— 98 RBI
1953—122 RBI 4th	1958— 64 RBI
1954—130 RBI 2nd	1959— 80 RBI
	Total: 1,001 RBI

Listed below are 12 pitchers who starred in the 1950's. They have led their league in statistical categories, won awards or accomplished some other noteworthy feat. The questions and answers will only concern statistics, awards and accomplishment from the years 1950—1959. Select the correct player for each question.

A. Lou Burdette   E. Billy Pierce   I. Bobby Shantz
B. Elroy Face   F. Allie Reynolds   J. Warren Spahn
C. Sal Maglie   G. Robin Roberts   K. Hoyt Wilhelm
D. Don Newcombe   H. Herb Score   L. Early Wynn

1. _____I had six consecutive 20-win seasons (1950-56), led my league in wins four straight times (1952-56), and my 28 wins in 1952 was the top mark of the decade.

2. _____My 45 consecutive scoreless innings in 1950 is the eighth best streak of all-time. An interesting fact about my career is that I pitched for all three New York City teams in three successive years: the Giants in 1955, the Dodgers in 1956, and the Yankees in 1957.

3. _____I never led my league in shutouts for a single season during the 1950's but my total of 33 shutouts is tied for the most in the decade. In 1959, I won the Cy Young Award.

4. _____I did quite well in the 1950's. I was the inaugural Gold Glove Award winner (1957), the first of three consecutive. I had my league's lowest ERA in 1957 (2.45), led my league in winning percentage in 1952 (.774), and was named league MVP that same season.

5. _____My time to shine was the 1957 World Series. I was named the Series MVP due to my three complete game victories, two shutouts, and a .067 ERA.

6. _____In 1951, I became the first pitcher since Johnny Vander Meer in 1938 to throw two no-hitters in the same season.

7. _____I was named Rookie of the Year in 1955, captured strikeout titles in 1955 and 1956, but a line drive ruined my career in 1957.

8. _____I was the first pitcher to win league MVP honors and win the Cy Young Award in the same season (1956).

9. _____In the 1950's, I led my league in victories five times (1950, 1953, 1957-59) and posted eight 20-win seasons. My 202 wins were the most of the decade.

10. _____I had 17 consecutive wins in 1959, the second-longest streak of all-time. My record that year was 18-1, and my winning percentage of .947 is the highest ever recorded for a single season (minimum 16 decisions).

11. _____I was the only pitcher of the decade to have an ERA under 2.00 (minimum 154 innings). I accomplished this in 1955 with an ERA of 1.97.

12. _____My career began in 1952, but it wasn't until 1958 that I pitched my first shutout. That happened on September 2 when I won the game 1-0. By the way, it was a no-hitter.

Answers to Pitchers of the 1950's

1. G—Robin Roberts—Philadelphia Phillies
1950—20 Wins 2nd (Tie)   1953—23 Wins 1st (Tie)
1951—21 Wins 5th   1954—23 Wins 1st
1952—28 Wins 1st   1955—23 Wins 1st

2. C—Sal Maglie—His scoreless inning streak was with the New York Giants

3. L—Early Wynn—Cleveland Indians
                              1950—57   24 Shutouts
Chicago White Sox   1958—59   9 Shutouts

4. I—Bobby Shantz—Philadelphia Athletics 1952 AL MVP 24 Wins—
                                               7 Losses .774 Pct.
              New York Yankees   1957, 58 & 59 Gold Glove

5. A—Lou Burdette—Milwaukee Braves

6. F—Allie Reynolds—New York Yankees   July 12   New York at
                                            Cleveland   1—0
                                          September 28   New York
                                            vs. Boston   8—0

7. H—Herb Score—Cleveland Indians
On May 7 Score was hit in the eye by a line drive off the bat of the New York Yankees' Gil McDougald.

8. D—Don Newcombe—Brooklyn Dodgers

9. J—Warren Spahn—Boston/Milwaukee Braves

1950—21 Wins 1st	1955—17 Wins 3rd (Tie)
1951—22 Wins 3rd (Tie)	1956—20 Wins 2nd (Tie)
1952—14 Wins	1957—21 Wins 1st
1953—23 Wins 1st (Tie)	1958—22 Wins 1st (Tie)
1954—21 Wins 2nd (Tie)	1959—21 Wins 1st (Tie)

10. B—Elroy Face—Pittsburgh Pirates

11. E—Billy Pierce—Chicago White Sox

12. K—Hoyt Wilhelm—Baltimore Orioles vs. New York Yankees

SECTION 4—EXCLUSIVE CLUBS

Exclusive Clubs

Baseball is a sport built upon numbers. It uses numbers to measure a player's success within the game. It uses numbers to measure players from different eras against those from both previous and future eras. Those players with similar numbers, who have reached certain milestones, are grouped together and put in certain clubs. For example, there is the 500 Home Run Club (17 members), the 300 Victory Club (20 members), the 3,000 Hit Club (24 members), and the 3,000 Strikeout Club (12 members). Some players have demonstrated abilities that are above the rest and have combined milestone numbers: 400 home runs and 3,000 hits (7 members), 300 victories and 3,000 strikeouts (7 members). Each of these very exclusive clubs tells fans where these players stand within the history of the game. They signify success. They signify excellence. They signify a career above the rest.

As we go up the numbers chart for any player's career, we find that the higher we go the more select the clubs become. Admittance is reserved for an elite few. One of the most exclusive clubs, one that receives extended applause, is 500 Home Runs and 3,000 Hits. This exclusive club has admitted only three players out of the thousands that have played Major League Baseball.

A question that I have pondered concerns those players whose accomplishments are so unique that they are the only ones to reach certain levels. Can you have a club with only one member? Three players and three achievements immediately come to mind. Cy Young is the only pitcher in Major League history with 500 wins. Nolan Ryan is the only pitcher in Major League history with 5,000 strikeouts. Barry Bonds is the only player in Major League history with 400 home runs and 400 stolen bases. These three career achievements are truly above the rest. Are they clubs of one? Will they ever have company? My guess is that Young and Ryan will remain alone. However, I believe that Bonds will be joined by others. As to who or when, only time will give us the answer.

Prior to the 2001 season, there were only 16 members in the 500 Home Run Club. Barry Bonds hit his 500th home run on April 17, 2001 to join Mark McGwire as the only active members; however, Bonds and his statistics will not be included. On the left are the career totals and on the right in (alphabetical order) are the 16 players. Match the career total with the correct player.

1.	755 _____		Hank Aaron
2.	714 _____		Ernie Banks
3.	660 _____		Jimmie Foxx
4.	586 _____		Reggie Jackson
5.	573 _____		Harmon Killebrew
6.	563 _____		Mickey Mantle
7.	554 _____		Eddie Mathews
8.	548 _____		Willie Mays
9.	536 _____		Willie McCovey
10.	534 _____		Mark McGwire
11.	521 _____		Eddie Murray
12.	521 _____		Mel Ott
13.	512 _____		Frank Robinson

14. 512 _____   Babe Ruth

15. 511 _____   Mike Schmidt

16. 504 _____   Ted Williams

500 Home Run Club Members in Order

1.	Hank Aaron	755	
2.	Babe Ruth	714	
3.	Willie Mays	660	
4.	Frank Robinson	586	
5.	Harmon Killebrew	573	
6.	Reggie Jackson	563	
7.	Mark McGwire	554	*Active*
8.	Mike Schmidt	548	
9.	Mickey Mantle	536	
10.	Jimmie Foxx	534	
11.	Ted Williams	521	
12.	Willie McCovey	521	
13.	Ernie Banks	512	
14.	Eddie Mathews	512	

| 15. | Mel Ott | 511 |
| 16. | Eddie Murray | 504 |

When did each one of these sluggers hit his 500th home run? Arrange from the earliest to the most recent, the date that each hit his milestone home run. On the left are the dates and on the right are the players (in alphabetical order). Match the date with the correct player.

August 11, 1929	_____	Hank Aaron
September 24, 1940	_____	Ernie Banks
August 1, 1945	_____	Jimmie Foxx
June 17, 1960	_____	Reggie Jackson
September 13, 1965	_____	Harmon Killebrew
May 14, 1967	_____	Mickey Mantle
July 14, 1967	_____	Eddie Mathews
June 14, 1968	_____	Willie Mays
May 12, 1970	_____	Willie McCovey
August 10, 1971	_____	Mark McGwire
September 13, 1971	_____	Eddie Murray
June 30, 1978	_____	Mel Ott
September 17, 1984	_____	Frank Robinson
April 18, 1987	_____	Babe Ruth

| September 6, 1996 | _____ | Mike Schmidt |
| August 5, 1999 | _____ | Ted Williams |

Answers: 500 Home Run Club —Chronological Order

August 11, 1929   Babe Ruth

September 24, 1940   Jimmie Foxx

August 1, 1945   Mel Ott

June 17, 1960   Ted Williams

September 13, 1965   Willie Mays

May 14, 1967   Mickey Mantle

July 14, 1967   Eddie Mathews

June 14, 1968   Hank Aaron

May 12, 1970   Ernie Banks

August 10, 1971   Harmon Killebrew

September 13, 1971   Frank Robinson

June 30, 1978   Willie McCovey

September 17, 1984   Reggie Jackson

April 18, 1987   Mike Schmidt

September 6, 1996   Eddie Murray

August 5, 1999   Mark McGwire

The following questions only concern members of the 500 Home Run Club. Match the player to the appropriate question.

A. Hank Aaron   G. Eddie Mathews   M. Frank Robinson
B. Ernie Banks   H. Willie Mays   N. Babe Ruth
C. Jimmie Foxx   I. Willie McCovey   O. Mike Schmidt
D. Reggie Jackson   J. Mark McGwire   P. Ted Williams
E. Harmon Killebrew   K. Eddie Murray
F. Mickey Mantle   L. Mel Ott

1. _____Consistency and durability were the hallmarks of my career as I had at least 75 RBI's for 20 consecutive seasons.

2. _____In this select group of power hitters I am first in career walks (2,056).

3. _____I certainly hit a lot of home runs, but there were also lots of times that I only got halfway around the bases. My 624 doubles are the most of anyone in the club and put me in the top ten of all-time.

4. _____I made more use of the stolen base than any other Club member. My 338 steals are tops in the group.

5. _____I hit home runs for my team, but unfortunately, I never got a chance to play in a World Series.

6. _____They say, "big things come in small packages." Well, I am the shortest member of the club (5'9") but that didn't prevent me from hitting home runs.

7. _____Managers couldn't play the percentages with me. I am the Major League leader for home runs by a switch hitter.

8. _____Hitting was my game. My career batting average (.344) is the highest of any member.

9. _____I packed a mighty wallop, but I also missed a lot. My career total of 2,597 strikeouts is a Major League record.

10. _____I am the only player in Major League history to be named MVP in both the American and National Leagues.

11. _____With me on deck, you would think National League pitchers would learn not to load the bases. I hold the career record for grand slams in the National League (18).

12. _____The heck with singles, my job was to hit home runs. My batting average suffered; I hit .256 for my career, the lowest average of any member.

13. _____I led my league in home runs eight times, more than any other right handed batter in Major League history.

14. _____Pitchers didn't intimidate me during my rookie season. I hold the Major League record for home runs by a rookie (49).

15. _____I was a consistent home run threat. I hold the Major League record with 30 or more home runs for 12 consecutive years.

16. _____The franchise I played for was on the mileage plan. I played for only one team, but it was located in three different cities during my career.

Answers: 500 Home Run Club

1. K   Eddie Murray (1977—1996)

2. N   Babe Ruth

3. A   Hank Aaron

4. H   Willie Mays

5. B   Ernie Banks

6. L   Mel Ott

7. F   Mickey Mantle

8. P   Ted Williams

9. D   Reggie Jackson

10. M   Frank Robinson   Cincinnati Reds—1961 (NL)
                          Baltimore Orioles—1966 (AL)

11. I   Willie McCovey

12. E   Harmon Killebrew

13. O   Mike Schmidt   (1974-76, 1980, 1981, 1983, 1984, 1986)

14. J   Mark McGwire (1987)

15. C   Jimmie Foxx (1929-40)

16. G   Eddie Mathews   Braves—Boston (1952), Milwaukee (1953-65), Atlanta (1966)

On April 15, 2000, Cal Ripken, Jr. entered the 3,000 Hit Club, joining 23 other players who have reached this milestone. The first player to reach to do so was Cap Anson in 1897. Anson played his entire career in the 19th century and finished his with exactly 3,000 hits. The second and third players to hit 3,000 were Honus Wagner and Napoleon Lajoie, both in 1914. These two had careers that started prior to 1901, the year generally accepted as the beginning of the modern era. Wagner finished his career with 3,418 hits, 649 of which came before 1901. Lajoie finished his career with 3,244 hits, having 721of those coming prior to 1901. Ripken and the twenty other players who gained entrance into the 3,000 Hit Club all had careers that started after 1901. Select the date that these twenty players recorded their milestone hit.

Aug. 19, 1921	_____	Hank Aaron
May 17, 1925	_____	Wade Boggs
June 3, 1925	_____	George Brett
June 19, 1942	_____	Lou Brock
May 13, 1958	_____	Rod Carew
May 17, 1970	_____	Ty Cobb
July 18, 1970	_____	Roberto Clemente
Oct. 5, 1972	_____	Eddie Collins
Sept. 24, 1974	_____	Tony Gwynn
May 5, 1978	_____	Al Kaline

Aug. 13, 1979	_____	Willie Mays
Sept. 12, 1979	_____	Paul Molitor
Aug. 4, 1985	_____	Eddie Murray
Sept. 9, 1992	_____	Stan Musial
Sept. 30, 1992	_____	Pete Rose
Sept. 16, 1993	_____	Tris Speaker
June 30, 1995	_____	Paul Waner
Sept. 16, 1996	_____	Dave Winfield
Aug. 6, 1999	_____	Carl Yastrzemski
Aug. 7, 1999	_____	Robin Yount

Answers: 3,000 Hits—Chronological Order

Aug. 19, 1921	Ty Cobb
May 17, 1925	Tris Speaker
June 3, 1925	Eddie Collins
June 19, 1942	Paul Waner
May 13, 1958	Stan Musial
May 17, 1970	Hank Aaron
July 18, 1970	Willie Mays
Oct. 5, 1972	Roberto Clemente
Sept. 24, 1974	Al Kaline
May 5, 1978	Pete Rose
Aug. 13, 1979	Lou Brock
Sept. 12, 1979	Carl Yastrzemski
Aug. 4, 1985	Rod Carew
Sept. 9, 1992	Robin Yount

Sept. 30, 1992	George Brett
Sept. 16, 1993	Dave Winfield
June 30, 1995	Eddie Murray
Sept. 16, 1996	Paul Molitor
Aug. 6, 1999	Tony Gwynn
Aug. 7, 1999	Wade Boggs

Prior to the 2001 season, there were only 24 members in the 3,000 Hit Club. On the left are the career totals and on the right (in alphabetical order) are the 24 players. Match the career total with the correct player.

1.   4,256 _____   Hank Aaron

2.   4,191 _____   Cap Anson

3.   3,771 _____   Wade Boggs

4.   3,630 _____   George Brett

5.   3,514 _____   Lou Brock

6.   3,419 _____   Rod Carew

7.   3,418 _____   Roberto Clemente

8.   3,319 _____   Ty Cobb

9.   3,313 _____   Eddie Collins

10.   3,283 _____   Tony Gwynn

11.   3,244 _____   Al Kaline

12.   3,154 _____   Napoleon Lajoie

13.   3,152 _____   Willie Mays

14.   3,142 _____   Paul Molitor

15.	3,110 _____	Eddie Murray
16.	3,108 _____	Stan Musial
17.	3,071 _____	Cal Ripken, Jr.
18.	3,070 _____	Pete Rose
19.	3,053 _____	Tris Speaker
20.	3,023 _____	Honus Wagner
21.	3,010 _____	Paul Waner
22.	3,007 _____	Dave Winfield
23.	3,000 _____	Carl Yastrzemski
23.	3,000 _____	Robin Yount

Baseball's All-Time Hit Leaders

Active Players

1. Pete Rose   4,256

2. Ty Cobb   4,191

3. Hank Aaron   3,771

4. Stan Musial   3,630

5. Tris Speaker   3,514

6. Carl Yastrzemski   3,419

7. Honus Wagner   3,418

8. Paul Molitor   3,319

9. Eddie Collins   3,313

10. Willie Mays   3,283

11. Napoleon Lajoie   3,244

12. George Brett   3,154

13. Paul Waner   3,152

14. Robin Yount	3,142
15. Dave Winfield	3,110
16. Tony Gwynn *	3,108
17. Eddie Murray	3,071
18. Cal Ripken, Jr. *	3,070
19. Rod Carew	3,053
20. Lou Brock	3,023
21. Wade Boggs	3,010
22. Al Kaline	3,007
23. Cap Anson	3,000
23. Roberto Clemente	3,000

On April 15, 2000, Cal Ripken, Jr. became the 24th player in Major League history to amass 3,000 hits. He became only the seventh player to combine those hits with 400 home runs. The members of this select group have demonstrated a unique ability and combination of batting skills; power to hit the long ball without sacrificing bat control. They are near the top of numerous offensive categories, and these questions will only deal with members of this exclusive club. Match the players to the appropriate descriptions.

A. Hank Aaron   C. Eddie Murray   F. Dave Winfield
B. Willie Mays   D. Stan Musial   G. Carl Yastrzemski
E. Cal Ripken, Jr.

1. _____I hit .300 seventeen times during my career. Believe it or not, this total only places me tied for fourth all-time.

2. _____I am the only switch-hitter in the group

3. _____I had 63 multiple home run games in my career, more than anyone excepting Babe Ruth. Well, I was second until Mark McGwire passed me in 2000.

4. _____My strikeout total is the most of the group and it puts me in the top 15 of all-time (1,686).

5. _____I played in a lot of baseball games (3,308), second only to Pete Rose on the all-time list.

6. _____I am the only member of this group to be the Major League leader for career home runs at my position.

7. _____My hits produced a lot of runs; I am number one in Major League history with 2,297 RBI's.

Answers to Players
with 3000 Hits & 400 Home Runs

1. D—Stan Musial

2. C—Eddie Murray

3. B—Willie Mays

4. F—Dave Winfield

5. G—Carl Yastrzemski

6. E—Cal Ripken, Jr.   Ripken is first in career home runs for a short-stop with 345.
Eddie Murray is fifth in career home runs for a first baseman with 409.
Hank Aaron is second in career home runs for outfielders with 661.
Willie Mays is third in career home runs for outfielders with 642.

7. A—Hank Aaron

Three players, Hank Aaron, Willie Mays, and Eddie Murray, form an extremely limited club: 500 home runs and 3,000 hits. The difficulty level of what these three have achieved in their careers speaks for itself. Twenty-four players have reached the 3,000 hit plateau, sixteen have reached the 500 home run plateau, but only three have had the unique ability to combine the two. Choose one of the three greats for each question.

A. Hank Aaron   B. Willie Mays   C. Eddie Murray

1. ____Which one had the highest career batting average (.305)?

2. ____Only Lou Gehrig's 23 grand slams top this player's total (19).

3. ____Which one received the most walks in his career and is 17th on the all-time list (1,464)?

4. ____Which one had the highest career slugging average (.557)?

5. ____All three played in more than one World Series in their careers. Which one had the highest World Series batting average (.364)?

6. ____Which one hit the most World Series home runs (4)?

7. ____Which is the only one to win both Rookie of the Year honors and be named Most Valuable Player
in his career?

8. ____Which one was the toughest to strike out in his career (11.18%)?

BONUS QUESTION

Both Aaron and Mays were outfielders and both played some games at first base in their careers. Murray was a first baseman who played a few games in the outfield. Additionally, there is another position on the diamond that all three played at some point in their careers. Which one?

A. Pitcher   B. Catcher   C. Second Base   D. Third Base   E. Shortstop

Answers: 3,000 Hits and 500 Home Runs

1. A—Hank Aaron   Willie Mays   .302
                       Eddie Murray   .287

2. C—Eddie Murray

3. B—Willie Mays

4. B—Willie Mays   Hank Aaron   .555
                       Eddie Murray   .476

5. A—Hank Aaron

6. C—Eddie Murray

7. B—Willie Mays
1951—Rookie of the Year   1954—Most Valuable Player
                             1965—Most Valuable Player
              Hank Aaron—1957—MVP
              Eddie Murray—1977—ROY

8. A—Hank Aaron   Eddie Murray 13.37%
                       Willie Mays   14.02%

BONUS QUESTION: D. Third Base

There are 20 pitchers who have won at least 300 games in their Major League careers, and they can be divided into two groups. The first group consists of those pitchers whose entire career was before 1901. They are: John Clarkson, Pud Galvin, Tim Keefe, Old Hoss Radburn and Mickey Welch. Included with these five are two others whose careers were spent in both the 1800's and the 1900's: Kid Nichols and Cy Young. The second group consists of all the other members of the club. The groups are separated because statistics from the two eras are not comparable. Before 1901, pitchers would typically have over 70 starts; over 70 complete games; over 600 innings and give up over 600 hits, all in a single season. Some scoring rules and playing conditions were different. For example, in 1887, walks were scored as hits, and it wasn't until 1893 that the current pitching distance of 60 feet 6 inches went into effect.

Listed here are these seven 300-club members and their win totals. Each of them is enshrined in the Hall of Fame, but aside from Cy Young, none of these are very well-known to the modern fan. A curious note about these seven "old timers" was that they were all righthanders. Try to match these astounding statistics to the appropriate pitchers.

A. Cy Young	511	286 Victories prior to 1901
B. Pud Galvin	361	
C. Kid Nichols	361	310 Victories prior to 1901
D. Tim Keefe	342	
E. John Clarkson	326	
F. Old Hoss Radburn	311	
G. Mickey Welch	308	

1. _____My seven 30-win seasons are the most by any pitcher of any era.

2. _____Does 1884 count twice for me when I add up my 30-win seasons? My record that year was 60-12.

3. _____I finished what I started; my resume includes an all-time best 750 complete games. No modern day pitcher is remotely close and even my contemporaries are over 100 games behind.

4. _____My single season record of 19 consecutive victories (1888) is good for any era. Only a fellow named Rube Marquard (New York Giants) in 1912 was able to match it.

5. _____I finished my career with a 2.87 ERA, despite my record 3,303 runs given up. This total is almost 1,000 more than the closest modern-day pitcher, Phil Niekro.

6. _____I led the league in complete games three times in my 12-year career, and in both 1885 and 1889 I had 68 complete games.

7. _____I have some rather dubious statistics: among these pitchers, I have the most career walks and in my first season (1880), I not only won 34 games, but lost 30 games as well.

Answers: Pitchers—1800's & 1900's

1. C—Kid Nichols

2. F—Old Hoss Radburn

3. A—Cy Young

4. D—Tim Keefe

5. B—Pud Galvin

6. E—John Clarkson

7. G—Mickey Welch

On the left are the career-win totals and on the right (in alphabetical order) are the 13 pitchers who won 300 games after 1901. Match the career total with the correct pitcher.
* Christy Mathewson did pitch in the 1900 season; his record was zero wins and three losses.

1. 417 _____   Grover Alexander

2. 373 _____   Steve Carlton

2. 373 _____   Lefty Grove

4. 363 _____   Walter Johnson

5. 329 _____   Christy Mathewson

6. 326 _____   Phil Niekro

7. 324 _____   Gaylord Perry

7. 324 _____   Eddie Plank

9. 318 _____   Nolan Ryan

10. 314 _____   Tom Seaver

11. 311 _____   Warren Spahn

12. 300 _____   Don Sutton

12. 300 _____   Early Wynn

300 Career Victories in Order

1.	417—Walter Johnson
2.	373—Grover Alexander
2.	373—Christy Mathewson
4.	363—Warren Spahn
5.	329—Steve Carlton
6.	326—Eddie Plank
7.	324—Nolan Ryan
7.	324—Don Sutton
9.	318—Phil Niekro
10.	314—Gaylord Perry
11.	311—Tom Seaver
12.	300—Lefty Grove
12.	300—Early Wynn

When did each one of these pitchers register his 300th victory? Arrange from the earliest to the most recent, the date that each recorded his milestone victory. On the left are the dates and on the right are the pitchers (in alphabetical order). Match the date with the correct pitcher.

June 13, 1912	_____	Grover Alexander
Sept. 11, 1915	_____	Steve Carlton
May 14, 1920	_____	Lefty Grove
Sept. 20, 1924	_____	Walter Johnson
July 25, 1941	_____	Christy Mathewson
August 11, 1961	_____	Phil Niekro
July 13, 1963	_____	Gaylord Perry
May 6, 1982	_____	Eddie Plank
September 23, 1983	_____	Nolan Ryan
August 4, 1985	_____	Tom Seaver
October 6, 1985	_____	Warren Spahn
June 18, 1986	_____	Don Sutton
July 31, 1990	_____	Early Wynn

Answers: 300 Victories—Chronological Order

June 13, 1912	Christy Mathewson
Sept. 11, 1915	Eddie Plank
May 14, 1920	Walter Johnson
Sept. 20, 1924	Grover Alexander
July 25, 1941	Lefty Grove
August 11, 1961	Warren Spahn
July 13, 1963	Early Wynn
May 6, 1982	Gaylord Perry
September 23, 1983	Steve Carlton
August 4, 1985	Tom Seaver
October 6, 1985	Phil Niekro
June 18, 1986	Don Sutton
July 31, 1990	Nolan Ryan

The following questions only concern pitchers with at least 300 victories starting with the 1901 season. Match the pitcher to the appropriate question.

A. Grover Alexander   E. Christy Mathewson   J. Tom Seaver
B. Steve Carlton   F. Phil Niekro   K. Warren Spahn
C. Lefty Grove   G. Gaylord Perry   L. Don Sutton
D. Walter Johnson   H. Eddie Plank   M. Early Wynn
I. Nolan Ryan

1. _____My career winning percentage of .680 is the fourth-best in Major League history and it is the highest among 300-game winners.

2. _____I only had one season with at least 20 victories (1976), but my consistency and longevity got me to the magic number.

3. _____I am the only pitcher with 300 wins to win the Cy Young Award in both the American and National Leagues.

4. _____My 16 shutouts in one season (1916) is a Major League record.

5. _____I am the only pitcher in Major League history to pass the century mark in shutouts (110).

6. _____My career total of 2,795 walks puts me 962 ahead of anyone else in Major League history.

7. _____No one in the club had a 20-win season later into their careers than I did. I posted 23 victories when I was 42 years old.

8. _____I struck out 4,136 batters in my career. This is the second-best total of all-time and the best for a lefthander.

9. _____I pitched in 864 games, more than anyone else in the club.

10. _____My career earned run average of 2.13 is the fifth-lowest of all-time and the lowest amongst 300-game winners.

11. _____I struck out the entire-line up plus one, 10 consecutive batters, a Major League record.

12. _____Included in my 300 victories are the 21 wins I earned in my one-year stint with the St. Louis Terriers of the Federal League in 1915. I am the only member of the club to pitch in the Federal League.

13. _____All those guys above me might have some noteworthy achievement besides their career victory total, but MY NAME means Victory!

Answers: 300 Career Victories

1. C—Lefty Grove

2. L—Don Sutton   1976—21 wins

3. G—Gaylord Perry   American League—1972—Cleveland Indians
                          National League—1978—San Diego Padres

4. A—Grover Alexander

5. D—Walter Johnson

6. I—Nolan Ryan

7. K—Warren Spahn   1963—23 wins

8. B—Steve Carlton

9. F—Phil Niekro

10. E—Christy Mathewson

11. J—Tom Seaver—New York Mets vs. San Diego Padres on April 22, 1970. He struck out 19 batters in a 2-1 victory.

12. H—Eddie Plank—One Federal League season with a 21—11 record and a 2.08 ERA.

13. M—Early Wynn

The counterpart to the home run is the strikeout. Only 12 pitchers have 3,000 strikeouts in their careers, a milestone that is more common to the last quarter of the 20th century. The early part of the 1900's had several 30-game winners, but only one pitcher reached the 3,000 strikeout plateau. On July 22, 1923, Walter Johnson became the sole member of the club and it was not until 1974 that another pitcher joined him with 3,000 strikeouts. What follows is a chronological timetable of when the other 11 pitchers reached their milestone strikeout. Match the correct pitcher with the date on which he joined the club.

July 17, 1974	_____	Bert Blyleven
Oct. 1, 1978	_____	Steve Carlton
July 4, 1980	_____	Roger Clemens
April 18, 1981	_____	Bob Gibson
April 29, 1981	_____	Ferguson Jenkins
May 25, 1982	_____	Randy Johnson
June 24, 1983	_____	Phil Niekro
July 4, 1984	_____	Gaylord Perry
Aug. 1, 1986	_____	Nolan Ryan
July 5, 1998	_____	Tom Seaver
Sept. 10, 2000	_____	Don Sutton

Answers: 3,000 Strikeouts —Chronological Order

July 17, 1974	Bob Gibson
Oct. 1, 1978	Gaylord Perry
July 4, 1980	Nolan Ryan
April 18, 1981	Tom Seaver
April 29, 1981	Steve Carlton
May 25, 1982	Ferguson Jenkins
June 24, 1983	Don Sutton
July 4, 1984	Phil Niekro
Aug. 1, 1986	Bert Blyleven
July 5, 1998	Roger Clemens
Sept. 10, 2000	Randy Johnson

Prior to the 2001 season, there were only 12 members in the 3,000 Strikeout Club. Randy Johnson is the newest member and he and Roger Clemens are the only active members. On the left are the career totals and on the right (in alphabetical order) are the 12 pitchers. Match the career total with the correct pitcher.

1.	5,714 _____	Bert Blyleven
2.	4,136 _____	Steve Carlton
3.	3,701 _____	Roger Clemens
4.	3,640 _____	Bob Gibson
5.	3,574 _____	Ferguson Jenkins
6.	3,534 _____	Randy Johnson
7.	3,509 _____	Walter Johnson
8.	3,504 _____	Phil Niekro
9.	3,342 _____	Gaylord Perry
10.	3,192 _____	Nolan Ryan
11.	3,117 _____	Tom Seaver
12.	3,040 _____	Don Sutton

Baseball's All-Time Strikeout Leaders

Active Players

1. Nolan Ryan   5,714

2. Steve Carlton   4,136

3. Bert Blyleven   3,701

4. Tom Seaver   3,640

5. Don Sutton   3,574

6. Gaylord Perry   3,534

7. Walter Johnson   3,509

8. Roger Clemens *   3,504

9. Phil Niekro   3,342

10. Ferguson Jenkins 3,192

11. Bob Gibson   3,117

12. Randy Johnson *   3,040

The pitcher's counterpart to 3,000 hits and 400 home runs is 3,000 strikeouts and 300 wins. A hurler must display pitching excellence for an extended period of time to reach these marks, and, like their hitting counterparts, only seven pitchers have ever achieved both. They are near the top in numerous pitching categories, and these questions will only deal with members of this exclusive club. Match the pitchers to the appropriate descriptions.

A. Steve Carlton   C. Phil Niekro   F. Tom Seaver
B. Walter Johnson   D. Gaylord Perry   G. Don Sutton
E. Nolan Ryan

1. _____A team usually starts its number one pitcher on opening day. My total of 16 starts on opening day is the best figure of all-time.

2. _____I didn't start as many times, but my total of nine victories on opening day is the most in Major League history.

3. _____Durability was a hallmark of my career; my 20 seasons with 200 or more innings pitched is the most of all-time.

4. _____When it comes to games started, only Cy Young tops my career mark of 773.

5. _____Unfortunately, I was no stranger to watching hitters circle the bases. I am third on the all-time list, behind Robin Roberts and Ferguson Jenkins in home runs allowed (482).

6. _____No one pitched more seasons in the National League than I did (22).

7. _____I struck out a lot of batters, but I traveled a great deal as well. I pitched for eight different teams during my 22-year career.

218 • So You Think You Know Baseball

Answers to Pitchers
with 300 Victories & 3000 Strikeouts

1. F—Tom Seaver   Opening day record: 7 Wins and 2 Losses

2. B—Walter Johnson

3. G—Don Sutton

4. E—Nolan Ryan

5. C—Phil Niekro

6. A—Steve Carlton

7. D—Gaylord Perry   San Francisco Giants, Cleveland Indians,
                      Texas Rangers, San Diego Padres, New York
                      Yankees, Atlanta Braves, Seattle Mariners,
                      and Kansas City Royals.

SECTION 5—TIMELINES

There are numerous events in baseball history that are quite memorable. Most fans know about Jackie Robinson breaking the color barrier and Pete Rose setting the new standard for career hits. But sometimes it isn't so easy to remember when these events happened. Sure, it's not difficult to figure out that Robinson began his career in the 1940's and Rose broke the record in the 1980's, but being more specific isn't always so easy.

1. Put these events that occurred between 1900 and 1909 in order from the earliest to the most recent.

1. April 24, 1901   _____   A. Jack Chesbro finishes the season with a Major League record 41 victories.

2. October 1, 1903   _____   B. Roger Bresnahan becomes the first catcher to wear shinguards.

3. October 10, 1904 _____   C. Chicago hosts and defeats Cleveland in the American League's first game, 8-2.

4. April 11, 1907   _____   D. Pittsburgh defeats Boston, 7-3, in the first World Series game.

2. Put these events that occurred between 1910 and 1919 in order from the earliest to the most recent.

1. September 22, 1911   _____   A. The Boston Braves end the New York Giants' record 26-game winning streak, 8-3.

2. April 13, 1914   _____   B. An unprecedented double no-hitter for nine innings: Fred Toney of the Cincinnati Reds and Hippo Vaughn of the Chicago Cubs both dominate opposing hitters. The Reds finally hit and win in the tenth, 1-0.

3. September 30, 1916   _____   C. The Federal League begins play as Baltimore defeats Buffalo, 3-2.

4. May 2, 1917   _____   D. Cy Young gets victory #511.

3. Put these events that occurred between 1920 and 1929 in order from the earliest to the most recent.

1. January 5, 1920   _____   A. Rogers Hornsby sets the single season Major League record with a .424 BA.

2. January 21, 1921   _____   B. The use of a resin bag during games by pitchers becomes legal.

3. September 28, 1924   _____   C. Judge Kenesaw Mountain Landis is appointed Baseball's first commissioner.

4. January 30, 1926   _____   D. The New York Yankees acquire Babe Ruth.

4. Put these events that occurred between 1930 and 1939 in order from the earliest to the most recent.

1. September 28, 1930   _____   A. Hack Wilson finishes the season with a Major League record 191 RBI's.

2. July 31, 1932   _____   B. Municipal Stadium opens in Cleveland before 76,979 fans; the Philadelphia Athletics defeat the Indians, 1-0.

3. May 25, 1935   _____   C. Lou Gehrig is honored in an emotional farewell at Yankee Stadium.

4. July 4, 1939   _____   D. Babe Ruth belts home run #714.

5. Put these events that occurred between 1940 and 1949 in order from the earliest to the most recent.

1. May 1, 1941   _____   A. Joe Nuxhall, at 15 years and 10 months, becomes the youngest player in Major League history.

2. June 10, 1944   _____   B. Joe DiMaggio signs Baseball's first $100,000 contract.

3. April 15, 1947   _____   C. Jackie Robinson makes his Major League debut with the Brooklyn Dodgers.

4. Febuary 7, 1949   _____   D. Brooklyn Dodgers' President Larry MacPhail submits a patent application for the first batting helmet.

6. Put these events that occurred between 1950 and 1959 in order from the earliest to the most recent.

1. August 19, 1951 _____ A. Roy Campanella suffers a broken neck in an automobile accident and is paralyzed from his shoulders down.

2. March 18, 1953 _____ B. Midget Eddie Gaedel pinch-hits for the St. Louis Browns in a game against the Detroit Tigers.

3. September 25, 1955 _____ C. The Boston Braves receive approval to move to Milwaukee.

4. January 28, 1958 _____ D. Al Kaline of the Detroit Tigers becomes the youngest player ever to win a batting title at 20 years old (.340).

7. Put these events that occurred between 1960 and 1969 in order from the earliest to the most recent.

1. October 1, 1961 _____ A. The first Major League game is played in Canada as Montreal defeats St.Louis, 8-7

2. October 3, 1962 _____ B. Roger Maris hits his record 61st home run.

3. April 12, 1965 _____ C. The first indoor Major League game is played at the Houston Astrodome. Final score: Phillies 2, Colt '45s 0.

4. April 14, 1969 _____ D. Maury Wills finishes the season with a record 104 stolen bases.

8. Put these events that occurred between 1970 and 1979 in order from the earliest to the most recent.

1. May 10, 1970 _____ A. Hank Aaron passes Babe Ruth with his 715th career home run.

2. April 13, 1972 _____ B. Hoyt Wilhelm becomes the first Major League pitcher to appear in 1,000 games.

3. April 8, 1974 _____ C. The first Major League players' strike is settled after 13 days.

4. June 18, 1976 _____ D. Oakland A's owner Charles O. Finley's fire sale of players is negated by Commissioner Bowie Kuhn.

9. Put these events that occurred between 1980 and 1989 in order from the earliest to the most recent.

1. July 24, 1983 _____ A. George Steinbrenner fires manager Billy Martin for a record fifth time.

2. September 11, 1985 _____ B. Nolan Ryan becomes the first Major League pitcher with 5,000 strikeouts.

3. June 23, 1988 _____ C. The infamous "Pine Tar" game is played between the New York Yankees and the Kansas City Royals.

4. August 22, 1989   _____   D. With a single, Pete Rose gets
                                           hit #4,192 and passes Ty Cobb for
                                           the ML record.

10. Put these events that occurred between 1990 and 1999 in order from
the earliest to the most recent.

1. May 1, 1991   _____   A. Cal Ripken, Jr. plays in his
                                           2,131st consecutive game and sets
                                           a new ironman streak.

2. September 14, 1994   _____   B. The remainder of the regular
                                           season is officially cancelled.

3. September 6, 1995   _____   C. Mark McGwire hits his record
                                           70th home run.

4. September 27, 1998   _____   D. Rickey Henderson steals base
                                           #939 and becomes baseball's all-
                                           time leader.

Answers: 20th Century Events

1. Events between 1900 and 1909:

1. April 24, 1901   C   Chicago hosts and defeats Cleveland in the American League's first game, 8-2.
2. October 1, 1903   D   Pittsburgh defeats Boston, 7-3, in the first World Series game.

3. October 10, 1904   A   Jack Chesbro finishes the season with a Major League record 41 victories.
4. April 11, 1907   B   Roger Bresnahan becomes the first catcher to wear shinguards.

2. Events between 1910 and 1919:

1. September 22, 1911   D   Cy Young gets victory #511.

2. April 13, 1914   C   The Federal League plays its first game as Baltimore defeats Buffalo, 3-2.
3. September 30, 1916   A   The Boston Braves end the N.Y. Giants record 26-game winning streak, 8-3.
4. May 2, 1917   B   An unprecedented double no-hitter for nine innings: Fred Toney of the Cincinnati Reds and Hippo Vaughn of the Chicago Cubs both. dominate opposing hitters. The Reds finally win in the tenth, 1-0.

3. Events between 1920 and 1929:

1. January 5, 1920   D   The New York Yankees acquire Babe Ruth.

2. January 21, 1921   C   Judge Kenesaw Mountain Landis is appointed Baseball's first commissioner.
3. September 28, 1924 A   Rogers Hornsby sets the single season Major League record with a .424 BA.
4. January 30, 1926   B   The use of a resin bag during games by pitchers becomes legal.

4. Events between 1930 and 1939:

1. September 28, 1930 A   Hack Wilson finishes the season with a Major League record 191 RBI's.
2. July 31, 1932   B   Municipal Stadium opens in Cleveland before 76,979 fans; the Philadelphia Athletics defeat the Indians, 1-0.
3. May 25, 1935   D   Babe Ruth belts home run #714.

4. July 4, 1939   C   Lou Gehrig is honored in an emotional farewell at Yankee Stadium.

5. Events between 1940 and 1949:

1. May 1, 1941   D   Brooklyn Dodgers' President Larry MacPhail submits a patent application for the first batting helmet.
2. June 10, 1944   A   Joe Nuxhall, at 15 years and 10 months, becomes the youngest player in Major League history.

3. April 15, 1947   C   Jackie Robinson makes his Major League debut with the Brooklyn Dodgers.

4. Febuary 7, 1949   B   Joe DiMaggio signs Baseball's first $100,000 contract.

6. Events between 1950 and 1959:

1. August 19, 1951   B   Midget Eddie Gaedel pinch-hits for the St. Louis Browns in a game against the Detroit Tigers.

2. March 18, 1953   C   The Boston Braves receive approval to move to Milwaukee.

3. September 25, 1955 D   Al Kaline of the Detroit Tigers becomes the youngest player ever to win a batting title at 20 years old (.340).

4. January 28, 1958   A   Roy Campanella suffers a broken neck in an automobile accident and is paralyzed from the shoulders down.

7. Events between 1960 and 1969:

1. October 1, 1961   B   Roger Maris hits his record 61st home run.

2. October 3, 1962   D   Maury Wills finishes the season with a record 104 stolen bases.

3. April 12, 1965   C   The first indoor game is played at the Houston Astrodome.
Final score: Phillies 2, Colt '45s 0

4. April 14, 1969   A   The first Major League game is played in Canada as Montreal defeats St.Louis, 8-7.

8. Events between 1970 and 1979:

1. May 10, 1970   B   Hoyt Wilhelm becomes the first Major League pitcher to appear in 1,000 games.

2. April 13, 1972   C   The first Major League players' strike is settled after 13 days.

3. April 8, 1974   A   Hank Aaron passes Babe Ruth with his 715th career home run.

4. June 18, 1976   D   Oakland A's owner Charles O. Finley's fire sale of players is negated by Commissioner Bowie Kuhn.

9. Events between 1980 and 1989:

1. July 24, 1983   C   The infamous "Pine Tar" game is played between the New York Yankees and the Kansas City Royals.

2. September 11, 1985 D   With a single, Pete Rose gets hit #4,192 and passes Ty Cobb for the ML record.

3. June 23, 1988   A   George Steinbrenner fires manager Billy Martin for a record fifth time.

4. August 22, 1989   B   Nolan Ryan becomes the first Major League pitcher with 5,000 strikeouts.

10. Events between 1990 and 1999:

1. May 1, 1991   D   Rickey Henderson steals base #939 and becomes baseball's all-time leader.
2. September 14, 1994 B   The remainder of the regular season is officially cancelled.

3. September 6, 1995 A   Cal Ripken, Jr. plays in his 2,131st consecutive game and sets a new ironman streak.
4. September 27, 1998 C   Mark McGwire hits his record 70th home run.

In 1947, the Rookie of the Year Award was instituted with Jackie Robinson of the Brooklyn Dodgers as the inaugural winner. Since 1949, Rookie of the Year Awards have been given to the outstanding first year player in both the National and American Leagues. What makes this award so special is that a player only has one chance to win the award, as he is only eligible in his first season of play. Listed below are 40 well-known players. Some are in the Hall of Fame and others are likely to be enshrined. Of the players listed, 20 won Rookie of the Year honors and 20 did not. Select the players that won the award and then match them with the years in which they won them.

1951	1963	1968	1981	1991
1956	1964	1970	1982	1993
1957	1967	1972	1986	1996
1959	1967	1977	1990	1997

	YES	NO		YES	NO
Hank Aaron	___	___	Mickey Mantle	___	___
Roberto Alomar	___	___	Don Mattingly	___	___
Felipe Alou	___	___	Willie Mays	___	___
Jeff Bagwell	___	___	Willie McCovey	___	___
Johnny Bench	___	___	Joe Morgan	___	___
George Brett	___	___	Thurman Munson	___	___
Jose Canseco	___	___	Eddie Murray	___	___

Rod Carew	___ ___		Tony Oliva	___ ___
Jack Clark	___ ___		Mike Piazza	___ ___
Will Clark	___ ___		Jim Rice	___ ___
Roger Clemens	___ ___		Dave Righetti	___ ___
Roberto Clemente	___ ___		Cal Ripken, Jr.	___ ___
Carlton Fisk	___ ___		Brooks Robinson	___ ___
Nomar Garciaparra	___ ___		Frank Robinson	___ ___
Ken Griffey, Sr.	___ ___		Alex Rodriguez	___ ___
Derek Jeter	___ ___		Pete Rose	___ ___
Andruw Jones	___ ___		Nolan Ryan	___ ___
David Justice	___ ___		Tom Seaver	___ ___
Harmon Killebrew	___ ___		Jim Thome	___ ___
Tony Kubek	___ ___		Robin Yount	___ ___

Answers: Rookie of the Year

PLAYER	TEAM	YEAR
Jeff Bagwell—Houston Astros		1991
Johnny Bench—Cincinnati Reds		1968
Jose Canseco—Oakland Athletics		1986
Rod Carew—Minnesota Twins		1967
Carlton Fisk—Boston Red Sox		1972
Nomar Garciaparra—Boston Red Sox		1997
Derek Jeter—New York Yankees		1996
David Justice—Atlanta Braves		1990
Tony Kubek—New York Yankees		1957
Willie Mays—New York Giants		1951
Willie McCovey—San Francisco Giants		1959
Thurman Munson—New York Yankees		1970
Eddie Murray—Baltimore Orioles		1977
Tony Oliva—Minnesota Twins		1964
Mike Piazza—Los Angeles Dodgers		1993
Dave Righetti—New York Yankees		1981
Cal Ripken, Jr.—Baltimore Orioles		1982
Frank Robinson—Cincinnati Reds		1956
Pete Rose—Cincinnati Reds		1963
Tom Seaver—New York Mets		1967

Since 1931, the Baseball Writers Association of America has selected a player from each league as the Most Valuable Player. This award is given to the player judged to have contributed the most to his team's success during the regular season. Match the player with the year in which he was named MVP.

American League—Most Valuable Player

Vida Blue	Dennis Eckersley	Mickey Mantle	Al Rosen
George Brett	Nellie Fox	Denny McLain	Mo Vaughn
Jeff Burroughs	Jason Giambi	Cal Ripken, Jr.	Zoilo Versalles
Rod Carew	Juan Gonzalez	Phil Rizzuto	Robin Yount
Roger Clemens	Mickey Mantle		

_____1950   _____1977

_____1953   _____1980

_____1956   _____1983

_____1959   _____1986

_____1962   _____1989

_____1965   _____1992

_____1968   _____1995

_____1971   _____1998

_____1974   _____2000

National League—Most Valuable Player

Ernie Banks	Bob Gibson	Kevin Mitchell	Mike Schmidt
Barry Bonds	Jeff Kent	Dale Murphy	Sammy Sosa
Roy Campanella	Jim Konstanty	Don Newcombe	Joe Torre
George Foster	Barry Larkin	Mike Schmidt	Maury Wills
Steve Garvey	Willie Mays		

_____1950

_____1953

_____1956

_____1959

_____1962

_____1965

_____1968

_____1971

_____1974

_____1977

_____1980

_____1983

_____1986

_____1989

_____1992

_____1995

_____1998

_____2000

Answers: American League MVP

PLAYER	TEAM	YEAR
Phil Rizzuto—New York Yankees		1950
Al Rosen—Cleveland Indians		1953
Mickey Mantle—New York Yankees		1956
Nellie Fox—Chicago White Sox		1959
Mickey Mantle—New York Yankees		1962
Zoilo Versalles—Minnesota Twins		1965
Denny McClain—Detroit Tigers		1968
Vida Blue—Oakland Athletics		1971
Jeff Burroughs—Texas Rangers		1974
Rod Carew—Minnesota Twins		1977
George Brett—Kansas City Royals		1980
Cal Ripken, Jr.—Baltimore Orioles		1983
Roger Clemens—Boston Red Sox		1986
Robin Yount—Milwaukee Brewers		1989
Dennis Eckersley—Oakland Athletics		1992
Mo Vaughn—Boston Red Sox		1995
Juan Gonzalez—Texas Rangers		1998
Jason Giambi—Oakland Athletics		2000

Answers: National League MVP

PLAYER	TEAM	YEAR
Jim Konstanty—Philadelphia Phillies		1950
Roy Campanella—Brooklyn Dodgers		1953
Don Newcombe—Brooklyn Dodgers		1956
Ernie Banks—Chicago Cubs		1959
Maury Wills—Los Angeles Dodgers		1962
Willie Mays—San Francisco Giants		1965
Bob Gibson—St. Louis Cardinals		1968
Joe Torre—St. Louis Cardinals		1971
Steve Garvey—Los Angeles Dodgers		1974
George Foster—Cincinnati Reds		1977
Mike Schmidt—Philadelphia Phillies		1980
Dale Murphy—Atlanta Braves		1983
Mike Schmidt—Philadelphia Phillies		1986
Kevin Mitchell—San Francisco Giants		1989
Barry Bonds—Pittsburgh Pirates		1992
Barry Larkin—Cincinnati Reds		1995
Sammy Sosa—Chicago Cubs		1998
Jeff Kent—San Francisco Giants		2000

Teams have been vying for a World Series Championship since 1903. However, it was not until 1955 that the most outstanding player in each Series was recognized for his play with a Most Valuable Player Award. Match the player with the year he was named World Series MVP.

Johnny Bench	Livan Hernandez	Paul Molitor	Brooks Robinson
Whitey Ford	Orel Hershiser	Jack Morris	Bret Saberhagen
Bob Gibson	Reggie Jackson	Johnny Podres	Willie Stargell
Bob Gibson	Derek Jeter	Darrell Porter	Bob Turley

_____1955 _____1979

_____1958 _____1982

_____1961 _____1985

_____1964 _____1988

_____1967 _____1991

_____1970 _____1993

_____1973 _____1997

_____1976 _____2000

Answers: World Series MVP

PLAYER	TEAM	YEAR
Johnny Podres—Brooklyn Dodgers		1955
Bob Turley—New York Yankees		1958
Whitey Ford—New York Yankees		1961
Bob Gibson—St. Louis Cardinals		1964
Bob Gibson—St. Louis Cardinals		1967
Brooks Robinson—Baltimore Orioles		1970
Reggie Jackson—Oakland Athletics		1973
Johnny Bench—Cincinnati Reds		1976
Willie Stargell—Pittsburgh Pirates		1979
Darrell Porter—St. Louis Cardinals		1982
Bret Saberhagen—Kansas City Royals		1985
Orel Hershiser—Los Angeles Dodgers		1988
Jack Morris—Minnesota Twins		1991
Paul Molitor—Toronto Blue Jays		1993
Livan Hernandez—Florida Marlins		1997
Derek Jeter—New York Yankees		2000

Since the first All-Star Game in 1933, baseball fans have enjoyed this mid-summer cavalcade of stars. It is a game for the fans, where the stars from both leagues are assembled on one diamond to showcase their skills. In each All-Star Game a Most Valuable Player is chosen. Sometimes he is a future Hall of Famer, other times a lesser-known player wins the award. Match the player with the year in which he was named All-Star MVP.

Jeff Conine	LaMarr Hoyt	Willie Mays	Red Schoendienst
Jimmie Foxx	Derek Jeter	Willie Mays	Max West
Julio Franco	Bill Madlock	Stan Musial	Ted Williams
Ken Griffey, Sr.	Juan Marichal	Babe Ruth	Carl Yastrzemski

_____1933   _____1965

_____1935   _____1970

_____1940   _____1975

_____1946   _____1980

_____1950   _____1985

_____1955   _____1990

_____1960 (Game 1)_____1995

_____1960 (Game 2)_____2000

Answers: All-Star Game MVP

PLAYER	TEAM	YEAR	
Babe Ruth—New York Yankees		1933	
Jimmie Foxx—Philadelphia Athletics		1935	
Max West—Boston Braves		1940	
Ted Williams—Boston Red Sox		1946	No All-Star Game in 1945
Red Schoendienst—St. Louis Cardinals		1950	
Stan Musial—St. Louis Cardinals		1955	
Willie Mays—San Francisco Giants		1960 (Game 1)	
Willie Mays—San Francisco Giants		1960 (Game 2)	
Juan Marichal—San Francisco Giants		1965	
Carl Yastrzemski—Boston Red Sox		1970	
Bill Madlock—Chicago Cubs		1975	
Ken Griffey, Sr.—Cincinnati Reds		1980	
LaMarr Hoyt—San Diego Padres		1985	
Julio Franco—Texas Rangers		1990	
Jeff Conine—Florida Marlins		1995	
Derek Jeter—New York Yankees		2000	

The Cy Young Award was instituted in 1956 to honor pitching excellence. From its inception until 1966, the award was a combined selection for both leagues and it was not until 1967 that the top pitcher in each league was bestowed with Cy Young honors. Match the pitcher with the year in which he won the Cy Young Award.

American League—Cy Young Award

Dean Chance	Mike Flanagan	Jim Palmer	Bob Turley
Roger Clemens	Whitey Ford	Jim Palmer	Frank Viola
Roger Clemens	Jim Lonborg	Jim Perry	Pete Vuckovich
David Cone	Pedro Martinez	Bret Saberhagen	Early Wynn

_____1958	_____1979
_____1959	_____1982
_____1961	_____1985
_____1964	_____1988
_____1967	_____1991
_____1970	_____1994
_____1973	_____1997
_____1976	_____2000

National League—Cy Young Award

Steve Carlton   Orel Hershiser   Sandy Koufax   Don Newcombe
Don Drysdale   Randy Johnson   Vernon Law   Tom Seaver
Bob Gibson   Randy Jones   Grag Maddux   Warren Spahn
Tom Glavine   Sandy Koufax   Pedro Martinez   Bruce Sutter
Dwight Gooden   Sandy Koufax   Mike McCormick

_____1956   _____1976

_____1957   _____1979

_____1960   _____1982

_____1962   _____1985

_____1963   _____1988

_____1965   _____1991

_____1966   _____1994

_____1967   _____1997

_____1970   _____2000

_____1973

Answers: American League Cy Young

PLAYER	TEAM	YEAR
Bob Turley—New York Yankees		1958
Early Wynn—Chicago White Sox		1959
Whitey Ford—New York Yankees		1961
Dean Chance—Los Angeles Angels		1964
Jim Lonborg—Boston Red Sox		1967
Jim Perry—Minnesota Twins		1970
Jim Palmer—Baltimore Orioles		1973
Jim Palmer—Baltimore Orioles		1976
Mike Flanagan—Baltimore Orioles		1979
Pete Vuckovich—Milwaukee Brewers		1982
Bret Saberhagen—Kansas City Royals		1985
Frank Viola—Minnesota Twins		1988
Roger Clemens—Boston Red Sox		1991
David Cone—Kansas City Royals		1994
Roger Clemens—Toronto Blue Jays		1997
Pedro Martinez—Boston Red Sox		2000

Answers: National League Cy Young

PLAYER	TEAM	YEAR
Don Newcombe—Brooklyn Dodgers		1956
Warren Spahn—Milwaukee Braves		1957
Vernon Law—Pittsburgh Pirates		1960
Don Drysdale—Los Angeles Dodgers		1962
Sandy Koufax—Los Angeles Dodgers		1963
Sandy Koufax—Los Angeles Dodgers		1965
Sandy Koufax—Los Angeles Dodgers		1966
Mike McCormick—San Francisco Giants		1967
Bob Gibson—St. Louis Cardinals		1970
Tom Seaver—New York Mets		1973
Randy Jones—San Diego Padres		1976
Bruce Sutter—Chicago Cubs		1979
Steve Carlton—Philadelphia Phillies		1982
Dwight Gooden—New York Mets		1985
Orel Hershiser—Los Angeles Dodgers		1988
Tom Glavine—Atlanta Braves		1991
Greg Maddux—Atlanta Braves		1994
Pedro Martinez—Montreal Expos		1997
Randy Johnson—Arizona Diamondbacks		2000

Listed here are 25 greats of the game, names that I think all fans recognize. Many are Hall-of-Famers; others have not been retired long enough to meet induction requirements. Choosing the era that each player starred in is not difficult, but identifying the last season in which they played is harder than it seems. Match the player with his final Major League season.

Hank Aaron   Joe DiMaggio   Sandy Koufax   Stan Musial
Grover Alexander Bob Feller   Mickey Mantle   Babe Ruth
Johnny Bench   Lou Gehrig   Christy Mathewson   Mike Schmidt
Wade Boggs   Lefty Gomez   Don Mattingly   Ted Williams
George Brett   Catfish Hunter Willie Mays   Smoky Joe Wood
Ty Cobb   Reggie Jackson Eddie Murray   Cy Young
Dizzy Dean

_____ 1911   _____ 1966

_____ 1916   _____ 1968

_____ 1922   _____ 1973

_____ 1928   _____ 1976

_____ 1930   _____ 1979

_____ 1935   _____ 1983

_____ 1939   _____ 1987

_____ 1943   _____ 1989

_____ 1947   _____ 1993

_____ 1951   _____ 1995

_____ 1956   _____ 1997

_____ 1960   _____ 1999

_____ 1963

Answers: When the Player Retired

Cy Young	1911	Sandy Koufax	1966
Christy Mathewson	1916	Mickey Mantle	1968
Smoky Joe Wood	1922	Willie Mays	1973
Ty Cobb	1928	Hank Aaron	1976
Grover Alexander	1930	Catfish Hunter	1979
Babe Ruth	1935	Johnny Bench	1983
Lou Gehrig	1939	Reggie Jackson	1987
Lefty Gomez	1943	Mike Schmidt	1989
Dizzy Dean	1947	George Brett	1993
Joe DiMaggio	1951	Don Mattingly	1995
Bob Feller	1956	Eddie Murray	1997
Ted Williams	1960	Wade Boggs	1999
Stan Musial	1963		

Many of today's players did not play their first game with the team they are currently with. In each group, seven current Major League players will be listed and the team they are now with. Every one of them played their first Major League game with a different team. The players and their present team (at the start of the 2001 season) are listed on the left. Match them with their original team.

1.
A. Kevin Brown (Los Angeles Dodgers)
B. Ellis Burks (Cleveland Indians)
C. Mike Hampton (Colorado Rockies)
D. Pat Hentgen (Baltimore Orioles)
E. J.T. Snow (San Francisco Giants)
F. Greg Vaughn (Tampa Bay Devil Rays)
G. Todd Zeile (New York Mets)

____Boston Red Sox
____Milwaukee Brewers
____New York Yankees
____Seattle Mariners
____St. Louis Cardinals
____Texas Rangers
____Toronto Blue Jays

2.
A. Sean Casey (Cincinnati Reds)
B. Carl Everett (Boston Red Sox)
C. Randy Johnson (Arizona Diamondbacks)
D. Tino Martinez (New York Yankees)
E. Raul Mondesi (Toronto Blue Jays)
F. Sammy Sosa (Chicago Cubs)
G. Robin Ventura (New York Mets)

____Chicago White Sox
____Cleveland Indians
____Florida Marlins
____Los Angeles Dodgers
____Montreal Expos
____Seattle Mariners
____Texas Rangers

3.
A. Sandy Alomar, Jr. (Chicago White Sox)   ____Boston Red Sox
B. Roger Clemens (New York Yankees)   ____Chicago Cubs
C. Darryl Kile (St. Louis Cardinals)   ____Cleveland Indians
D. Fred McGriff (Tampa Bay Devil Rays)   ____Houston Astros
E. Rafael Palmeiro (Texas Rangers)   ____Los Angeles Dodgers
F. Mike Piazza (New York Mets)   ____San Diego Padres
G. Richie Sexson (Milwaukee Brewers)   ____Toronto Blue Jays

4.
A. Albert Belle (Baltimore Orioles)   ____California Angels
B. Andy Benes (St. Louis Cardinals)   ____Chicago Cubs
C. Dante Bichette (Boston Red Sox)   ____Cleveland Indians
D. Chuck Knoblach (New York Yankees)   ____Los Angeles Dodgers
E. Greg Maddux (Atlanta Braves)   ____Minnesota Twins
F. David Wells (Chicago White Sox)   ____San Diego Padres
G. John Wetteland (Texas Rangers)   ____Toronto Blue Jays

5.
A. Barry Bonds (San Francisco Giants)   ____Baltimore Orioles
B. David Cone (Boston Red Sox)   ____Houston Astros
C. Shawn Green (Los Angeles Dodgers)   ____Kansas City Royals
D. Marquis Grissom (Milwaukee Brewers)   ____Montreal Expos
E. Kenny Lofton (Cleveland Indians)   ____Pittsburgh Pirates
F. Mike Mussina (New York Yankees)   ____Seattle Mariners
G. Alex Rodriguez (Texas Rangers)   ____Toronto Blue Jays

6.
A. Roberto Alomar (Cleveland Indians)   ____Atlanta Braves
B. Will Clark (St. Louis Cardinals)   ____Baltimore Orioles
C. Andres Galarraga (Texas Rangers)   ____Boston Red Sox
D. David Justice (New York Yankees)   ____Montreal Expos
E. John Olerud (Seattle Mariners)   ____San Diego Padres
F. Curt Schilling (Arizona Diamondbacks)   ____San Francisco Giants
G. Mo Vaughn (Anaheim Angels)   ____Toronto Blue Jays

7.
A. Jose Canseco (Anaheim Angels)   ____Atlanta Braves
B. Steve Finley (Arizona Diamondbacks)   ____Baltimore Orioles
C. Jeff Kent (San Francisco Giants)   ____Cincinnati Reds
D. Ryan Klesko (San Diego Padres)   ____Los Angeles Dodgers
E. Pedro Martinez (Boston Red Sox)   ____Oakland Athletics
F. Paul O'Neill (New York Yankees)   ____Seattle Mariners
G. Omar Vizquel (Cleveland Indians)   ____Toronto Blue Jays

8.
A. Moises Alou (Houston Astros)   ____Cincinnati Reds
B. Jeromy Burnitz (Milwaukee Brewers)   ____Detroit Tigers
C. Eric Davis (San Francisco Giants)   ____Los Angeles Dodgers
D. Scott Erickson (Baltimore Orioles)   ____Minnesota Twins
E. Travis Fryman (Cleveland Indians)   ____New York Mets
F. Hideki Irabu (Montreal Expos)   ____New York Yankees
G. Hideo Nomo (Boston Red Sox)   ____Pittsburgh Pirates

9.

A. Brady Anderson (Baltimore Orioles)   ____Boston Red Sox
B. Jay Buhner (Seattle Mariners)   ____Milwaukee Brewers
C. Juan Gonzalez (Cleveland Indians)   ____Montreal Expos
D. Mark McGwire (St. Louis Cardinals)   ____New York Yankees
E. B. J. Surhoff (Atlanta Braves)   ____Oakland Athletics
F. Larry Walker (Colorado Rockies)   ____San Francisco Giants
G. Matt Williams (Arizona Diamondbacks)   ____Texas Rangers

10.

A. Scott Brosius (New York Yankees)   ____Baltimore Orioles
B. Ken Caminiti (Texas Rangers)   ____California Angels
C. Jim Edmonds (St. Louis Cardinals)   ____Cleveland Indians
D. Pete Harnisch (Cincinnati Reds)   ____Houston Astros
E. Manny Ramirez (Boston Red Sox)   ____Milwaukee Brewers
F. Gary Sheffield (Los Angeles Dodgers)   ____Oakland Athletics
G. Todd Stottlemyre (Arizona Diamondbacks)____Toronto Blue Jays

11.

A. Derek Bell (Pittsburgh Pirates)   ____Atlanta Braves
B. Johnny Damon (Oakland Athletics)   ____California Angels
C. Chuck Finley (Cleveland Indians)   ____Florida Marlins
D. Livan Hernandez (San Francisco Giants)   ____Kansas City Royals
E. Todd Hundley (Chicago Cubs)   ____Los Angeles Dodgers
F. Jose Offerman (Boston Red Sox)   ____New York Mets
G. Mike Stanton (New York Yankees)   ____Toronto Blue Jays

12.

A. Jeff Conine (Baltimore Orioles)	____California Angels
B. Brian Giles (Pittsburgh Pirates)	____Cleveland Indians
C. Ben Grieve (Tampa Bay Devil Rays)	____Florida Marlins
D. Ken Griffey, Jr. (Cincinnati Reds)	____Kansas City Royals
E. Al Leiter (New York Mets)	____New York Yankees
F. Edgar Renteria (St. Louis Cardinals)	____Oakland Athletics
G. Devon White (Los Angeles Dodgers)	____Seattle Mariners

Answers: Name That Team

1.

A—Kevin Brown	Texas Rangers (1986)
B—Ellis Burks	Boston Red Sox (1987)
C—Mike Hampton	Seattle Mariners (1993)
D—Pat Hentgen	Toronto Blue Jays (1991)
E—J.T. Snow	New York Yankees (1992)
F—Greg Vaughn	Milwaukee Brewers (1989)
G—Todd Zeile	St. Louis Cardinals (1989)

2.

A—Sean Casey	Cleveland Indians (1997)
B—Carl Everett	Florida Marlins (1993)
C—Randy Johnson	Montreal Expos (1988)
D—Tino Martinez	Seattle Mariners (1990)
E—Raul Mondesi	Los Angeles Dodgers (1993)
F—Sammy Sosa	Texas Rangers (1989)
G—Robin Ventura	Chicago White Sox (1989)

3.

A—Sandy Alomar, Jr.	San Diego Padres (1988)
B—Roger Clemens	Boston Red Sox (1984)
C—Darryl Kile	Houston Astros (1991)
D—Fred McGriff	Toronto Blue Jays (1986)
E—Rafael Palmeiro	Chicago Cubs (1986)
F—Mike Piazza	Los Angeles Dodgers (1992)
G—Richie Sexson	Cleveland Indians (1997)

4.

A—Albert Belle	Cleveland Indians (1989)
B—Andy Benes	San Diego Padres (1989)
C—Dante Bichette	California Angels (1988)
D—Chuck Knoblach	Minnesota Twins (1991)
E—Greg Maddux	Chicago Cubs (1986)
F—David Wells	Toronto Blue Jays (1987)
G—John Wetteland	Los Angeles Dodgers (1989)

5.

A—Barry Bonds	Pittsburgh Pirates (1986)
B—David Cone	Kansas City Royals (1986)
C—Shawn Green	Toronto Blue Jays (1993)
D—Marquis Grissom	Montreal Expos (1989)
E—Kenny Lofton	Houston Astros (1991)
F—Mike Mussina	Baltimore Orioles (1991)
G—Alex Rodriguez	Seattle Mariners (1994)

6.

A—Roberto Alomar	San Diego Padres (1988)
B—Will Clark	San Francisco Giants (1986)
C—Andres Galarraga	Montreal Expos (1985)
D—David Justice	Atlanta Braves (1989)
E—John Olerud	Toronto Blue Jays (1989)
F—Curt Schilling	Baltimore Orioles (1988)
G—Mo Vaughn	Boston Red Sox (1991)

7.

A—Jose Canseco	Oakland Athletics (1985)
B—Steve Finley	Baltimore Orioles (1989)
C—Jeff Kent	Toronto Blue Jays (1992)
D—Ryan Klesko	Atlanta Braves (1992)
E—Pedro Martinez	Los Angeles Dodgers (1992)
F—Paul O'Neill	Cincinnati Reds (1985)
G—Omar Vizquel	Seattle Mariners (1989)

8.

A—Moises Alou	Pittsburgh Pirates (1990)
B—Jeromy Burnitz	New York Mets (1993)
C—Eric Davis	Cincinnati Reds (1974)
D—Scott Erickson	Minnesota Twins (1990)
E—Travis Fryman	Detroit Tigers (1990)
F—Hideki Irabu	New York Yankees (1997)
G—Hideo Nomo	Los Angeles Dodgers (1995)

9.

A—Brady Anderson	Boston Red Sox (1988)
B—Jay Buhner	New York Yankees (1987)
C—Juan Gonzalez	Texas Rangers (1989)
D—Mark McGwire	Oakland Athletics (1986)
E—B. J. Surhoff	Milwaukee Brewers (1987)
F—Larry Walker	Montreal Expos (1989)
G—Matt Williams	San Francisco Giants (1987)

10.

A—Scott Brosius	Oakland Athletics (1991)
B—Ken Caminiti	Houston Astros (1987)
C—Jim Edmonds	California Angels (1993)
D—Pete Harnisch	Baltimore Orioles (1988)
E—Manny Ramirez	Cleveland Indians (1993)
F—Gary Sheffield	Milwaukee Brewers (1988)
G—Todd Stottlemyre	Toronto Blue Jays (1988)

11.

A—Derek Bell	Toronto Blue Jays (1991)
B—Johnny Damon	Kansas City Royals (1995)
C—Chuck Finley	California Angels (1986)
D—Livan Hernandez	Florida Marlins (1996)
E—Todd Hundley	New York Mets (1990)
F—Jose Offerman	Los Angeles Dodgers (1990)
G—Mike Stanton	Atlanta Braves (1989)

12.

A—Jeff Conine	Kansas City Royals (1990)
B—Brian Giles	Cleveland Indians (1995)
C—Ben Grieve	Oakland Athletics (1997)
D—Ken Griffey, Jr.	Seattle Mariners (1989)
E—Al Leiter	New York Yankees (1987)
F—Edgar Renteria	Florida Marlins (1996)
G—Devon White	California Angels (1985)

Many Hall of Fame players are associated with a particular team. In several of these cases, however, that team is not the one that the Hall of Famer played his last game for. For each player listed, select the team whose uniform he wore in his final game. Remember, **all** the players listed played their last game with a team that they are not normally associated with.

A. Hank Aaron (Milwaukee/Atlanta Braves)   _____Boston Braves

B. Yogi Berra (New York Yankees)   _____Boston Red Sox

C. Lou Boudreau (Cleveland Indians)   _____Boston Red Sox

D. Steve Carlton (Philadelphia Phillies)   _____Cincinnati Reds

E. Ty Cobb (Detroit Tigers)   _____Cleveland Indians

F. Dizzy Dean (St. Louis Cardinals)   _____Detroit Tigers

G. Nellie Fox (Chicago White Sox)   _____Houston Astros

H. Jimmie Foxx (Philadelphia Athletics)   _____Kansas City Royals

I. Lefty Gomez (New York Yankees)   _____Los Angeles Dodgers

J. Hank Greenberg (Detroit Tigers)   _____Milwaukee Braves

K. Harmon Killebrew (Minnesota Twins)   _____Milwaukee Brewers

L. Ralph Kiner (Pittsburgh Pirates)   _____Minnesota Twins

M. Juan Marichal (San Francisco Giants) _____New York Mets

N. Eddie Mathews (Milwaukee/Atlanta Braves) _____New York Mets

O. Christy Mathewson (New York Giants) _____Oakland Athletics

P. Willie Mays (New York/San _____Philadelphia
Francisco Giants) Athletics

Q. Joe Morgan (Cincinnati Reds) _____Philadelphia Phillies

R. Babe Ruth (New York Yankees) _____Pittsburgh Pirates

S. Tom Seaver (New York Mets) _____San Francisco Giants

T. Enos Slaughter (St. Louis Cardinals) _____San Francisco Giants

U. Warren Spahn (Milwaukee Braves) _____St. Louis Browns

V. Duke Snider (Brooklyn/Los _____Washington
Senators Angeles Dodgers)

Answers: Hall of Fame Players—Last Team

A—Hank Aaron   Milwaukee Brewers (1976)

B—Yogi Berra   New York Mets (1965)

C—Lou Boudreau   Boston Red Sox (1952)

D—Steve Carlton   Minnesota Twins (1988)

E—Ty Cobb   Philadelphia Athletics (1928)

F—Dizzy Dean   St. Louis Browns (1947)

G—Nellie Fox   Houston Astros (1965)

H—Jimmie Foxx   Philadelphia Phillies (1945)

I—Lefty Gomez   Washington Senators (1943)

J—Hank Greenberg   Pittsburgh Pirates (1947)

K—Harmon Killebrew   Kansas City Royals (1975)

L—Ralph Kiner   Cleveland Indians (1955)

M—Juan Marichal   Los Angeles Dodgers (1975)

N—Eddie Mathews   Detroit Tigers (1968)

O—Christy Mathewson   Cincinnati Reds (1916)

P—Willie Mays   New York Mets (1973)

Q—Joe Morgan   Oakland Athletics (1984)

R—Babe Ruth   Boston Braves (1935)

S—Tom Seaver   Boston Red Sox (1986)

T—Enos Slaughter   Milwaukee Braves (1959)

U—Warren Spahn   San Francisco Giants (1965)

V—Duke Snider   San Francisco Giants (1964)

Sometimes, nicknames take the form of a phrase in describing a player. When we hear this phrase, we immediately know who the player is. For example, "Mr. Cub," is Ernie Banks. Below are more of these nickname phrases. Match the player with his nickname.

Luke Appling   Lou Gehrig   Dennis Martinez   Duke Snider
Orlando Cepeda   Charlie Gehringer   Willie Mays   Don Stanhouse
Jack Clark   Reggie Jackson   John Montefusco   Rusty Staub
Will Clark   Randy Johnson   Dave Parker   Casey Stengel
Andre Dawson   Walter Johnson   Vic Raschi   Dick Stuart
Leo Durocher   Tony Lazzeri   Brooks Robinson   Frank Thomas
Frankie Frisch   Greg Luzinski   Nolan Ryan   Honus Wagner
Andres Galarraga   Sal Maglie   Ozzie Smith   Eddie Yost

_____The Mechanical Man   _____The Ripper

_____The Cobra   _____The Big Hurt

_____The Old Professor   _____The Lip

_____Mr. October   _____The Wizard

_____The Big Unit   _____Poosh 'Em Up

_____The Flying Dutchman _____The Iron Horse

_____The Thrill   _____The Baby Bull

_____The Walking Man   _____Dr. Strangeglove

_____The Hawk   _____The Say Hey Kid

_____Old Aches and Pains   _____El Presidente

_____The Big Train   _____The Barber

_____The Count   _____The Big Cat

_____The Express   _____The Fordham Flash

_____Le Grand Orange   _____The Silver Fox

_____Stan the Man Unusual _____The Springfield Rifle

_____The Bull   _____The Human Vacuum
                                       Cleaner

Answers: Phrases as Nicknames

Luke Appling—Old Aches and Pains

Orlando Cepeda—The BabyBull

Jack Clark—The Ripper

Will Clark—The Thrill

Andre Dawson—The Hawk

Leo Durocher—The Lip

Frankie Frisch—The Fordham Flash

Andres Galarraga—The Big Cat

Lou Gehrig—The Iron Horse

Charlie Gehringer—
The Mechanical Man

Reggie Jackson—Mr. October

Randy Johnson—The Big Unit

Walter Johnson—The Big Train

Tony Lazzeri—Poosh 'Em Up

Dennis Martinez—El Presidente

Willie Mays—The Say Hey Kid

John Montefusco—The Count

Dave Parker—The Cobra

Vic Raschi—The Springfield Rifle

Brooks Robinson—The Human Vacuum
Cleaner

Nolan Ryan—The Express

Ozzie Smith—The Wizard

Duke Snider—The Silver Fox

Don Stanhouse—Stan the Man Unusual

Rusty Staub—Le Grand Orange

Casey Stengel—The Old Professor

Dick Stuart—Dr. Strangeglove

Frank Thomas—The Big Hurt

Greg Luzinski—The Bull

Sal Maglie—The Barber

Honus Wagner—The Flying Dutchman

Eddie Yost—The Walking Man

Sometimes a player is better known by his nickname than his given name. Below are sixteen such players. Select the correct nickname for each player.

Babe	Cookie	Pepper	Red
Boog	Ducky	Pie	Smoky
Chipper	Dusty	Pudge	Whitey
Choo Choo	Pee Wee	Rabbit	Yogi

Johnnie B. _____Baker, Jr.

Lawrence Peter _____Berra

Forrest Harrill _____Burgess

Clarence _____Coleman

Carlton Ernest _____Fisk

Dorrel Norman Elvert _____Herzog

Larry Wayne _____Jones

Henry Arthur _____Lavagetto

Walter James Vincent _____Maranville

John Leonard Roosevelt _____Martin

Joseph Michael _____Medwick

John Wesley _____ Powell

Harold Henry _____ Reese

George Herman _____ Ruth

Albert Fred _____ Schoendienst

Harold Joseph _____ Traynor

Answers: Players' Nicknames

Johnnie B. **'Dusty'** Baker, Jr.

Lawrence Peter **'Yogi'** Berra

Forrest Harrill **'Smoky'** Burgess

Clarence **'Choo Choo'** Coleman

Carlton Ernest **'Pudge'** Fisk

Dorrel Norman Elvert **'Whitey'** Herzog

Larry Wayne **Chipper'** Jones

Henry Arthur **'Cookie'** Lavagetto

Walter James Vincent **'Rabbit'** Maranville

John Leonard Roosevelt **'Pepper'** Martin

Joseph Michael **'Ducky'** Medwick

John Wesley ' **Boog'** Powell

Harold Henry **'Pee Wee'** Reese

George Herman **'Babe'** Ruth

Albert Fred **'Red'** Schoendienst

Harold Joseph **'Pie'** Traynor

Sometimes a pitcher is better known by his nickname than his given name. Below are sixteen such pitchers. Select the correct nickname for each one.

Blue Moon	Dizzy	Mudcat	Storm
Bobo	Doc	Oil Can	Three Finger
Catfish	Hippo	Preacher	Vinegar Bend
Daffy	Lefty Red	Whitey	

Dennis Ray _____Boyd

Mordecai Peter Centennial _____Brown

George Earl _____Davis

Jay Hanna _____Dean

Paul Dee _____Dean

Edward Charles _____Ford

James Timothy _____Grant

Dwight Eugene _____Gooden

Robert Moses _____Grove

James Augustus _____Hunter

Wilmer David _____Mizel

Louis Norman _____Newsom

Johnny Lee _____Odom

Elwin Charles _____Roe

Charles Herbert _____Ruffing

James Leslie _____Vaughn

Answers: Pitchers' Nicknames

Dennis Ray ' **Oil Can**" Boyd

Mordecai Peter Centennial '**Three Finger**' Brown

George Earl '**Storm**' Davis

Paul Dee '**Daffy**' Dean

Jay Hanna '**Dizzy**' Dean

Edward Charles '**Whitey**' Ford

James Timothy '**Mudcat**" Grant

Dwight Eugene '**Doc**' Gooden

Robert Moses '**Lefty**' Grove

James Augustus '**Catfish**' Hunter

Wilmer David '**Vinegar Bend**' Mizel

Louis Norman '**Bobo**" Newson

Johnny Lee '**Blue Moon**' Odom

Elwin Charles **'Preacher'** Roe

Charles Herbert **'Red'** Ruffing

James Leslie **'Hippo'** Vaughn

SECTION 6—RANK THE PLAYERS

Baseball is a sport that enables fans to compare players from different eras. We can compare their stats and place them on the all-time list. We can see not only where they stood in their own era, but against both previous and future eras as well. Balls hit over the fence have been a home run in any generation. How do the retired greats of the game stack up against each other? Match the player with his career home run total.

1. Joe DiMaggio   493 _____
    Lou Gehrig   407 _____
    Brooks Robinson   361 _____
    Pete Rose   268 _____
    Duke Snider   160 _____

2. Rod Carew   475 _____
    Dale Murphy   398 _____
    Stan Musial   220 _____
    Tony Oliva   137 _____
    Jackie Robinson   92 _____

3. Wade Boggs   438 _____
    George Brett   317 _____
    Andre Dawson   222 _____
    Don Mattingly   118 _____
    Ozzie Smith   28 _____

4. Johnny Bench   465 _____
    Steve Garvey   389 _____
    Keith Hernandez   272 _____
    Thurman Munson   162 _____
    Dave Winfield   113 _____

5. Frank Howard   442 _____
    Dave Kingman   382 _____
    Roger Maris   275 _____
    Bill Mazeroski   207 _____
    Kirby Puckett   138 _____

6. Roberto Clemente   370 _____
    Ty Cobb   301 _____
    Ken Griffey, Sr.   240 _____
    Gil Hodges   152 _____
    Rogers Hornsby   118 _____

7. Lou Brock   452 _____
    Al Kaline   399 _____
    Joe Morgan   268 _____
    Lou Piniella   149 _____
    Carl Yastrzemski   102 _____

8. Felipe Alou   379 _____
   Roy Campanella   306 _____
   Fred Lynn   242 _____
   Tony Perez   206 _____
   Honus Wagner   101 _____

9. Luis Aparicio   475 _____
   Richie Ashburn   324 _____
   Gary Carter   245 _____
   Ryne Sandberg   83 _____
   Willie Stargell   29 _____

10. Yogi Berra   379 _____
    Orlando Cepeda   358 _____
    Billy Martin   251 _____
    Pee Wee Reese   126 _____
    Robin Yount   64 _____

11. Bobby Bonds   382 _____
    Bill Buckner   332 _____
    Mario Mendoza   234 _____
    Paul Molitor   174 _____
    Jim Rice   4 _____

12. Carlton Fisk   376 _____
    Charlie Gehringer 331 _____
    Hank Greenberg   264 _____
    Bobby Thomson   184 _____
    Maury Wills   20 _____

13. Joe Cronin   369 _____
    Ralph Kiner   279 _____
    Ted Kluszewski   205 _____
    Joe Medwick   170 _____
    George Sisler   102 _____

14. Dwight Evans   385 _____
    Nellie Fox   252 _____
    Bobby Murcer   154 _____
    Bill Terry   35 _____
    Bob Uecker   14 _____

15. Dave Concepion   359 _____
    Bill Dickey   339 _____
    Kirk Gibson   255 _____
    Johnny Mize   202 _____
    Boog Powell   101 _____

Answers: Career Home Runs—Retired Players

1.	Lou Gehrig	493 HR's
	Duke Snider	407 HR's
	Joe DiMaggio	361 HR's
	Brooks Robinson	268 HR's
	Pete Rose	160 HR's
2.	Stan Musial	475 HR's
	Dale Murphy	398 HR's
	Tony Oliva	220 HR's
	Jackie Robinson	137 HR's
	Rod Carew	92 HR's
3.	Andre Dawson	438 HR's
	George Brett	317 HR's
	Don Mattingly	222 HR's
	Wade Boggs	118 HR's
	Ozzie Smith	28 HR's
4.	Dave Winfield	465 HR's
	Johnny Bench	389 HR's
	Steve Garvey	272 HR's
	Keith Hernandez	162 HR's
	Thurman Munson	113 HR's

5.	Dave Kingman	442 HR's
	Frank Howard	382 HR's
	Roger Maris	275 HR's
	Kirby Puckett	207 HR's
	Bill Mazeroski	138 HR's
6.	Gil Hodges	370 HR's
	Rogers Hornsby	301 HR's
	Roberto Clemente	240 HR's
	Ken Griffey, Sr.	152 HR's
	Ty Cobb	118 HR's
7.	Carl Yastrzemski	452 HR's
	Al Kaline	399 HR's
	Joe Morgan	268 HR's
	Lou Brock	149 HR's
	Lou Piniella	102 HR's
8.	Tony Perez	379 HR's
	Fred Lynn	306 HR's
	Roy Campanella	242 HR's
	Felipe Alou	206 HR's
	Honus Wagner	101 HR's
9.	Willie Stargell	475 HR's
	Gary Carter	324 HR's
	Ryne Sandberg	245 HR's
	Luis Aparicio	83 HR's
	Richie Ashburn	29 HR's

10.	Orlando Cepeda	379 HR's
	Yogi Berra	358 HR's
	Robin Yount	251 HR's
	Pee Wee Reese	126 HR's
	Billy Martin	64 HR's
11.	Jim Rice	382 HR's
	Bobby Bonds	332 HR's
	Paul Molitor	234 HR's
	Bill Buckner	174 HR's
	Mario Mendoza	4 HR's
12.	Carlton Fisk	376 HR's
	Hank Greenberg	331 HR's
	Bobby Thomson	264 HR's
	Charlie Gehringer	184 HR's
	Maury Wills	20 HR's
13.	Ralph Kiner	369 HR's
	Ted Kluszewski	279 HR's
	Joe Medwick	205 HR's
	Joe Cronin	170 HR's
	George Sisler	102 HR's
14.	Dwight Evans	385 HR's
	Bobby Murcer	252 HR's
	Bill Terry	154 HR's
	Nellie Fox	35 HR's
	Bob Uecker	14 HR's

15.

Johnny Mize	359 HR's
Boog Powell	339 HR's
Kirk Gibson	255 HR's
Bill Dickey	202 HR's
Dave Concepion	101 HR's

In today's game, home runs are being hit faster they you can say, "It's outta here." So how do today's ballplayers stack up against each other? Match the player with his career home run total at the start of the 2001 season.

1.   Jose Canseco   554 _____

      Barry Larkin   446 _____

      Mark McGwire   417 _____

      Cal Ripken, Jr.   344 _____

      Frank Thomas   179 _____

2.   Barry Bonds   494 _____

      Jay Buhner   386 _____

      Manny Ramirez   308 _____

      Sammy Sosa   236 _____

      Bernie Williams   181 _____

3.   Albert Belle   438 _____

      Ken Griffey, Jr.   381 _____

      Chipper Jones   271 _____

      Jim Thome   233 _____

      Larry Walker   189 _____

4.   Ken Caminiti   400 _____

      Rafael Palmeiro   346 _____

      Mike Piazza   278 _____

      Alex Rodriguez   224 _____

      Matt Williams   189 _____

5. Jeff Bagwell   417 _____
    Carlos Delgado   362 _____
    Juan Gonzalez   310 _____
    Fred McGriff   260 _____
    Paul O'Neill   190 _____

6. Harold Baines   384 _____
    Will Clark   284 _____
    Jim Edmonds   235 _____
    Tony Gwynn   163 _____
    Edgar Martinez   134 _____

7. Andres Galarraga   360 _____
    Jason Giambi   282 _____
    Todd Helton   194 _____
    Rickey Henderson   149 _____
    Jeff Kent   107 _____

8. Roberto Alomar   299 _____
    Vladimir Guerrero   229 _____
    Tino Martinez   170 _____
    Scott Rolen   136 _____
    Mo Vaughn   108 _____

9. Nomar Garciaparra   276 _____
    Mark Grace   187 _____
    Derek Jeter   148 _____
    David Justice   117 _____
    Raul Mondesi   78 _____

10.   Eric Davis   278 _____
       Darin Erstad   227 _____
       Andruw Jones   171 _____
       Ivan Rodriguez   116 _____
       Robin Ventura   77 _____

Answers: Career Home Runs—Active Players

1.

Mark McGwire	554 HR's
Jose Canseco	446 HR's
Cal Ripken, Jr.	417 HR's
Frank Thomas	344 HR's
Barry Larkin	179 HR's

2.

Barry Bonds	494 HR's
Sammy Sosa	386 HR's
Jay Buhner	308 HR's
Manny Ramirez	236 HR's
Bernie Williams	181 HR's

3.

Ken Griffey, Jr.	438 HR's
Albert Belle	381 HR's
Larry Walker	271 HR's
Jim Thome	233 HR's
Chipper Jones	189 HR's

4.

Rafael Palmeiro	400 HR's
Matt Williams	346 HR's
Mike Piazza	278 HR's
Ken Caminiti	224 HR's
Alex Rodriguez	189 HR's

5.

Fred McGriff	417 HR's
Juan Gonzalez	362 HR's
Jeff Bagwell	310 HR's

| | Paul O'Neill | 260 HR's |
| | Carlos Delgado | 190 HR's |

6.	Harold Baines	384 HR's
	Will Clark	284 HR's
	Edgar Martinez	235 HR's
	Jim Edmonds	163 HR's
	Tony Gwynn	134 HR's

7.	Andres Galarraga	360 HR's
	Rickey Henderson	282 HR's
	Jeff Kent	194 HR's
	Jason Giambi	149 HR's
	Todd Helton	107 HR's

8.	Mo Vaughn	299 HR's
	Tino Martinez	229 HR's
	Roberto Alomar	170 HR's
	Vladimir Guerrero	136 HR's
	Scott Rolen	108 HR's

9.	David Justice	276 HR's
	Raul Mondesi	187 HR's
	Mark Grace	148 HR's
	Nomar Garciaparra	117 HR's
	Derek Jeter	78 HR's

10.	Eric Davis	278 HR's
	Robin Ventura	227 HR's
	Ivan Rodriguez	171 HR's
	Andruw Jones	116 HR's
	Darin Erstad	77 HR's

Many of baseball's top career batting averages were compiled by players of previous eras. How do players throughout the century compare with each other? Match the following greats of the game with their career batting averages.

1.   Ty Cobb   .367 _____
        Roger Maris   .342 _____
        Pete Rose   .327 _____
        Babe Ruth   .303 _____
        Honus Wagner   .260 _____

2.   Roberto Clemente   .358 _____
        Rogers Hornsby   .344 _____
        Mickey Mantle   .317 _____
        Ted Williams   .298 _____
        Dave Winfield   .283 _____

3.   Hank Aaron   .328 _____
        Rod Carew   .305 _____
        Nellie Fox   .288 _____
        Eddie Mathews   .271 _____
        Bill Mazeroski   .260 _____

4.   Andre Dawson   .338 _____
        Al Kaline   .312 _____
        Napoleon Lajoie   .297 _____
        Johnny Mize   .279 _____
        Ozzie Smith   .262 _____

5.   Wade Boggs   .340 _____
       George Brett   .328 _____
       Lou Gehrig   .305 _____
       Brooks Robinson   .294 _____
       Frank Robinson   .267 _____

6.   Reggie Jackson   .343 _____
       Willie Keeler   .304 _____
       Thurman Munson   .292 _____
       Mel Ott   .282 _____
       Willie Stargell   .262 _____

7.   Joe Jackson   .356 _____
       Willie Mays   .331 _____
       Stan Musial   .318 _____
       Kirby Puckett   .302 _____
       Mike Schmidt   .267 _____

8.   Jimmie Foxx   .340 _____
       Paul Molitor   .325 _____
       Dale Murphy   .306 _____
       George Sisler   .285 _____
       Carl Yastrzemski   .265 _____

9.   Joe Medwick   .341 _____
       Jackie Robinson   .324 _____
       Duke Snider   .311 _____
       Bill Terry   .295 _____
       Robin Yount   .285 _____

10. Johnny Bench .345 _____
    Yogi Berra .325 _____
    Joe DiMaggio .307 _____
    Don Mattingly .285 _____
    Tris Speaker .267 _____

11. Carlton Fisk .333 _____
    Hank Greenberg .313 _____
    Harmon Killebrew .287 _____
    Eddie Murray .269 _____
    Paul Waner .256 _____

12. Ed Delahanty .346 _____
    Dom DiMaggio .316 _____
    Frankie Frisch .298 _____
    Deion Sanders .284 _____
    Casey Stengel .266 _____

13. Cecil Fielder .316 _____
    Steve Garvey .294 _____
    Gil Hodges .273 _____
    Bob Uecker .255 _____
    Lloyd Waner .200 _____

14. Cap Anson .329 _____
    Luke Appling .310 _____
    Dave Kingman .297 _____
    Willie McCovey .270 _____
    Joe Torre .236 _____

15. Lou Boudreau   .295 _____
     Bo Jackson   .279 _____
     Mario Mendoza   .250 _____
     Tony Perez   .237 _____
     Marv Throneberry   .215 _____

Answers: Career Batting Average
—Retired Players

1. Ty Cobb   .367
   Babe Ruth   .342
   Honus Wagner   .327
   Pete Rose   .303
   Roger Maris   .260

2. Rogers Hornsby   .358
   Ted Williams   .344
   Roberto Clemente   .317
   Mickey Mantle   .298
   Dave Winfield   .283

3. Rod Carew   .328
   Hank Aaron   .305
   Nellie Fox   .288
   Eddie Mathews   .271
   Bill Mazeroski   .260

4. Napoleon Lajoie   .338
   Johnny Mize   .312
   Al Kaline   .297
   Andre Dawson   .279
   Ozzie Smith   .262

5.	Lou Gehrig	.340
	Wade Boggs	.328
	George Brett	.305
	Frank Robinson	.294
	Brooks Robinson	.267
6.	Willie Keeler	.343
	Mel Ott	.304
	Thurman Munson	.292
	Willie Stargell	.282
	Reggie Jackson	.262
7.	Joe Jackson	.356
	Stan Musial	.331
	Kirby Puckett	.318
	Willie Mays	.302
	Mike Schmidt	.267
8.	George Sisler	.340
	Jimmie Foxx	.325
	Paul Molitor	.306
	Carl Yastrzemski	.285
	Dale Murphy	.265
9.	Bill Terry	.341
	Joe Medwick	.324
	Jackie Robinson	.311
	Duke Snider	.295
	Robin Yount	.285

10.	Tris Speaker	.345
	Joe DiMaggio	.325
	Don Mattingly	.307
	Yogi Berra	.285
	Johnny Bench	.267

11.	Paul Waner	.333
	Hank Greenberg	.313
	Eddie Murray	.287
	Carlton Fisk	.269
	Harmon Killebrew	.256

12.	Ed Delahanty	.346
	Frankie Frisch	.316
	Dom DiMaggio	.298
	Casey Stengel	.284
	Deion Sanders	.266

13.	Lloyd Waner	.316
	Steve Garvey	.294
	Gil Hodges	.273
	Cecil Fielder	.255
	Bob Uecker	.200

14.	Cap Anson	.329
	Luke Appling	.310
	Joe Torre	.297
	Willie McCovey	.270
	Dave Kingman	.236

15. Lou Boudreau .295
    Tony Perez .279
    Bo Jackson .250
    Marv Throneberry .237
    Mario Mendoza .215

In today's game, home runs are being hit in record numbers. But what about batting averages? Home runs do not automatically translate into higher averages. How do today's ballplayers stack up against each other in this category? Match the player with his career batting average at the start of the 2001 season.

1. Jose Canseco   .338 _____
    Tony Gwynn   .321 _____
    Barry Larkin   .300 _____
    Frank Thomas   .284 _____
    Jim Thome   .266 _____

2. Edgar Martinez   .320 _____
    Paul O'Neill   .309 _____
    Alex Rodriguez   .298 _____
    Sammy Sosa   .289 _____
    Mo Vaughn   .273 _____

3. Jeff Bagwell   .322 _____
    Vladimir Guerrero .305 _____
    Rickey Henderson   .296 _____
    Andruw Jones   .282 _____
    Rafael Palmeiro   .272 _____

4. Jeromy Burnitz   .306 _____
    Andres Galarraga   .291 _____
    Jeff Kent   .284 _____
    Kenny Lofton   .273 _____
    Tino Martinez   .259 _____

5.	Roberto Alomar	.313	_____
	Harold Baines	.304	_____
	Jay Buhner	.291	_____
	Mark McGwire	.267	_____
	Manny Ramirez	.254	_____
6.	Darin Erstad	.308	_____
	Juan Gonzalez	.301	_____
	Mark Grace	.295	_____
	Fred McGriff	.286	_____
	Omar Vizquel	.276	_____
7.	Albert Belle	.328	_____
	Eric Davis	.304	_____
	Mike Piazza	.295	_____
	Scott Rolen	.284	_____
	Bernie Williams	.271	_____
8.	Craig Biggio	.312	_____
	Sean Casey	.303	_____
	Carlos Delgado	.291	_____
	Chipper Jones	.282	_____
	Greg Vaughn	.247	_____
9.	Ken Griffey, Jr.	.334	_____
	Todd Helton	.311	_____
	David Justice	.296	_____
	Larry Walker	.283	_____
	Matt Williams	.269	_____

10. Barry Bonds .333 _____
    Nomar Garciaparra .322 _____
    Derek Jeter .304 _____
    Cal Ripken, Jr. .289 _____
    Ivan Rodriguez .277 _____

Answers: Career Batting Averages
—Active Players

1. Tony Gwynn   .338
   Frank Thomas   .321
   Barry Larkin   .300
   Jim Thome   .284
   Jose Canseco   .266

2. Edgar Martinez   .320
   Alex Rodriguez   .309
   Mo Vaughn   .298
   Paul O'Neill   .289
   Sammy Sosa   .273

3. Vladimir Guerrero   .322
   Jeff Bagwell   .305
   Rafael Palmeiro   .296
   Rickey Henderson   .282
   Andruw Jones   .272

4. Kenny Lofton   .306
   Andres Galarraga   .291
   Jeff Kent   .284
   Tino Martinez   .273
   Jeromy Burnitz   .259

5. Manny Ramirez   .313
    Roberto Alomar   .304
    Harold Baines   .291
    Mark McGwire   .267
    Jay Buhner   .254

6. Mark Grace   .308
    Darin Erstad   .301
    Juan Gonzalez   .295
    Fred McGriff   .286
    Omar Vizquel   .276

7. Mike Piazza   .328
    Bernie Williams   .304
    Albert Belle   .295
    Scott Rolen   .284
    Eric Davis   .271

8. Sean Casey   .312
    Chipper Jones   .303
    Craig Biggio   .291
    Carlos Delgado   .282
    Greg Vaughn   .247

9. Todd Helton   .334
    Larry Walker   .311
    Ken Griffey, Jr. .296
    David Justice   .283
    Matt Williams   .269

10. Nomar Garciaparra .333
     Derek Jeter   .322
     Ivan Rodriguez   .304
     Barry Bonds   .289
     Cal Ripken, Jr.   .277

How do pitchers throughout the century compare? They all threw a little round ball from a distance of 60'6". Three strikes is an out. Three outs is an inning. One measure of a pitcher's success is how many victories he recorded in his career. So how do the retired pitchers of the game stack up against each other? Match the pitcher with his career victory total.

1.　Jim Bunning　　273 _____
　　Sparky Lyle　　224 _____
　　Red Ruffing　　143 _____
　　Lee Smith　　　99 _____
　　Hoyt Wilhelm　68 _____

2.　Jim Bouton　　236 _____
　　Ryne Duren　　182 _____
　　Whitey Ford　　132 _____
　　Vic Raschi　　　62 _____
　　Allie Reynolds　27 _____

3.　Dennis Eckersley　224 _____
　　Catfish Hunter　197 _____
　　Ron Perranoski　119 _____
　　Dan Quisenberry　79 _____
　　Bobby Shantz　　56 _____

4.　Lefty Gomez　　229 _____
　　Goose Gossage　189 _____
　　Sam McDowell　141 _____
　　Bruce Sutter　　124 _____
　　Luis Tiant　　　68 _____

302 • So You Think You Know Baseball

5. Vida Blue   209 _____
    Elroy Face   173 _____
    Dave Righetti   139 _____
    Johnny Sain   104 _____
    Fernando Valenzuela   82 _____

6. Don Drysdale   270 _____
    Burleigh Grimes   209 _____
    Don Larsen   148 _____
    Johnny Podres   107 _____
    J.R. Richard   81 _____

7. Bert Blyleven   287 _____
    Jack Chesbro   243 _____
    Juan Marichal   198 _____
    Tug McGraw   131 _____
    Denny McLain   96 _____

8. Ralph Branca   284 _____
    Bob Gibson   251 _____
    Ferguson Jenkins   166 _____
    Eddie Lopat   119 _____
    Sal Maglie   88 _____

9. Daffy Dean   288 _____
    Dizzy Dean   254 _____
    Tommy John   150 _____
    Jack Morris   94 _____
    Babe Ruth   50 _____

10. Lou Burdette 283 _____
    Carl Hubbell 253 _____
    Jim Kaat 203 _____
    Sandy Koufax 165 _____
    Smoky Joe Wood 116 _____

11. Steve Barber 268 _____
    Dennis Martinez 231 _____
    Tippy Martinez 184 _____
    Dave McNally 121 _____
    Jim Palmer 55 _____

12. Ron Guidry 286 _____
    Bob Feller 266 _____
    Rollie Fingers 217 _____
    Mickey Lolich 170 _____
    Robin Roberts 114 _____

13. Eddie Cicotte 240 _____
    Harvey Haddix 208 _____
    Satchel Paige 164 _____
    Mel Stottlemyre 136 _____
    Frank Tanana 28 _____

14. Roger Craig 240 _____
    Mike Flanagan 201 _____
    Rube Marquard 167 _____
    Herb Pennock 119 _____
    Johnny Vander Meer 74 _____

304 •   So You Think You Know Baseball

15.   Johnny Antonelli   239 _____
       Three Finger Brown   207 _____
       Hugh Casey   171 _____
       Bob Lemon   126 _____
       Rick Sutcliffe   75 _____

16.   Dean Chance   220 _____
       Don Gullett   196 _____
       Don Newcombe   149 _____
       Claude Osteen   128 _____
       Jerry Reuss   109 _____

17.   Moe Drabowsky   211 _____
       Mike Garcia   186 _____
       Rick Honeycutt   142 _____
       Jimmy Key   107 _____
       Bob Welch   88 _____

18.   Al Hrabosky   222 _____
       Jerry Koosman   207 _____
       Hal Newhouser   168 _____
       Joe Nuxhall   135 _____
       Dave Stewart   64 _____

Answers: Career Victories—Retired Pitchers

1. Red Ruffing   273 Wins
    Jim Bunning   224 Wins
    Hoyt Wilhelm   143 Wins
    Sparky Lyle   99 Wins
    Lee Smith   68 Wins

2. Whitey Ford   236 Wins
    Allie Reynolds   182 Wins
    Vic Raschi   132 Wins
    Jim Bouton   62 Wins
    Ryne Duren   27 Wins

3. Catfish Hunter   224 Wins
    Dennis Eckersley   197 Wins
    Bobby Shantz   119 Wins
    Ron Perranoski   79 Wins
    Dan Quisenberry   56 Wins

4. Luis Tiant   229 Wins
    Lefty Gomez   189 Wins
    Sam McDowell   141 Wins
    Goose Gossage   124 Wins
    Bruce Sutter   68 Wins

5. Vida Blue   209 Wins
    Fernando Valenzuela   173 Wins
    Johnny Sain   139 Wins
    Elroy Face   104 Wins
    Dave Righetti   82 Wins

6. Burleigh Grimes   270 Wins
    Don Drysdale   209 Wins
    Johnny Podres   148 Wins
    J.R. Richard   107 Wins
    Don Larsen   81 Wins

7. Bert Blyleven   287 Wins
    Juan Marichal   243 Wins
    Jack Chesbro   198 Wins
    Denny McLain   131 Wins
    Tug McGraw   96 Wins

8. Ferguson Jenkins   284 Wins
    Bob Gibson   251 Wins
    Eddie Lopat   166 Wins
    Sal Maglie   119 Wins
    Ralph Branca   88 Wins

9. Tommy John   288 Wins
    Jack Morris   254 Wins
    Dizzy Dean   150 Wins
    Babe Ruth   94 Wins
    Daffy Dean   50 Wins

10.	Jim Kaat	283 Wins
	Carl Hubbell	253 Wins
	Lou Burdette	203 Wins
	Sandy Koufax	165 Wins
	Smoky Joe Wood	116 Wins
11.	Jim Palmer	268 Wins
	Dennis Martinez	231 Wins
	Dave McNally	184 Wins
	Steve Barber	121 Wins
	Tippy Martinez	55 Wins
12.	Robin Roberts	286 Wins
	Bob Feller	266 Wins
	Mickey Lolich	217 Wins
	Ron Guidry	170 Wins
	Rollie Fingers	114 Wins
13.	Frank Tanana	240 Wins
	Eddie Cicotte	208 Wins
	Mel Stottlemyre	164 Wins
	Harvey Haddix	136 Wins
	Satchel Paige	28 Wins
14.	Herb Pennock	240 Wins
	Rube Marquard	201 Wins
	Mike Flanagan	167 Wins
	Johnny Vander Meer	119 Wins
	Roger Craig	74 Wins

15. Three Finger Brown   239 Wins
     Bob Lemon   207 Wins
     Rick Sutcliffe   171 Wins
     Johnny Antonelli   126 Wins
     Hugh Casey   75 Wins

16. Jerry Reuss   220 Wins
     Claude Osteen   196 Wins
     Don Newcombe   149 Wins
     Dean Chance   128 Wins
     Don Gullett   109 Wins

17. Bob Welch   211 Wins
     Jimmy Key   186 Wins
     Mike Garcia   142 Wins
     Rick Honeycutt   107 Wins
     Moe Drabowsky   88 Wins

18. Jerry Koosman   222 Wins
     Hal Newhouser   207 Wins
     Dave Stewart   168 Wins
     Joe Nuxhall   135 Wins
     Al Hrabosky   64 Wins

Do any of today's pitchers have a chance for 300 victories? Where do they stand in relation to the greats of previous eras? Where do they stand in relation to each other? Match the following active pitchers with their career win totals at the start of the 2001 season.

1. Bartolo Colon   240 _____
    Tom Glavine   208 _____
    Darryl Kile   157 _____
    Greg Maddux   112 _____
    John Smoltz   51 _____

2. Rick Ankiel   181 _____
    Chuck Finley   125 _____
    Pedro Martinez   85 _____
    Tim Wakefield   21 _____
    Kerry Wood   11 _____

3. John Franco   179 _____
    Randy Johnson   138 _____
    Curt Schilling   110 _____
    Todd Stottlemyre   82 _____
    John Wetteland   48 _____

4. Andy Benes   161 _____
    Mike Hampton   143 _____
    Hideki Irabu   85 _____
    Hideo Nomo   69 _____
    David Wells   31 _____

5.   Roger Clemens   260 _____
      David Cone   184 _____
      Orlando Hernandez   147 _____
      Mike Mussina   100 _____
      Andy Pettite   41 _____

Answers: Career Victories—Active Pitchers

1. Greg Maddux   240 Wins
    Tom Glavine   208 Wins
    John Smoltz   157 Wins
    Darryl Kile   112 Wins
    Bartolo Colon   51 Wins

2. Chuck Finley   181 Wins
    Pedro Martinez   125 Wins
    Tim Wakefield   85 Wins
    Kerry Wood   21 Wins
    Rick Ankiel   11 Wins

3. Randy Johnson   179 Wins
    Todd Stottlemyre   138 Wins
    Curt Schilling   110 Wins
    John Franco   82 Wins
    John Wetteland   48 Wins

4. David Wells   161 Wins
    Andy Benes   143 Wins
    Mike Hampton   85 Wins
    Hideo Nomo   69 Wins
    Hideki Irabu   31 Wins

5. Roger Clemens   260 Wins
    David Cone   184 Wins
    Mike Mussina   147 Wins
    Andy Pettite   100 Wins
    Orlando Hernandez   41 Wins

SECTION 7—TRUE OR FALSE?

True or False

1. _____Babe Ruth had over 100 victories in his pitching career.

2. _____The New York Yankees have never lost 100 games in a season.

3. _____In his career as manager, Casey Stengel only managed teams that played in New York City.

4. _____The only pitcher to ever lose three games in a single Word Series was Lefty Williams of the infamous 1919 Chicago White Sox. Williams was paid off by gamblers to lose the World Series, which he so expertly did.

5. _____The last pitcher to go 3-0 in a single World Series was Mickey Lolich of the 1968 Detroit Tigers.

6. _____Tom Seaver pitched one no-hitter in his career and it came while he was a member of the New York Mets.

7. _____Wade Boggs is the only player in Major League history to have 200 singles in a one season.

8. _____The National League leads the American League in All-Star Game victories.

9. _____No team has ever won a World Series after being down three games to none.

10. _____No player has ever won a League MVP with three different teams.

11. _____No player has ever won consecutive Rookie of the Year Awards.

12. _____New York City is the only city to have a "subway series," in which both teams played their home games in the same city.

13. _____Excluding the strike shortened 1981, 1994, and 1995 seasons, there has never been a season in which there were no 20-game winners in either league.

14. _____In 1999, an incredible 57 players had 100-RBI seasons and every team had at least one player with 100 RBI's.

15. _____No player has ever led his league in doubles, triples and home runs in the same season.

16. _____Steve Carlton is the only lefthanded pitcher with more than 3,000 career strikeouts.

17. _____Mickey Mantle appeared in three games as a pitcher for the New York Yankees.

18. _____The Major League record for the fewest home runs hit in a season by one team is three (minimum 140 games).

19. _____The record for most World Series losses is eight and is held by Whitey Ford.

20. _____Willie Mays is third on the all-time home run list; however, he holds the record for most home runs hit for one franchise.

21. _____The only season Ty Cobb hit below .300 was his first season, 1905 (41 games—.240 BA).

22. _____Due to World War II, there were no All-Star Games played from 1942-45.

23. _____Nolan Ryan pitched more seasons in the National League than in the American League.

24. _____The record for most teams played for in one season is four. In 1977, Dave Kingman became the last player to do so.

25. _____Minnie Minoso was the oldest player (59) to play in a Major League game.

26. _____The National League (Senior Circuit) began play in 1888.

27. _____Ted Williams holds the record for most plate appearances in one inning (4).

28. _____Pete Rose holds the record for hits in a season by a switch-hitter (230).

29. _____Eddie Murray is the only switch-hitter to have hit a home run from both sides of the plate in a game in each league.

30. _____Stan Musial is the career leader in extra-base hits.

31. _____The Monteal Expos have never changed their name in any form.

32. _____At the start of the 2001 season, the last Naional League team to win the World Series was the Atlanta Braves.

33. _____At the start of the 2001 season, the last American League team to win the World Series (excluding the New York Yankees) was the Minnesota Twins.

34. _____Babe Ruth is the only lefthanded batter to hit 50 home runs in a season.

35. _____Mickey Mantle is the only switch-hitter to hit 50 home runs in a season.

36. _____Mike Schmidt holds the record for home runs by an infielder (48).

37. _____Nolan Ryan is the only pitcher with 400 strikeouts in one season.

38. _____The modern record for runs scored in one game by one team is 29.

39. _____The record for being shut out the most times in one season is 33.

40. _____In today's game, managers are quick to go to the bullpen. The record for the fewest complete games by a pitching staff in one season is two.

41. _____In 1996, the Cleveland Indians became the first team to play an entire season (min. 140 games) and not be shutout.

42. _____With no errors in 1990, Cal Ripken, Jr. set the fielding record for shortstops (min.140 games).

43. _____Honus Wagner was the first hitter to receive the ultimate compliment: to be intentionally walked with the bases loaded.

44. _____Jackie Robinson is the last player, on a straight steal, to steal home in the World Series.

45. _____The longest game in Major League history went 26 innings and it resulted in a 1-1 tie.

46. _____Reggie Jackson is the only player to have more than 2,000 career strikeouts.

47. _____Lonnie Smith is the only non-Yankee to appear in the World Series for five consecutive years.

48. _____The record for home runs in a game by one team is ten. Thanks to the launching pad called Coors Field, the Colorado Rockies set this mark during the 1998 season.

49. _____Nolan Ryan is the all-time leader in grand slams allowed (10).

50. _____Jim Palmer never gave up a grand slam during his 19-year career.

51. _____In 1978, the Los Angeles Dodgers were the first team to reach 3,000,000 in home attendance.

52. _____In 1995, The Colorado Rockies were the first team to reach 4,000,000 in home attendance.

53. _____Babe Ruth stole home ten times in his career.

54. _____The St. Louis Cardinals have played in more World Series games than any other National League franchise.

55. _____The record for home runs in All-Star competition is six, and it is held by George Brett.

56. _____No player has ever hit for the cycle in an All-Star Game.

57. _____No player has appeared in more All-Star Games than Hank Aaron (24).

58. _____Johnny Bench is the career leader in home runs by a catcher.

59. _____Don Baylor is the career leader in home runs by a designated hitter (219).

60. _____There are more lefthanded hitters with 500 home runs than righthanded hitters.

61. _____The Kansas City Royals (AL) and the San Diego Padres (NL) both began play in the same season.

62. _____The Brooklyn Dodgers and the New York Giants both moved to Los Angeles and San Francisco, respectively, in the same season.

63. _____The New York Mets began play in 1962, and have compiled more victories than losses.

64. _____Frank Robinson is the only person to win Most Valuable Player and Manager of the Year honors.

65. _____Mario Mendoza had more career strikeouts than base hits.

Answers: True or False

1. False   Ruth had 94 victories

2. False   The New York Yankees lost 100 games twice: 1908 (103 games) and 1912 (102 games).

3. False   Stengel also managed the Boston Braves from 1938-43.

4. False   George Frazier of the New York Yankees went 0-3 in the 1981 World Series.

5. True   Only six other pitchers ever went 3-0 in a single
World Series.
1905—Christy Mathewson—New York Giants
1909—Babe Adams—Pittsburgh Pirates
1910—Jack Coombs—Philadelphia Athletics
1920—Stan Covelski- Cleveland Indians (Best of nine)
1946—Harry Brecheen—St. Louis Cardinals
1967—Bob Gibson—St. Louis Cardinals
All of these pitchers and their teams, including Lolich, won the Series.

6. False   Tom Seaver was a member of the Cincinnati Reds when he pitched his no-hitter on June 16, 1978 against the St. Louis Cardinals.

7. False   No player has ever had 200 singles in one season. The highest total was by Lloyd Waner of the Pittsburgh Pirates in 1927, with 198 singles. Pete Rose had 181 singles while with the Cincinnati Reds in 1973.

8. True   The Natonal League leads the series: 40-30-1

9. True

10. True   Many players have won the award with two different teams.

11. True   A player is only eligible to win the award once.

12. False   Chicago 1906   The White Sox defeated the Cubs, 4- 2.
                St. Louis 1944   The   Cardinals   defeated   the Browns, 4-2.

13. True

14. False   Three teams did not have a 100 RBI player: Minnesota, Florida and San Diego.

15. True

16. False   Randy Johnson had 3,040 career strikeouts as of the start of the 2001 season.

17. False   Mantle never took the mound for the Yankees.

18. True   The Chicago White Sox in 1908.

19. True

20. False   Mays (Giants) is third on the list with 646 home runs. Hank Aaron (Braves) is first with 733 and Babe Ruth (Yankees) is second with 659.

21. True

22. False   The only year in which there was no All-Star Game due to World War II was 1945.

23. True   NL—14 seasons   AL—13 seasons

24. True   Kingman played for the Mets (58 games), Padres (56), Angels (10), and Yankees (8).

25. False   Satchel Paige was 59 years, 2 months, and 18 days old when he pitched for the Kansas City Athletics on September 25, 1965.

26. False   The NL began play in 1876.

27. False   No player has ever had four plate appearences in one inning, although several, including Williams, have had three.

28. True   Rose (Reds, 1973) is tied with Willie Wilson (Royals, 1980).

29. False   Other switch-hitters who have done so are: Reggie Smith, Ted Simmons, Chili Davis, Tim Raines, Dale Sveum, and Bobby Bonilla.

30. False   Hank Aaron holds the record with 1,477 extra-base hits. Musial is second with 1,377.

31. True

32. False   The Florida Marlins defeated the Cleveland Indians in 1997.

33. False   The Toronto Blue Jays defeated the Philadelphia Phillies in 1993.

34. False   Others include: Roger Maris, 61 HR's (1961); Johnny Mize, 51 HR's (1947); Ken Griffey, Jr., 56 HR's (1997, 1998); Brady Anderson, 50 HR's (1996).

35. True   52 HR's (1956); 54 HR's (1961)

36. False   Mark McGwire 70 HR's (1998)

37. False   No pitcher has 400 strikeouts in one season. The ML record is 383, held by Ryan (1973).

38. True   June 8, 1950, at Boston   Boston Red Sox 29—St. Louis Browns 4

        April 23, 1955 at Chicago   Chicago White Sox 29—Kansas City Athletics 6

39. True   St. Louis Cardinals (1933)

40. True   Oakland Athletics (1997); Milwaukee Brewers
(1998, 1999)

41. False   No team has ever played an entire season (min. 140
games) without being shutout.

42. False   Ripken did establish a Major League record with a
.996 fielding percentage, but he committed three errors in his 161 games.

43. False   Napoleon Lajoie (Philadelphia Athletics) was the
first to be intentionally walked with the bases loaded. It happened in the
9th inning on May 23, 1901.

44. True   On September 28, 1955, vs. the New York Yankees.
Tim McCarver (Cardinals) was the last player to steal home in the Series,
but it was part of a double-steal (10/15/64 vs. NYY).

45. True   On May 1, 1920 at Boston   Boston Braves 1—
                                                    Brooklyn Dodgers
                                                    1

46. True   Jackson has 2,597 career strikeouts.

47. False   However, Smith does hold the record for playing in
the World Series with the most different teams (4): Philadelphia Phillies
(1980), St. Louis Cardinals (1982). Kansas City Royals (1985), Atlanta
Braves (1991, 1992).

48. False   The record is ten, but it was set by the Toronto Blue
Jays on 9/14/87, at Baltimore.

49. True

50. True

51. True   3,347,527

52. False   In 1991, Toronto was the first team to reach the
mark (4,001,527).

53. True

54. True   96 Games: 48 Wins—48 Losses

55. False   Stan Musial holds the All-Star home run record

56. True

57. True   Willie Mays and Stan Musial have also appeared in
24 All-Star Games. Aaron has also been selected to the most games (25).

58. False   Carlton Fisk is first with 351 home runs as a
catcher. Bench hit 327 HR's and is second.

59. True

60. False   There are eight righthanded hitters (Aaron, Mays,
Robinson, Killebrew, Schmidt, Foxx, McGwire, and Banks), seven left-
handed hitters (Ruth, Jackson, McCovey, Williams, Mathews, Ott,
Bonds), and two switch-hitters (Mantle, Murray).

61. True   Both began play in 1969.

62. True   Both began play on the west coast in 1958.

63. False   The Mets did begin play in 1962, but they have a record of 2,934 and 3,246.

64. True   Robinson won the NL MVP in 1961 with Cincinnati, the AL MVP in 1966 with Baltimore, and the Manager of the Year Award in 1989, also with Baltimore.

65. False   The namesake of the infamous "Mendoza Line" had 287 hits and 219 strikeouts.

SECTION 8—ALL-STAR TEAMS

Baseball fans like to pick all-star teams from different eras and compare them to see which is the best. It's fun and it makes for some lively conversation. I thought it would be fun in this section to pick an alphabet team: players from any era whose last names start with the same letter. I have selected teams from all letters except I, Q, U, X, Y, and Z. Some selections were very tough. For example, who is the first baseman for the M team? Do you pick Mattingly, McCovey, McGwire, Murray, or someone else? Conversely, some were very easy. Who is an outfielder for the R team? Ruth is a no-brainer. Do you agree or disagree with my teams? Can you come up with your own? Have a little fun with these alphabet teams.

There will be a right handed and left handed pitcher and no DH. Outfielders were selected regardless of which field they played. An asterisk denotes a Hall of Fame player.

A

1B	Joe Adcock
2B	Roberto Alomar
3B	Dick (Richie) Allen
SS	Luis Aparicio*
OF	Hank Aaron*
OF	Richie Ashburn*
OF	Earl Averill*
C	Sandy Alomar, Jr.
RHP	Grover Alexander*
LHP	Johnny Antonelli

B

1B	Jeff Bagwell
2B	Craig Biggio
3B	George Brett*
SS	Ernie Banks*
OF	Cool Papa Bell*
OF	Barry Bonds
OF	Lou Brock*
C	Johnny Bench*
RHP	Three Finger Brown*
LHP	Vida Blue

C

1B	Rod Carew*
2B	Eddie Collins*
3B	Ken Caminiti
SS	Joe Cronin*
OF	Oscar Charleston*
OF	Roberto Clemente*
OF	Ty Cobb*
C	Mickey Cochrane*
RHP	Roger Clemens
LHP	Steve Carlton*

D

1B	Carlos Delgado
2B	Bobby Doerr*
3B	Ray Dandridge*
SS	Shawon Dunston
OF	Eric Davis
OF	Andre Dawson
OF	Joe DiMaggio*
C	Bill Dickey*
RHP	Dizzy Dean*
LHP	Al Downing

E

1B	Darin Erstad
2B	Johnny Evers*
3B	Darrell Evans
SS	Kevin Elster
OF	Jim Edmonds
OF	Dwight Evans
OF	Carl Everett
C	Johnny Edwards
RHP	Dennis Eckersley
LHP	Dick Ellsworth

F

1B	Jimmie Foxx*
2B	Nellie Fox*
3B	Travis Fryman
SS	Tony Fernandez
OF	Steve Finley
OF	Curt Flood
OF	George Foster
C	Carlton Fisk*
RHP	Bob Feller*
LHP	Whitey Ford*

G

1B	Lou Gehrig*
2B	Charlie Gehringer*
3B	Troy Glaus
SS	Nomar Garciaparra
OF	Juan Gonzalez
OF	Ken Griffey, Jr.
OF	Tony Gwynn
C	Josh Gibson*
RHP	Bob Gibson*
LHP	Lefty Grove*

H

1B	Gil Hodges
2B	Rogers Hornsby*
3B	Bob Horner
SS	Ron Hansen
OF	Harry Heilmann*
OF	Rickey Henderson
OF	Harry Hooper*
C	Gabby Hartnett*
RHP	Catfish Hunter*
LHP	Carl Hubbell*

J

1B	Joe Judge
2B	Davey Johnson
3B	Chipper Jones
SS	Derek Jeter
OF	Joe Jackson
OF	Reggie Jackson*
OF	Andruw Jones
C	Charles Johnson
RHP	Walter Johnson*
LHP	Randy Johnson

K

1B	Harmon Killebrew*
2B	Jeff Kent
3B	George Kell*
SS	Don Kessinger
OF	Al Kaline*
OF	Ralph Kiner*
OF	Chuck Klein*
C	Jason Kendall
RHP	Darryl Kile
LHP	Sandy Koufax*

L

1B	Dale Long
2B	Nap Lajoie*
3B	Carney Lansford
SS	Barry Larkin
OF	Kenny Lofton
OF	Greg Luzinski
OF	Fred Lynn
C	Ernie Lombardi*
RHP	Bob Lemon*
LHP	Eddie Lopat

M

1B	Eddie Murray
2B	Joe Morgan*
3B	Eddie Mathews*
SS	Rabbit Maranville*
OF	Mickey Mantle*
OF	Willie Mays*
OF	Stan Musial*
C	Thurman Munson
RHP	Christy Mathewson*
LHP	Rube Marquard*

N

1B	Irv Noren
2B	Charlie Neal
3B	Graig Nettles
SS	Skeeter Newsome
OF	Bill Nicholson
OF	Otis Nixon
OF	Jim Northrup
C	Matt Nokes
RHP	Phil Niekro*
LHP	Hal Newhouser*

O

1B	John Olerud
2B	Jose Offerman
3B	Ken Oberkfell
SS	Rey Ordonez
OF	Tony Oliva
OF	Paul O'Neill
OF	Mel Ott*
C	Mickey Owen
RHP	Blue Moon Odom
LHP	Claude Osteen

P

1B	Rafael Palmeiro
2B	Tony Phillips
3B	Tony Perez*
SS	Johnny Pesky
OF	Dave Parker
OF	Lou Piniella
OF	Kirby Puckett*
C	Mike Piazza
RHP	Jim Palmer*
LHP	Eddie Plank*

R

1B	Pete Rose
2B	Jackie Robinson*
3B	Brooks Robinson*
SS	Cal Ripken, Jr.
OF	Jim Rice
OF	Frank Robinson*
OF	Babe Ruth*
C	Ivan Rodriguez
RHP	Nolan Ryan*
LHP	Dave Righetti

S

1B	George Sisler*
2B	Ryne Sandberg
3B	Mike Schmidt*
SS	Ozzie Smith
OF	Al Simmons*
OF	Duke Snider*
OF	Tris Speaker*
C	Ray Schalk*
RHP	Tom Seaver*
LHP	Warren Spahn*

T

1B	Bill Terry*
2B	Manny Trillo
3B	Pie Traynor*
SS	Alan Trammell
OF	Frank Thomas (1951-1966)
OF	Gorman Thomas
OF	Bobby Thomson
C	Joe Torre
RHP	Luis Tiant
LHP	John Tudor

V

1B	Mo Vaughn
2B	Bobby Valentine
3B	Robin Ventura
SS	Omar Vizquel
OF	Andy Van Slyke
OF	Greg Vaughn
OF	Bobby Veach
C	Ozzie Virgil
RHP	Dazzy Vance*
LHP	Fernando Valenzuela

W

1B	Vic Wertz
2B	Lou Whitaker
3B	Matt Williams
SS	Honus Wagner*
OF	Paul Waner*
OF	Ted Williams*
OF	Hack Wilson*
C	Dan Wilson
RHP	Smoky Joe Wood*
LHP	David Wells

Carrying our all-star teams one step farther; you are captain of the ultimate pick-up game. Every player who has ever played baseball is standing in front of you. You get to pick your dream team. Whom do you select? Who is on you all-time team? There are no reservations. Select an all-time 30-man roster for both the American and National Leagues: two players from each infield position, ten outfielders, two catchers, and ten pitchers. Once you have made your selections, name your starting lineup for each league. Finally, select your All-Time Major League team. Please note that players who played in both leagues will be selected for the league they are best associated with or where their most noted accomplishments occurred.

AMERICAN LEAGUE

1B	Jimmie Foxx*	OF	Ty Cobb*	C	Carlton Fisk*
1B	Lou Gehrig*	OF	Joe DiMaggio*	C	Ivan Rodriguez
		OF	Ken Griffey, Jr.		
2B	Roberto Alomar	OF	Joe Jackson	RHP	Roger Clemens
2B	Nellie Fox*	OF	Kirby Puckett*	RHP	Bob Feller*
		OF	Frank Robinson*	RHP	Rollie Fingers*
3B	George Brett*	OF	Babe Ruth*	LHP	Whitey Ford*
3B	Brooks Robinson*	OF	Tris Speaker*	LHP	Lefty Gomez*
		OF	Ted Williams*	LHP	Lefty Grove*
SS	Cal Ripken, Jr.	OF	Carl Yastrzemski*	RHP	Walter Johnson*
SS	Alex Rodriguez			RHP	Pedro Martinez
				RHP	Jim Palmer*
				RHP	Nolan Ryan*

AMERICAN LEAGUE
STARTERS/BATTING LINEUP

OF	Ty Cobb*
2B	Roberto Alomar
OF	Babe Ruth*
1B	Lou Gehrig*
OF	Ted Williams*
SS	Cal Ripken, Jr.
C	Ivan Rodriguez
3B	Brooks Robinson*
RHP	Walter Johnson*
LHP	Lefty Grove*

NATIONAL LEAGUE

1B	Willie McCovey*	OF	Hank Aaron*	C	Johnny Bench*
1B	Bill Terry*	OF	Barry Bonds	C	Mike Piazza
		OF	Roberto Clemente*		
2B	Rogers Hornsby*	OF	Tony Gwynn	RHP	Grover Alexander*
2B	Joe Morgan*	OF	Willie Mays*	LHP	Steve Carlton*
		OF	Stan Musial*	RHP	Dizzy Dean*
3B	Eddie Mathews*	OF	Pete Rose	RHP	Bob Gibson*
3B	Mike Schmidt*	OF	Duke Snider*	LHP	Carl Hubbell*
		OF	Sammy Sosa	LHP	Sandy Koufax*
SS	Ozzie Smith	OF	Hack Wilson*	RHP	Greg Maddux
SS	Honus Wagner*			RHP	Christy Mathewson*
				RHP	Tom Seaver*
				LHP	Warren Spahn*

NATIONAL LEAGUE STARTERS/BATTING LINEUP

OF	Willie Mays*
2B	Rogers Hornsby*
OF	Stan Musial*
OF	Hank Aaron*
1B	Willie McCovey*
SS	Honus Wagner*
3B	Mike Schmidt*
C	Johnny Bench*
RHP	Christy Mathewson*
LHP	Warren Spahn*

ALL-TIME TEAM/BATTING LINEUP

OF	Willie Mays*
2B	Rogers Hornsby*
OF	Babe Ruth*
1B	Lou Gehrig*
OF	Stan Musial*
SS	Honus Wagner*
C	Johnny Bench*
3B	Brooks Robinson*
RHP	Walter Johnson*
LHP	Warren Spahn*

SECTION 9—DID YOU KNOW?

Did You Know?

In this section I have tried to present one fact, event, or record from each of the 100 years in the 20th century. You might already know some of this information, but hopefully these facts will be something new, something that you will find interesting. What follows for each year might be about a record-setting season, a career achievement, a well-known game, a World Series, or possibly even something that occurred off the field such as a new rule. It could also be about the not so good. Whatever it may be, I hope you enjoy reading "Did You Know."

Did You Know?

1900—The National League, with eight teams, is the only "Major" league. The teams were (in the order that they finished): the Brooklyn Superbas, Pittsburgh Pirates, Phildelphia Philllies, Boston Beaneaters, Chicago Orphans, St. Louis Cardinals, Cincinnati Reds, and the New York Giants.

1901—The American League begins play and, together with the National League, forms the Major Leagues. The AL was comprised of eight teams, which finished in the following order: the Chicago White Stockings, Boston Somersets, Detroit Tigers, Phildelphia Athletics, Baltimore Orioles, Washington Nationals, Cleveland Blues, and the Milwaukee Brewers. (This year is regarded as the start of the modern era of Major League Baseball.)

1902—The entire National League hits only 99 home runs. Tommy Leach of the Pittsburgh Pirates was the league leader with an astounding 6 home runs. As a team, both the Pittsburgh Pirates and the Brooklyn Dodgers tied for the league lead with 19 home runs. These totals pale in comparison to those of the end of the century, when players and teams matched them in one week.

1903—The New York Giants have two pitchers win 30 games: Joe McGinnity (31-20) and Christy Mathewson (30-13). The pair duplicated this pitching feat the following season; McGinnity went 35-8 and Mathewson went 33-12. The National League has only had a 30-game winner six other times: Mathewson (1905, 1908), Grover Alexander (1915, 1916, 1917), and Dizzy Dean (1934).

1904—Owner John T. Brush and manager John McGraw of the National League champion New York Giants declare the Giants world champions, refusing to play the American League champion Boston Pilgrims. Both Brush and McGraw claimed that Boston was from a "minor league," and that as champions of the National League, the Giants had nothing more to prove and were indeed the World Champions. Fortunately for baseball fans, Brush and McGraw's way of thinking would be pushed aside the following year, as the World Series would become an American sports tradition unlike any other.

1905—The World Series resumes in October when the National Commission adopts New York Giants owner John T. Brush's rules for Series play: a seven game format, a total of four umpires (two from each league) and revenue sharing for the teams involved. The Series opened on October 9 in Philadelphia, as the Athletics hosted the New York Giants. The Giants won the Series in five games and every game was a shutout. The pitching performance of Giants' ace Christy Mathewson was truly remarkable. Mathewson pitched three games, all complete game shutouts! The World Series records that Mathewson established in 1905 that still stand at the end of the century are: most innings pitched in a five game series (27), most wins in a five game series (3—tie), lowest earned-run average in a minimum of 14 innings (0.00), most shutouts in one series (3), most consecutive scoreless innings in one series (27), fewest hits allowed in three consecutive complete games (14), and most strikeouts in a five game series (18). In addition (although it is not an official record) Mathewson only issued one base on balls. Mathewson's performance in the World Series was truly one for the ages.

1906—The Chicago Cubs post a record of 116 wins and 36 losses, finishing the season with an incredible .763 winning percentage. This was the most wins and the highest winning percentage in the regular season for any Major League team in the 20th century. But in true Cub form, they lost the World Series to the Chicago White Sox. As a baseball fan, I see a lot of irony in the fact that those lovable losers from the Windy City hold the all-time best record in Major League Baseball.

1907—Ty Cobb hits .350, winning the first of nine consecutive American League batting titles. During this streak, Cobb hit .400 in two consecutive seasons, and his .420 average in 1911 is the third-highest mark ever. The streak was broken in 1916, when Cobb *only* hit .371, finishing second to Tris Speaker (.386). Undaunted, Cobb won the next three batting titles, giving him 12 for his career, a Major League record.

1908—The sacrifice fly rule is implemented. The rule states that if a runner tags up after a fly ball has been caught and scores, the batter will not be charged with a time at bat.

1909—The Chicago Cubs post a record of 104 wins and 49 losses for a .680 percentage. However, they still finish 6.5 games out of first place. The Pittsburgh Pirates won 110 games (the fourth-highest total of all time), allowing the Cubs' paltry 104 wins to set a new record: best record by a second-place team.

1910—On April 14, President William Howard Taft starts an American tradition by throwing out the first ball in the Washington Nationals' home opener.

1911—Shoeless Joe Jackson hits .408, but only finishes second in the American League batting race as Ty Cobb hits .420. Cobb would also prove to be Jackson's nemesis the next two seasons. In 1912, Jackson hit .395 and finished second to Cobb's .410 and in 1913, Jackson hit .373 and again finished second to Cobb's .390. In his 13-year career, Jackson had a lifetime batting average of .356 (third-best of all-time), but thanks to Ty Cobb, he never won a batting title.

1912—Owen "Chief" Wilson of the Pittsburgh Pirates sets the all-time season record for triples with 36. This mark far outdistances any other, as the next-highest total is 26 (three players), a full ten less than Wilson's incredible total. In addition, no player has even approached the second-place mark since 1925, making Wilson's record one that is unlikely to ever be broken.

1913—Christy Mathewson wins 25 games while issuing only 21 walks. A baseball axiom that has always been true is that walks will be a pitcher's undoing. Mathewson was one of the greatest pitchers ever, and no starting pitcher has been able to equal his extreme level of control. Mathewson's feat of more victories than walks has only been duplicated once: he did it again the following season (24/23).

1914—The Federal League is formed as a third "Major" league with eight teams: the Indianapolis Hoosiers (became the Newark Peppers in 1915), Chicago Chi-Feds, Baltimore Terrapins, Buffalo Buffeds, Brooklyn Tip-Tops, Kansas City Packers, Pittsburgh Rebels and the St. Louis Terriers. The Federal League was short-lived, as it folded after the 1915 season, and its threat to the existing order of the National and American Leagues was quickly over.

1915—Ty Cobb of the Detroit Tigers steals a record 96 bases, establishing a single season standard against which future base stealers would be measured. Cobb broke the old record of 88 steals, set in 1912 by Clyde Milan, and far outdistanced second-place Fritz Maisel, who had 51 steals. No one would challenge Cobb's record for almost a half-century. In 1962, Maury Wills of the Los Angeles Dodgers would be the first to hit the century mark with 104 thefts. A new age of base thievery had begun, with the likes of Lou Brock, Vince Coleman and Rickey Henderson, who in 1982 established a new standard of 130 thefts in a single season. Cobb's mark of 96 steals still places him in the single season top ten and his career total of 892 steals leaves him fourth all-time.

1916—Herman John (Jack) Nabors of the Philadelphia Athletics sets a single-season Major League record with 19 consecutive losses, finishing the season with a record of 1 win and 20 losses. Nabors was quite possibly one of the worst pitchers of all-time, but was it the pitcher or the team? The Athletics won only 36 games and lost 117, finishing last (8th). They ended the season a mere 40 games behind 7th-place Washington, and only 54.5 games behind first-place Boston. Philadelphia had three pitchers lose 20 games and the team had a season-high winning streak of 2! Nabors would end his career in 1917 with a three-year record of 1 win and 25 losses, truly one of the most storied careers in Major League history.

1917—The Chicago White Sox defeat the New York Giants in the World Series, four games to two. This was the last year in which a team from the city of Chicago (either the Cubs or the White Sox) won the World Series. Boston has its famous "Curse of the Bambino," but the city of Chicago has known baseball futility for a year longer. Chicago has had a team in both the National and American Leagues since 1901 but fans in Chicago have waited longer for a World Series parade than anyone else. Even fans in expansion cities of Kansas City, Toronto and Miami (Florida Marlins) have celebrated a World Series championship. To make matters worse, the White Sox (aka the Black Sox) conspired with gamblers and threw the 1919 Series. A combined 200 seasons of baseball and only four championships truly gives the baseball fans of Chicago a right to cry in their beers.

1918—Paced by pitchers Carl Mays (2-0 and a 1.00 ERA) and Babe Ruth (2-0 and a 1.06 ERA), the Boston Red Sox defeat the Chicago Cubs, four games to two, and claim their fifth World Series (1903, 1912, 1915, 1916, 1918). Boston was riding high; five Championships in five trips to the Series. Little did Red Sox fans know that this would be their last hurrah, the beginning of the end. The 1919 season saw the appearance of Babe Ruth as an everyday player and hopes for continued Red Sox dominance. Ruth responded with a .322 avg., led the league in home runs (29), runs scored (103), and RBI's (114). Despite these numbers, the Red Sox had a losing record and finished in fifth place. Things would only get worse, as on January 5, 1920, the "Curse of the Bambino" came into being. Boston Red Sox owner Harry Frazee, to cover some bad Broadway investments, sold Babe Ruth to the New York Yankees for $125,000. Boston fans have been crying in their chowder ever since. In 1946, there was Enos Slaughter's mad dash for home in Game Seven, giving the Cardinals a Series victory over the Red Sox. In 1967, St. Louis once again defeated Boston in seven games, this time paced by Bob Gibson's 3-0 record. In 1976, the Red Sox were derailed by the Big Red Machine of Cincinnati, again in seven games. And in 1986, defeat was snatched from the jaws of victory when, in Game Six, Mookie Wilson's grounder went under Bill Buckner's glove and so did the Series. A seventh game was necessary, and (you guessed it) the Red Sox lost the Series four games to three.

1919—On September 28, the New York Giants and the Philadelphia Phillies play the shortest nine-inning game in Major League history. The contest took less than an hour, as the Giants won 6 to 1 in a scant 51 minutes. Thanks to fussy batters, slow pitchers, a wandering strike zone, and Madison Ave. admen, some *innings* in today's game take 51 minutes!

1920—Babe Ruth hits 54 home runs to lead the Major Leagues. What makes this total so astounding is that Ruth hit more home runs than every other *team* except the Philadelphia Phillies, who hit 64 home runs.

1921—Determined to clean up Major League Baseball, Commissioner Kenesaw Landis bans eight members of the 1919 Chicago White Sox from Major League Baseball for life. Landis cited their association with gamblers and their conspiracy to throw the 1919 World Series as reasons for their lifetime ban. Although the players were acquitted in a court of law, Commissioner Landis, with his absolute power, banned them anyway. The players were Eddie Cicotte, Happy Felsch, Chick Gandil, Joe Jackson, Fred McMullin, Swede Risberg, Buck Weaver, and Lefty Williams. With this lifetime ban, Landis established gambling as the most serious offense for Major League ballplayers.

1922—The Philadelphia Phillies and the Chicago Cubs set a Major League record by combining for 49 runs in a single game. On August 25, this baseball game was disguised as a slow pitch softball game. Philadelphia outhit Chicago 26-25, setting a new record for most hits (combined) in a nine-inning game. However, the Cubs won 26 to 23. This high-scoring affair would lead one to think that either the wind was blowing out that day at Wrigley Field or that both pitching staffs decided to take a vacation. Nearly six decades later, on May 17, 1979, the Phillies and the Cubs re-enacted their long-ago slugfest. This time the score was only 23-22, and there were only 50 hits (including 11 home runs). Philadelphia won the rematch. Perhaps baseball fans will witness Round Three sometime in 2036?

Line score for August 25, 1922:

	1	2	3	4	5	6	7	8	9	Total
Phillies	0	3	2	1	3	0	0	8	6	23
Cubs	1	10	0	14	0	1	0	0	x	26

Line score for May 17, 1979:

	1	2	3	4	5	6	7	8	9	10	Total
Phillies	7	0	8	2	4	0	1	0	0	1	23
Cubs	6	0	0	3	7	0	3	0	0		22

1923—The most famous ballpark in the world, Yankee Stadium, opens on April 18. The first game in The House that Ruth Built set a Major League record for attendance, as 74,217 fans witnessed the Yankees defeat the rival Boston Red Sox, 4-1. The new stadium hosted its first World Series game on October 10, and ironically, it was a future Yankee legend, Casey Stengel, who hit the game-winning inside-the-park home run for the New York Giants. However, the Yanks went on to defeat the Giants in six games, capturing their first Series title. Since that inaugural season of 1923, Yankee Stadium has been home to more World Series (37) and more Series games (94) than any other ballpark. The Stadium was refurbished in 1974, and with its classic architectural lines and Monument Park, it remains a symbol of the sport itself into the new millennium.

1924—The nation's capital celebrates its only World Series Championship as the Washington Senators defeat the New York Giants, four games to three. The Series proved to be an exciting one, with four games decided by one run and a 6-2 Giants win in Game Five the largest margin of victory. Game One was a 4-3 Giants victory in 12 innings and thereafter, the teams alternated wins, forcing a winner-take-all Game Seven. Game Seven was another 12-inning affair, which ended when a ground ball hit by the Senators' Earl McNeely found a well-placed pebble and bounced over the head of Giants third baseman Fred Lindstrom. Washington won the game 4-3 and claimed their first and only World Series Title.

1925—Rogers Hornsby hits .403, giving him his sixth consecutive National League batting title and joining him with Ty Cobb as the only players to have back-to-back .400 seasons. The previous year, Hornsby hit an incredible .424, a National League record. During the years 1921-1925, Hornsby collected 1078 hits and his average for those five seasons was an astounding .402!

1921—235 Hits—.397 BA
1922—250 Hits—.401 BA
1923—163 Hits—.384 BA
1924—227 Hits—.424 BA
1925—203 Hits—.403 BA

1926—On August 28, Emil "Dutch" Levsen of the Cleveland Indians hurls two complete game victories. Levsen led the Indians to a double-header sweep of the Boston Red Sox at Fenway Park by scores of 6-1 and 5-1, limiting the Red Sox to only four hits in each game. Levsen's feat has not been duplicated since.

1927—One of the rarest occurrences in baseball, the unassisted triple play, happens twice in the 24-hour period of May 30-31. On May 30, Jimmy Cooney, shortstop for the Chicago Cubs, accomplished this amazing feat and Detroit Tigers first baseman Johnny Neun duplicated it the next day. The next unassisted triple play would not occur for another four decades, when shortstop Ron Hansen of the Washington Senators recorded one on July 30, 1968. With all the baseball games throughout the years, the unassisted triple play has happened just eleven times; the most recent occurred on May 29, 2000 by Randy Velarde of the Oakland Athletics. Furthermore, this fielding masterpiece has occurred only once in World Series play, by second baseman Bill Wambganss of the Cleveland Indians on October 10, 1920.

1928—National League President John Heydler proposes adding a designated hitter, contending that fans were tired of watching the futility of pitchers trying to hit. The rule was voted down but the idea never died; the American League would adopt the designated hitter rule in 1973.

1929—The New York Yankees announce that they will put permanent numbers on the backs of player uniforms, a sight that baseball fans now take for granted. The Yankees assigned numbers according to their batting lineup, giving number three to Babe Ruth and number four to Lou Gehrig.

1930—The National League finishes the regular season with an astounding .303 composite batting average. This is the only time in history that a league terrorized pitchers to the tune of a .300 average. The Philadelphia Phillies finished second in team batting with a .315 average, but managed to win only 52 games, a number good enough to qualify them for last place, a mere 40 games behind the first-place Cardinals.

1931—Journeyman Earl Webb of the Boston Red Sox breaks a five-year old record by hitting 67 doubles. During the next five seasons, four Hall of Famers would come close to eclipsing Webb's mark: Paul Waner (62 doubles in 1932), Hank Greenberg (63 in 1934), Joe Medwick (64 in 1936), and Charlie Gehringer (60 in 1936). None could top Webb's total, and the little-known outfielder is still in the record books with the highest mark ever. What is even more amazing about Webb's explosive season is that he only hit 155 doubles over the course of his seven-year career. In addition, with the exception of the four players listed above, no player came within 10 of reaching Webb's record for 70 years, until Todd Helton of the Colorado Rockies hit 59 in the 2000 season.

1932—Shortstop Johnny Burnett of the Cleveland Indians goes nine for eleven in an 18-inning slugfest with the Philadelphia Athletics on July 10. Burnett's record nine hits included another record, seven singles, as well as two doubles. No other player has ever recorded eight hits in a game, and only three have had seven hits: Rocky Colavito (22 innings), Cesar Gutierrez (12 innings), and Rennie Stennett (9 innings). Also, only 45 players in American League history have ever had six hits in a game. This number includes Jimmie Foxx, who did so in the same game that Burnett did. Foxx rapped two singles and a double, in addition to blasting three home runs, giving him 16 total bases for his nine at-bats. Another record was set that day, as the teams combined for 58 hits, the most ever for a single game. And yes, there were pitchers that day. Philadelphia's Eddie Rommel relieved starter Lew Krause in the second inning and pitched 17 innings, giving up 14 runs on 29 hits. However, he was still credited with the victory, as the Athletics defeated the Indians, 18-17.

1933—Chuck Klein of the Phillies wins the National League Triple Crown with a .368 batting average, 28 home runs and 120 runs batted in. At the same time, cross-town rival Jimmie Foxx of the Athletics wins the American League Triple Crown, posting numbers of a .356 BA, 48 HR's and 163 RBI's. Only 14 Triple Crowns have ever been won, and 1933 is the only season in which both leagues had a player do so. Amazingly, both Klein and Foxx played in the same city, Philadelphia.

1934—On April 29, the city of Pittsburgh becomes the last Major League city to lift its "Blue Laws" and allow the playing of baseball on Sundays. Forbes Field was now allowed to come alive on the day of rest, and in this first Sunday game, the Pirates showed their gratitude by defeating the Cincinnati Reds 9-5. "Blue Laws" are admittedly outdated and they do make us chuckle, but just imagine no baseball on Sundays.

1935—A new era in Major League baseball begins, as the first night game is played. Cincinnati's Crosley Field was the scene where the hometown Reds defeated the Philadelphia Phillies, on May 24, 2-1. However, light bulb salesmen would have awhile to wait before the next stadium became ready for night play. Ebbets Field in Brooklyn was lit up on June 15, 1938, and most franchises followed suit during the next decade. Exactly ten years after the Dodgers played under the lights for the first time, Tiger Stadium in Detroit was lighted, making 15 out of 16 Major League stadiums capable of hosting baseball games under the stars. However, one team still thought the game was meant to be played before dinnertime, and it wasn't until August 9, 1988 that the Chicago Cubs played a night game at Wrigley Field. Incidentally, Wrigley was supposed to be lit up on the previous night, but Mother Nature rained on the Cubs' parade and the game had to be postponed.

1936—The National Baseball Hall of Fame opens in Cooperstown, New York with an initial class of five. Ty Cobb, Walter Johnson, Christy Mathewson, Babe Ruth and Honus Wagner were the first inductees, with Cobb receiving 222 of a possible 226 votes, the highest total of the group.

1937—Joe Medwick of the St. Louis Cardinals becomes the fourth player in the National League to win the Triple Crown. Medwick compiled a .374 batting average, belted 34 home runs and drove in 154 runs in this, the NL's last Triple Crown season. Since 1937, several players have led the league in two categories, but not the required three. The closest any National Leaguer has come to a Triple Crown season was Stan Musial in 1948, when he led the league with a .376 BA, topped the RBI list with 131 but his 39 HR's were one behind league leaders Ralph Kiner and Johnny Mize

1938—Johnny Vander Meer of the Cincinnati Reds etches his name in baseball lore by pitching no-hitters in two consecutive starts. On June 11 vs. Boston and on June 15 at Brooklyn, Vander Meer shut down opposing hitters, winning by scores of 3-0 and 6-0. Most pitchers never throw a no-hitter in their careers, and no one else has ever pitched two consecutive.

1939—On August 26, a Major League game is televised for the first time. Television, something that today's fans take for granted, was introduced as the station W2XBS broadcast the second game of a doubleheader between the Brooklyn Dodgers and the Cincinnati Reds at Ebbets Field. Brooklyn won the game, 6-1. The line score for that read:

Dodgers	6 Runs 9 Hits 2 Errors	WP—Hugh Casey
Reds	1 Run 8 Hits 1 Error	LP—Johnny Niggeling

Many years and thousands of games later, the information generation cannot imagine not looking at the television listings to see when their favorite team will be on.

1940—On September 24, in the sixth inning of a 16-8 Boston victory over the Philadelphia Athletics, Jimmie Foxx of the Red Sox hits his 35th home run of the season and joins Babe Ruth in the 500 Home Run Club. In addition, three of Foxx's teammates joined him in celebration with home runs of their own. Ted Williams, Joe Cronin, and Jim Tabor also cleared the fences, as the Red Sox became the first American League team and third overall to hit four home runs in the same inning. As a franchise, the Boston Red Sox hold the record for most four home run innings as they have done so seven times.

1941—Joe DiMaggio of the New York Yankees hits safely in 56 consecutive games. DiMaggio started the streak on May 15 against the Chicago White Sox, and it wasn't until two months later that he was held hitless by the Cleveland Indians on July 17. During this remarkable streak, DiMaggio had 22 multiple hit games, amassing 91 base hits and a .408 BA. At the end of the season, DiMaggio was honored with the MVP Award, and his phenomenal accomplishment remains a record that is thought to be untouchable. Other players have put together hit streaks of their own, but none has ever come close to DiMaggio's mark. The second-longest streak belongs to Pete Rose, who hit safely for 44 straight games in 1978. A high mark to be sure, but still two weeks' worth of games out of first place! During the time that DiMaggio was putting together his streak, another one of the all-time greats was carving a place for himself in baseball history. Ted Williams of the Boston Red Sox finished the season with a .406 average, and he remains the last player to hit over .400 for an entire season. Entering the last day of the season, Williams was informed that if he sat out the doubleheader, his average (as it was just below .400) would be rounded off to .400. Williams said "no way" and went 6 for 8, giving him his .406 average. Baseball has some very exclusive clubs and in 1941, Ted Williams became just the eighth player to join the exclusive.400 club.

1942—On May 13, Jim Tobin of the Boston Braves defeats the Chicago Cubs, 6-5, limiting the Cubs to five hits and only two earned runs. However, someone forgot to tell Tobin that pitchers aren't supposed to be able to hit. Tobin had four RBI's and hit an incredible three home runs, becoming the only pitcher ever to do so in a single game. Tobin was less than stellar on the mound that season, finishing with a record of 12 wins and a league-leading 21 losses. Conversely, Tobin was quite productive at the plate, finishing with a .246 batting average, 15 RBI's, and 6 home runs, tying the National League record for home runs in a season by a pitcher.

1943—The ultimate "dead" ball is introduced. With the United States fully immersed in World War II, shortages were everywhere, as materials were needed for the war effort and Major League Baseball was not immune. Rubber was in short supply, so a new balata baseball was produced (balata is the seepage from the rubber tree). Pitchers found their best friend in the form of these new baseballs; for the first 11 games of the season not one home run was hit and 11 of the first 29 games resulted in shutouts. To appease fans (and hitters), leftover baseballs from the previous season were used until a better solution could be found.

1944—St. Louis becomes the third city (Chicago and New York previously) to have a cross-town World Series. The Browns captured their only American League pennant and play in their only World Series. They faced their rivals, the Cardinals, and lost the Series in 6 games. Travel costs were further reduced, as both teams played their home games in Sportsman's Park.

1945—Tommy Holmes of the Boston Braves compiles a batting average of .352 with a league leading 224 hits. Incredibly, he struck out only nine times in 636 at-bats!

1946—Ted Williams plays in his only World Series, a Boston loss to the St. Louis Cardinals in seven games. Williams hit only .200 (5 for 25) with no extra base hits and only one RBI. (What curse?) How else could a Red Sox fan explain why one of the greatest hitters in baseball history had such a futile World Series?

1947—The complexion of Major League Baseball (literally) changes as Jackie Robinson breaks the color barrier by playing for the Brooklyn Dodgers. Although it was too late for many of the older players in the Negro Leagues, Robinson's admittance would pave the way for future generations. He played 151 games at first base for the Dodgers, hitting .297 with 175 hits, 12 home runs, 29 stolen bases and a .989 fielding average. This performance earned Robinson the Rookie of the Year; an award instituted that same year.

1948—Baseball fans, the New York Yankees, and all of America mourn the death of George Herman (Babe) Ruth on August 16. Ruth was a legend in his own time and arguably baseball's greatest, most beloved, and best-known player ever. The Bambino established numerous hitting and slugging records (although some would be broken). He is still the standard by which all other players are measured. Ruth was also an outstanding pitcher, as he collected 94 victories and was a perfect 3-0 in World Series play. Ruth was a member of the first Hall of Fame class in 1936, and what many fans might not know is that he compiled a lifetime batting average of .342. Babe Ruth was not only a great baseball player, but an American icon as well. He remains an inspiration and hero to the kid in all of us.

1949—The New York Yankees outdo themselves by winning the first of five consecutive World Series Titles. This streak bested the previous standard of four consecutive titles set by the 1936-39 Yankees. The National League would prove no match for the Yanks as they defeated both of their cross-town rivals, the Giants and Dodgers, twice and the Phillies once during the streak. The Yanks would be stopped in 1954 by the Indians' 111-win season, thus allowing another team to claim the Series title (the Giants did). Incidentally, the Oakland Athletics are the only other Major League franchise to claim three consecutive World Series triumphs (1972-74).

1950—Connie Mack, born Cornelius Alexander McGillicuddy, ends his incredible 53-year managerial career. Mack's trademark suit and tie spent three years (1894-96) with the Pittsburgh Pirates and an astounding 50 seasons (1901-50) with the Philadelphia Athletics. Also, until 1950, Mack was the only manager the Athletics ever had. Mack piled up some untouchable career stats: 7,755 games, 3,731 wins and 3,948 losses. He managed in eight World Series, winning five: 1910, 1911, 1913, 1929, and 1930. In addition, he was one of only three managers to have his team win 100 games for three consecutive seasons: 1929 (104 wins), 1930 (102), and 1931 (107). Connie Mack was enshrined in the Baseball Hall of Fame in 1937, 13 years before his retirement.

1951—One of Major League Baseball's most memorable games is played on October 3, as the New York Giants defeat the Brooklyn Dodgers 5-4 to capture the National League pennant and a spot in the World Series. The final score of the game is not what is so remarkable; rather it is the game itself and the events leading up to it that are noteworthy. On August 11, the Dodgers had a 13.5 game lead over the Giants, but New York would not say die. The rest of the season saw the Giants post a record of 39 wins and 8 losses. When the National League's regular season was over, the Dodgers and the Giants stood tied atop the standings with identical records of 96 wins and 58 losses. Now these hated cross-town rivals would meet in a three game playoff to determine who would meet that other New York team, the Yankees, in the World Series. After two games, nothing was settled, leaving one more game, winners take all. The Dodgers led 4-1 in the bottom of the ninth; all they needed were three more outs. Unfortunately for Brooklyn, they only got one more. In the ninth, singles by Al Dark and Don Mueller and a double by Whitey Lockman produced one run. Brooklyn brought in pitcher Ralph Branca to relieve Don Newcombe and face Bobby Thomson. The rest, as they say, is history. Thomson hit a three-run home run and "The Giants win the Pennant! The Giants win the Pennant!"

	123	456	789	
Dodgers	100	000	030	4
Giants	010	000	004	5

1952—In three consecutive games on July 14 and 15 (doubleheader), Walt Dropo of the Detroit Tigers hits safely in 12 consecutive trips to the plate. Baseball has all kinds of streaks, but Dropo's is one of the more remarkable ones. On July 14, at Yankee Stadium, he had five singles in five plate appearances in an 8-2 victory over New York. The following day in Detroit, the Tigers were swept in a doubleheader by the visiting Washington Senators, 8-2 and 9-8, but Dropo did not make things easy for the visitors. He got four more singles in four trips to the plate in the first game, and in the nightcap, he collected a triple, a single and a double before pitcher Lou Sleater got him to foul out to catcher Mickey Grasso and end the streak at 12 for 12. On his next at-bat, his "slump" ended as he started a new streak with a single. Officially, the record books list Walt Dropo as tying Pinky Higgins of the 1938 Boston Red Sox, but Higgins also had two walks interspersed with his 12 hits. Dropo had 12 hits in 12 consecutive plate appearances!

1953—On May 6, rookie pitcher Bobo Holloman of the St. Louis Browns makes one of the grandest entrances to the Big Leagues, becoming the first and the only pitcher in Major League history to toss a no-hitter in his very first start. Holloman no-hit the Philadelphia Athletics 6-0 on his way to a grand career of one season in which he appeared in 22 games and compiled a lifetime record of 3 wins and 7 losses. Bobo may not have lasted long, but on May 6, 1953, he was on top of the baseball world.

1954—A rule is made that requires players to take their gloves with them to the dugout instead of leaving them on the field of play. One wonders if prior to this, players worried that they might lose their gloves if they brought them into the dugout? Perhaps they tried to sabotage an opposing fielder by placing the glove in just the right spot? Or was it just plain laziness? Future generations may never know.

1955—The Brooklyn Dodgers not only win the World Series, but do so by defeating the rival New York Yankees. Finally, there is joy in Mudville! Brooklyn fans had suffered through seven World Series losses, five of which coming at the hands of the Yankees (1941, 1947, 1949, 1952, 1953). Pitcher Johnny Podres was named the Series MVP with a 2-0 record and the Series clinching 2-0 shutout at Yankee Stadium in Game 7. However, this Series triumph was short-lived, as in 1956 things were back to normal as the Dodgers lost once again to the Yankees, and after the 1957 season the beloved "Bums" were gone forever, thousands of miles away in Los Angeles.

1956—It has been said that everyone gets 15 minutes of fame, but this is not completely true. On October 8, in Game Five of the World Series, New York Yankee pitcher Don Larsen got slightly more than fifteen minutes. For two hours and six minutes, Larsen was in the national spotlight, as he not only pitched a shutout, but a perfect game as well. The Yankees defeated the Brooklyn Dodgers 2-0, and Larsen's performance was only the fourth perfect game in Major League history (there have been 14 total) and is still the only perfect game in World Series play. Larsen needed only 97 pitches to complete his masterpiece. His only scare came in the second inning, when a ground ball off the bat of Jackie Robinson deflected off the glove of Yankee third baseman Andy Carey. Fortunately, the ball went right to shortstop Gil McDougald, who threw to first just in time to beat Robinson. In the ninth inning, when pinch-hitter Dale Mitchell (batting for Sal Maglie) took a called third strike for the final out, Yankee Stadium erupted in celebration and Don Larsen's place in baseball history was secured forever.

	123	456	789	R H E
Dodgers	000	000	000	0 0 0
Yankees	000	101	00x	2 5 0

1957—The American League decides that a player getting beaned without any form of protection is not a good thing and makes the wearing of batting helmets mandatory. Many players had already begun to wear batting helmets, but some resisted the change. One wonders if those players who resisted this rule or thought a batting helmet unmanly would go without a protective cup?

1958—Nellie Fox of the Chicago White Sox establishes a new Major League record by playing in 98 consecutive games without striking out. Fox broke the old record of 89 games, set in 1932 by another White Sox player, Carey Selph. In his 19-year Hall of Fame career, Fox only fanned an incredible 216 times in 9,232 career at bats, a .023 career percentage! Fox never struck out more than 18 times in a season, and in 1958, he whiffed only 11 times!

1959—On July 21, the Boston Red Sox finally integrate their team, inserting infielder Pumpsie Green into the lineup. The Red Sox were the last team to break the color barrier.

1960—In one of the more bizarre World Series, the New York Yankees defeat the Pittsburgh Pirates by scores of 16-3, 10-0, and 12-0. The Yankees outscored the Pirates 55-27 for the Series and compiled a team ERA of 3.54 to the Pirates' 7.11. However, Pittsburgh won the Series on Bill Mazeroski's dramatic home run in the bottom of the ninth in Game Seven. This was first time in World Series history that a team captured the title with a walk-off home run.

1961—New York Yankee teammates Roger Maris and Mickey Mantle stage a home run battle to see if either could break Babe Ruth's single season home run record of 60. Fan sentiment lies with the very popular Mantle, but unfortunately for the fans, the Mick fell short with 54 homers. Maris not only beat Mantle, but also topped Ruth's record. Maris hit his record-breaking 61st home run in the last (162nd) game of the season, but commissioner Ford Frick put an asterisk on the record. When Ruth set the record, the season was only 154 games long and since Maris had only 59 home runs after 154 games, Frick asserted that Maris did not break Ruth's record. Maris would be forever haunted by this asterisk; he broke the record but he didn't. It would not be until 1998, when Mark McGwire and Sammy Sosa assaulted the single season home run mark, that Maris' record of 61 finally received the acclaim that it richly deserved.

1962—The National League returns to New York City with an expansion team called the Mets. During their first seven seasons the Mets would turn losing into an art form. Their best season would come in 1968, when they would lose 89 games and be only 24 games out of first. In the years 1962-68 the Mets would finish last five times and second last twice, compiling a record of 394-737 for a .348 winning percentage, or rather, a .652 LOSING pct.! In 1969, while everyone was still laughing, the Mets would win their division, defeat the Atlanta Braves for the National League crown and win the World Series over the Baltimore Orioles, ultimately giving themselves the last laugh.

1963—What is a strike (not the work stoppage kind)? Pitchers, hitters, and fans alike want to know. In January of 1963, a strike was defined as the area from the top of the shoulders to the bottom of the knees. In 1968, the Rules Committee shrank the strike zone to the area from the armpits to the top of the knees. Still not satisfied with their own definition of a strike, in 1995 the Rules Committee changed the strike zone again by lowering it from the top of the knees to "a line at the hollow beneath the kneecap." All these changes allowed umpires a leeway in interpreting what is a strike, thus giving an umpire his own personal strike zone. However, in meetings following the 2000 season, the league changed the rules again, this time reverting to the 1963 definition of the strike zone.

1964—The April 24 newspaper reads, "Houston pitcher Ken Johnson tosses no-hitter and losses." Neither the headline nor the box score of April 23 game was a misprint, as the Cincinnati Reds got no hits but still managed one run and defeated the Colts .45's, 1-0. The Reds scored their run in the top of the ninth. Johnson caused his own downfall, as he threw wildly to first on a bunt by Pete Rose, who took second on the play. Rose moved to third on a fielder's choice and scored the game's only run when second baseman Nellie Fox booted Vada Pinson's two-out grounder. Houston failed to score in the bottom of the ninth and Ken Johnson won the dubious distinction of being the first pitcher in Big League history to pitch nine innings, give up no hits, and still lose the game.

1965—Major League franchises decide to try to even up the playing field by instituting an amateur player draft. Teams would now select free-agent players in reverse order of how they finished the previous season. For obvious reasons, the New York Yankees were not in favor of this proposal but their protests fell upon deaf ears. Yankee haters rejoiced, as for the first time since 1925 the Yanks finish the season with a losing record and a place in the second division. The New Yorkers would suffer at this gross misuse of democracy until 1976, when they would once again finish at the top of the league.

1966—Sandy Koufax of the Los Angeles Dodgers retires. Koufax's last four seasons (1963-66) were so dominating that they earned him a Hall of Fame plaque and established Koufax as one of the best left-handers of all time. Below is a composite of his statistics for those four seasons (parentheses indicate the number of times Koufax led the league). Koufax was named National League MVP in 1963, and he won the Cy Young in 1963, 1965, and 1966, during which time only one Cy Young Award given out.

Wins	Losses	Pct.	ERA	GS	CG	ShO	IP	BB	SO	Hits
97	27	.782	1.85	150	89	31	1192.	2259	122	825
(3)		(2)	(4)	(1)	(2)	(3)	(2)		(3)	

1967—Future Hall of Famer and super-thief Lou Brock of the St. Louis Cardinals sets a new World Series record for stolen bases. Brock abused Red Sox catching, as he swiped seven bases, scored a Series-leading eight runs, compiled a .414 batting average and served as a catalyst in the Cardinals' triumph over Boston. Brock equaled his own Series record with seven more thefts the following year against the Detroit Tigers, and in the process established himself (along with Eddie Collins) as the top base stealer in World Series history with 14.

1968—Carl Yastrzemski of the Boston Red Sox wins the American League batting title with a .301 average. As the season wound down, fans feared that for the first time in history a batting champion would hit under .300. Fortunately, Yastrzemski came through, and he was the only player in the American League to hit .300, with Danny Cater of the Oakland Athletics finishing a distant second at .290. Yastrzemski's .301 batting average is the lowest ever compiled by a batting champion in either the American or National League.

1969—Divisional playoffs begin in both leagues, with division winners scheduled to meet in a best of five series and the winners advancing to the World Series. In the American League, the Baltimore Orioles (East) defeated the Minnesota Twins (West), 3-0, and in the National League, the New York Mets (East) bested the Atlanta Braves (West) 3-0. The 'Miracle' Mets won the World Series by defeating the Orioles, four games to one.

1970—Curt Flood refuses to report to the Philadelphia Phillies after being traded from the St. Louis Cardinals. Flood filed a federal lawsuit challenging baseball's reserve clause, a condition that binds a player to a certain team for the duration of a player's career, and got the ball rolling in the players' fight to do away with it. This fight would culminate on December 23, 1975, when labor arbitrator Peter Seitz decided on unqualified free agency for pitchers Andy Messersmith and Dave McNally. It is somewhat ironic that when the 1975 season ended, so had McNally's career. Messersmith would sign a lifetime contract with the Atlanta Braves the following April; however, he would pitch just two seasons with the Braves and his career would end in 1979.

1971—A new chapter in World Series history is written as the Series moves into television's prime time. The first night game was played on October 13 in Pittsburgh's Three Rivers Stadium, as the Pirates defeated the Baltimore Orioles, 4-3. Pittsburgh's Roberto Clemente was named Series MVP, shining in the televised spotlight. Clemente hit .414 for the

Series with a .759 slugging percentage, two home runs, and four RBI's, numbers that confirmed his superstar status.

1972—Steve Carlton of the Philadelphia Phillies wins the Cy Young Award with a 27-10 record and a 1.97 ERA. An excellent season by any standard, but Carlton did it for a Phillies team that won only 59 games and finished 37 games behind the first place Pittsburgh Pirates, facts that make Carlton's year truly incredible.

1973—Baseball's Hall of Fame enshrines Roberto Clemente of the Pittsburgh Pirates as the Hall waves its requisite five-year waiting period for the first and only time. During the offseason, Clemente was on his way to Nicaragua to aid earthquake victims. However, on December 31, 1972, Clemente's plane crashed and the superstar's life was tragically cut short. Clemente played 18 years, compiling a lifetime .317 batting average and exactly 3,000 hits. He was named the National League's MVP in 1966, but it was his unforgettable performance in the 1971 Word Series that earned Clemente the accolades that he so richly deserved.

1974—The Los Angeles Dodgers put together an infield consisting of Steve Garvey at first, Davey Lopes at second, Ron Cey at third, and Bill Russell at short. The four would play together for eight seasons, setting a record for consistency, longevity, and cohesiveness.

1975—On September 16, Rennie Stennett of the Pittsburgh Pirates puts himself in the record books by going seven for seven, becoming the only modern-era player to do so in a nine inning game. Stennett had four singles, two doubles and a triple in the Pirates 22-0 victory over the Chicago Cubs.

1976—In one of the closest races in Major League history, teammates George Brett and Hal McRae of the Kansas City Royals fight it out for the

American League's batting title right down to the last at-bat of the season. Going into the last game, McRae was leading Brett by the slimmest of margins, .3308 to .3307. After three at-bats, each player had collected two more hits, so McRae still led Brett, .3326 to .3323. Each player had one more at-bat. Brett, who hit right before McRae, came up first. He hit an inside-the-park home run, a hit that would prove to be controversial. McRae contended that Minnesota Twins left-fielder Steve Brye intentionally misplayed Brett's routine fly ball and that his misplay was racially motivated (both Brett and Brye are white and McRae is black). Brett's average was now .3333, and McRae had one more at-bat. A hit would give McRae the title, and an out would give it to Brett. McRae grounded out, giving him a final average of .3321 and Brett the batting title. Twins manager Gene Mauch took exception to McRae's accusation, saying he didn't want either Royal to win the batting crown but that he wanted his own player Rod Carew (who is black) to take it. The final averages in this batting title race were: Brett—.3333, McRae—.3321 and Carew—.3306.

1977—Inside-the-park home runs are rare, but for one day they were common. On August 27, at Yankee Stadium, Toby Harrah and Bump Wills of the Texas Rangers both hit inside-the-park home runs. Fans don't generally like to see home runs hit by the visiting team, but an inside-the-park one is still exciting. It is truly thrilling to see a player race around the bases, trying to make it home before the ball does, even if he plays for the other team. Amazingly, Harrah and Wills hit their homers on consecutive pitches, spoiling the game for those fans who got up to get a hot dog and a beer that inning. And the Rangers won the game 8-2, spoiling it for all the other Yankee fans.

1978—A one-game playoff is needed to decide the winner of the American League's Eastern Division, as the Boston Red Sox and the New York Yankees finish the regular season tied for first place. At one point during the year, the Yankees were as far back as 14 games, and as late as

August 21, the Bombers were 8.5 games out, still firmly in Boston's rearview mirror. Yet at the conclusion of the season on October 1, the teams stood tied with identical records of 99 wins and 63 losses. Things looked promising for Boston, as they won the coin toss and the right to host the game, winner-take-all. The Red Sox led 2-0 through six innings, but light-hitting shortstop Bucky Dent (.243 avg. and 5 HR's) crushed a three-run home run in the seventh inning to give the Yankees the lead, one that they would not relinquish. The Sox had one last chance; in the bottom of the ninth with two outs they had the tying and winning runs on base with Carl Yastrzemski at the plate. But alas, Yaz fouled out to Graig Nettles, and the game was over. No pennant for the Red Sox as the final score was New York 5, Boston 4. 'The Curse' struck again, and Boston fans again cursed the 'Damn Yankees.' The Yankees then went on to defeat the Kansas City Royals in the American League Championship Series, 3 games to 1, and collected their 22nd World Series Title with a victory over the Los Angeles Dodgers in six games.

1979—For the first time in Major League history, siblings share league leadership in a pitching category. The brothers Niekro, Phil of the Atlanta Braves and Joe of the Houston Astros, led the National League in wins with 21. Incidentally, they were the only two pitchers in the National League to win 20 games that season.

1980—With a World Series victory over the Kansas City Royals, the Philadelphia Phillies get a big monkey off of their back. Since its inception in 1903, the World Series was never won by the Phillies, and in fact, the franchise had only appeared in the championship two times previous to 1980. In 1915, the Phillies won Game One against the Boston Red Sox, but then lost the next four games. In 1950, Philadelphia didn't even win a game, as they were swept by the New York Yankees. Finally, in 1980, the Phillies defeated KC in six games to claim the Series. Their win in Game One (on October 14) ended an eight game Series losing streak, with their last win coming 65 years earlier. In addition, the win allowed the Phillies to drop their distinction of being the only franchise (of the 16 franchises that have been vying for a Series title since 1903) to never claim a Series Trophy. With a history like this, it is no wonder that Phillies fans have an attitude.

1981—Due to a players' strike, Major League Baseball plays a split season. The Cincinnati Reds had the best combined record in the National League, but since the Reds did not finish first in either half of the split season, they did not qualify for the playoffs. The Los Angeles Dodgers, first half leaders, defeated the Houston Astros, second half leaders, three games to two to claim the Western Division title.

1982—Rickey Henderson of the Oakland Athletics sets a new standard by stealing 130 bases. Henderson shattered Lou Brock's record of 118 stolen bases set in 1974, stealing at least one base in 84 games, including 25 games in which he stole two bases and six games in which he stole three. Henderson also stole four bases in a game on three separate occasions. He accomplished all this despite missing 13 games during the season. What Babe Ruth was to home run hitters, Rickey Henderson is to base stealers. Henderson is baseball's all-time stolen base leader and in 1998, at the age of 39, he would claim his twelfth league title with 66 stolen bases.

1983—The infamous "Pine Tar Game" is played on July 24. In the top of the ninth, the Kansas City Royals trailed the rival New York Yankees 4-3, when George Brett hit a two-run homer off of pitcher Goose Gossage. Seemingly up 5-4, the Royals celebrated until Yankee manager Billy Martin appealed to the umpire, claiming that the pine tar on Brett's bat extended too far up the handle. Upon measurement of the bat, Brett was called out and New York declared the winner. However, the Royals appealed to American League President Lee MacPhail, and the call was reversed. On August 18, the ninth inning was replayed, with Brett's home run counting.

Martin appealed each base, but to no avail, as Brett was ruled to have touched them all. The Yankees went down 1-2-3 in the bottom of the inning to end one of the strangest games in Major League history.

1984—Red Sox outfielder Jim Rice grounds into 36 double plays, a mark which gives Rice a rather dubious record, most double plays in a single season. In addition, Rice is tied with catcher Ernie Lombardi for most seasons for leading the league in twin killings. Both did so four times, with Rice's coming in consecutive years (1982-85). Despite these unpleasant numbers, Rice had an excellent career. He finished with a career average of .298, 382 home runs, and 1451 RBI's, and was honored with the American League MVP Award in 1978.

1985—Players and fans from any team all have a similar refrain concerning umpires: "We was robbed." This sentiment was never more evident for St. Louis Cardinals players and fans than in the 1985 World Series against the Kansas City Royals. In Game Six, the Cardinals were up three games to two in the Series and were leading 1 to 0 in the bottom of the ninth with the champagne ready to be savored, when the baseball world exploded for St. Louis right before their very eyes. Defeat was snatched from the jaws of victory by umpire Don Denkinger. Denkinger's call at first base on runner Jorge Orta was beyond belief. Both Cardinal and Royal alike, fans in the stadium and those watching on television thought they were seeing things: Denkinger signaled Orta safe. Cardinals manager Whitey Herzog went ballistic, yelling and screaming at Denkinger. Pitcher Todd Worrell had the ball, so how could Orta be safe when he stepped on Worrell's foot before he touched first base? One can only guess at how big the smile was on Kansas City manager Dick Howser. The Cardinals lost their argument, and the Royals scored two runs in the inning to even the Series at three games apiece. With the defeated Cardinals emotionally spent, Game Seven was a 11-0 Royal blowout. To Cardinal players and fans alike, umpire Don Denkinger lived up the that refrain, "We was robbed!"

1986—The Boston Red Sox are one out away from defeating the New York Mets and claiming a World Series championship when the Curse strikes again. A ground ball by the Mets' Mookie Wilson went through the legs of Red Sox first baseman Bill Buckner and Boston's title hopes were dashed. The Mets rallied to win Game Six and then captured their second World Series with a 8-5 victory in Game Seven.

Somewhat less well-known but interesting nonetheless, is what befell on October 4 in the Metrodome. The Chicago White Sox and the Minnesota Twins were playing out the season and the Twins won the game 7-3 to end the year on a happy note. During the game, Twins' shortstop Greg Gagne put his name in the record books by hitting two inside-the-park home runs, becoming the most recent player to accomplish this unusual feat.

1987—Two rookies show no fear in playing their first full season in the Major Leagues. Both Mark McGwire of the Oakland Athletics and Benito Santiago of the San Diego Padres put up numbers that any veteran would like to have and in the process established a Major League record. McGwire won Rookie of the Year honors in the American League and became the first rookie in Major League history to have a 40-home run season. He ended the year with a league-leading 49 home runs and in the process shattered the old rookie record of 38 set in 1930 by Wally Berger and tied in 1956 by Frank Robinson. McGwire also led the American League with a .618 slugging percentage and finished the season with 161 hits and a .289 batting average. Meanwhile, Benito Santiago captured the National League's Rookie of the Year Award, finishing the season with a .300 batting average, 164 hits, 18 home runs and 64 runs batted in. What set Santiago apart was that from August 25 to October 2, he hit safely in 34 consecutive games, a new record for rookies. Santiago's streak eclipsed the old mark of 26 games set by Guy Curtright in 1943 and tied him for the eighth-longest streak of all-time. Not a bad year for these two rookies.

1988—Sometimes a team can hang around in the pennant race until Labor Day. Bad teams are out by July 4th. Really horrible teams are out of it by Memorial Day, but the Baltimore Orioles were out of the pennant race in April! The Orioles set a Major League record for losses at the start of a season with 21, and they did not win their first game until April 29 against the Chicago White Sox. Baltimore went on to finish the season with a club record 107 losses.

1989—On October 17, fans get ready to watch Game Three of the World Series between the Oakland Athletics and the San Francisco Giants when the television screen goes black. Mother Nature was at her awful worst, striking the Bay Area with a devastating earthquake. Fans across the country got a first-hand look at what an earthquake is like, as it measured 7.1 on the Richter scale and brought havoc and chaos to the Bay Area. The Series had to be postponed for ten days, and when it resumed it was an afterthought. On October 27, Game Three was played, with the A's winning 13-7 on their way to a four-game sweep of the Giants.

1990—On June 29, Dave Stewart of the Oakland Athletics and Fernando Valenzuela of the Los Angeles Dodgers both throw no-hitters. Stewart held the Toronto Blue Jays hitless in a 5-0 victory and Valenzuela no-hit the St. Louis Cardinals in a 6-0 win. This was the first and only time in Major League history that two no-hitters were thrown on the same day.

1991—What a difference a year makes. In 1990, the Minnesota Twins finished in last place in the AL West, 29 games behind the first place Oakland Athletics. In the NL West, the Atlanta Braves finished 26 games behind the front-running Cincinnati Reds. But all that changed in 1991, as both teams captured their respective pennants and met in the World Series. This turnaround marked the first time that either league had a team go from worst to first in successive seasons. The Series proved to be one of the most exciting ever, with five one-run decisions, four games ending on the home team's last at-bat, and a Game Seven that went 10 innings with the Twins winning 1-0, capturing their second World's Championship.

1992—For the first time, a new national anthem is played before the World Series. *Oh, Canada* was heard as the Toronto Blue Jays were the first non-American team to appear in the Series. The Jays defeated the Atlanta Braves 4 games to 2, and went on to repeat as World Series champs in 1993, this time defeating the Philadelphia Phillies.

1993—For the second time in history, a walk off home run wins the World Series, as Blue Jays' outfielder Joe Carter joins Bill Mazeroski of the 1960 Pittsburgh Pirates as the only players to perform these heroics. In the bottom of the ninth of Game Six, Carter's three run homer off Philadelphia Phillies' pitcher Mitch Williams propelled the Blue Jays to an 8-6 triumph and a Series celebration. Blue Jay fans cheered as Carter circled the bases and when he touched home plate the game and Series were over. Also, this was the first time that a team losing in the ninth inning won the Series on a home run.

1994—A players' strike forces the cancellation of the World Series, the first time in 91 years that no Series is played. For baseball fans everywhere this was indeed a tough pill to swallow, but for the fans of the divisional winners and wild card teams it was even worse, for there would be no post season. The playoff positioning at the close of the season looked like this:

	National League	American League
East	Montreal Expos	New York Yankees
Central	Cincinnati Reds	Chicago White Sox
West	Los Angeles Dodgers	Texas Rangers
Wild Card	Atlanta Braves	Cleveland Indians

1995—The Braves become the first franchise to win World Series titles in three different cities. Incidentally, the Braves have won the Series only three times.

1914—Boston Braves 4	Philadelphia Athletics 0
1957—Milwaukee Braves 4	New York Yankees 3
1995—Atlanta Braves 4	Cleveland Indians 2

1996—On September 27 in Toronto, home plate umpire John Hirschbeck throws Baltimore Oriole second baseman Roberto Alomar out of the game. This, in itself, is not a big deal; players get tossed all the time by umpires. Maybe the player gets upset and curses the ump; maybe he knocks over the water jug or, in a rare case, he throws dugout paraphernalia onto the field. Not so this time, as Alomar became so enraged that he spit in Hirschbeck's face. Vilified across the country, Alomar received only a five-game suspension, further enraging fans. Additionally, the suspension would begin the following season, allowing Alomar to participate in the playoffs. Eventually, Alomar and Hirschbeck made up, but Alomar could not turn back the clock and retract his actions of September 27, 1996.

1997—Baseball purists cry "foul" as the baseball owners decide on interleague play. The teams in each league's corresponding divisions would play each other; east vs. east, central against central, and west versus west. Some were delighted, however. Fans in New York could see the Yankees and Mets play each other, and other natural rivalries could develop, such as in Chicago, Los Angeles and the Bay Area. Fans in each league would now get a chance to see stars from the 'other' league. Still, purists claimed that it would cheapen the World Series. But like it or hate it, interleague play has become a staple of the baseball season.

1998—Baseball fans eagerly watch as both Mark McGwire and Sammy Sosa chase after Roger Maris's single-season home run record of 61.

McGwire eclipsed the mark first by hitting number 62 on September 8; Sosa soon followed with his 62nd five days later. The focus then switched to who would set the new mark, with the battle lasting right up until the last week of play. McGwire ultimately won the title, hitting his 70th home run on the final day of the season. It should be noted that Sosa's 66 did not even earn him a home run title, as both he and McGwire played in the National League. However, Sosa did set a Major League record of his own by hitting the most home runs in a month when he blasted 20 in June.

1999—The century ends with the New York Yankees winning another World Series by sweeping the Atlanta Braves. What a fitting way to end the 1900's, as professional sport's most successful franchise added another championship to its already illustrious record. The franchise moved from Baltimore in 1903 and became known as the Highlanders. In 1912, the name Yankees was adopted, and the team won their first World Series in 1923. A dynasty was begun, as the franchise knew success like no other in professional sports. The Yankees appeared in 36 World Series during the 1900's, winning the title 25 times. Since the 1920's, no decade passed without the Bronx Bombers appearing in at least one World's Championship, and excluding the 1980's, the Yanks won the Series at least once in every decade. Wearing Yankee pinstripes is a badge of honor, with so many great players breaking and establishing all sorts of records. Love 'em or hate 'em, the New York Yankees are the team of the century. And, they've started the new one in the same manner; in 2000, the Yankees defeated their cross-town rivals, the New York Mets, 4 games to 1 to win yet another World Series.

2000—Baseball enters its third century. What is in store for baseball and its fans? Only time will tell. This book deals with the Major Leagues and its players, but baseball is much more than the professional kind, played before screaming fans in huge stadiums on national television. Baseball is the game played at family picnics; by tee-ballers who don't know which base to run to; by little leaguers, high school kids, American Legion players, and thousands of other summertime competitors who play the game, simply because it's fun. Who can forget the simple joy of a backyard game of catch between a father and his child? No matter your age, baseball is a game that brings out the little kid in all of us. Let us hope that baseball never stops being the National Pastime.

ABOUT THE AUTHOR

David Parks is an avid baseball fan. He grew up idolizing Brooks Robinson and the Baltimore Orioles, despite living in a Yankee-dominated neighborhood. He currently resides in Depew, NY with his wife, Patricia.

0-595-20300-0